Church leaders are saying . . .

A sleeping giant is slowly awakening as our people understand and live out their personal calling in community. Younique has become central to our discipleship culture.

—David Loveless, pastor of Disciple and Leadership Initiatives,
First Baptist Orlando, Orlando, FL

It's amazing to watch a room full of people discover their special calling and put it work almost instantly. In just a few months we will have more than one thousand people involved with Younique.

—Scott Kindig, pastor of Kingdom Initiatives,
Community Bible Church, San Antonio, TX

Three years ago I came to a church with incredible depth of leadership experience and corporate training. After installing Younique I regularly hear our leaders say that it is the best training they have ever experienced.

—Dr. Richard Kannwischer, senior pastor,
Peachtree Church, Atlanta, GA

We needed a catalyst to awaken and activate our people, and the Younique process is delivering beyond what we could imagine. Our people are living with freedom and leading with focus because of personal clarity. The breakthrough process is transforming our people, our leadership dynamics, and the DNA of our church culture. We use the personal Vision Frame and language from the Younique toolbox every day.

—Jay Cull, pastor of Leadership Movement,
and Craig Cheney, pastor of Strategy and Leadership
Development, Heartland Church, Kansas City, KS

We believe training is vital to our future, and Younique is the first step. We are using Younique as our foundational training for missional communities as we train hundreds to launch thousands to fulfill our mission: living the adventure-filled good life in Jesus every day.

—Caleb Panter, executive minister,
Campus Church of Christ, Atlanta, GA

One year after installing Younique in our congregation, it has been extraordinarily transformational for our church family. The Younique experience is now the foundation of our discipleship strategy.

—Dr. Jody Ray, senior pastor,
Mt. Bethel United Methodist Church, Marietta, GA

Participants are saying . . .

The Younique experience bridged the gap between who I am and who God has called me to be. I now live with confidence knowing God created me on purpose, and I look forward to living out my specific purpose every day.

—Jeff J., 40-something

When you are young, going through life transition is just hard; but the entire Younique journey powerfully clarified the call on my life.

—Sydney H., 20-something

As a senior pastor of thirty years, the week I went through a Younique accelerator was the best week of my life.

—Ken W., 60-something

I am "all in" on Younique! As someone who has spent my entire career coaching and developing people for high performance, I think Younique is THE best approach to life design.

—Elizabeth P., 50-something

I've always thought of myself as someone who had clarity about his life. But by going through Younique, I learned that there's a difference between having a feeling of clarity about your life and being able to articulate that clarity in a memorable and meaningful way.

—Chad P., 40-something

As a professional in transition, Younique provided great clarity for my next career decision. Not only did it help me to articulate my calling, it highlighted roles in my life that had been neglected.

—Liz H., 40-something

The journey of Younique has brought light to the depth of God's hand in my life—through my past as he's written my story and through a fresh vision for my future!

—Marci H., 30-something

As a seasoned believer, the greatest benefit of Younique for me was to refine my focus into accepting who I am in Christ and committing to finishing life well.

—Don C., 60-something

God has used the Younique process to enable me to see his works prepared in advance for me to do with the greatest clarity ever!

—Dan W., 50-something

The Younique toolbox helped me get clarity on where to focus my time, how to invest in relationships, and guided a big next step in my vocation.

—Travis J., 30-something

The Younique journey awakened me to the people who've influenced me. As I looked back on my experiences, a revelation emerged—now I'm the one called to influence. Younique helped me realize my gifting and how to best utilize it.

—Wisdom A., 40-something

Younique definitely awakened me. God showed me how much more there is to my life. And ministry is now much more than my weekly volunteer role at church.

—Debbie C., 60-something

Through Younique, I was able to navigate and claim my own story—both the mountains and valleys—anchored in God's story. The incredible Master Tools provided such singular clarity that I now have a filter and lens with which I can make confident decisions, sift through my yeses and nos, and boldly step into the calling that God has placed over my life.

—Brooke H., 30-something

Previously I struggled with the feeling that I have a professional calling and a personal calling, and they were constantly at odds. Younique gave me tools and strategies to look at myself and ask the Lord what I am called to do all the time and everywhere, at work and at home. I can stop trying to be someone I'm not!

—Elise B., 30-something

The beauty of Younique is that the process employs simple, successful tools to take you from surviving to thriving in a gospel-centered life design.

—Terri H., 50-something

Younique reaffirmed that God has been a part of my life the entire time—no matter when I've gotten off course, he's always been there to get me back on track. Seeing this has truly changed how I work, worship, and interact with others, including my family and marriage.

—Scott B., 40-something

I constantly felt pulled in two directions, caught between two vocational passions. Younique helped me to recognize the one-of-a-kind way God has designed me to do both, and it helped me put a plan in place to live out that calling.

—Dennis B., 50-something

Younique has given me the courage to fully step into my calling and to never settle for less than what God has intended for me. This has been the most amazing ride ever!

—Diane H., 50-something

Younique really helped me understand myself. But months later I am surprised by how much I appreciate the differences of others as well, giving me more patience in my daily interactions.

—Danica K., teenager

YOUNIQUE

WILL MANCINI

with Dave Rhodes and Cory Hartman

YOUNIQUE

Designing the Life
that God Dreamed for You

B&H
PUBLISHING
NASHVILLE, TENNESSEE

Published by B&H Publishing Group
Nashville, Tennessee

Dewey Decimal Classification: 248.84
Subject Heading: SELF / CHRISTIAN LIFE / INDIVIDUALITY /
PERSONALITY

Author photo by Shanon Bell.

2 3 4 5 6 7 8 • 24 23 22 21 20

To Poema Rose Mancini

You are God's miracle child and during the writing of this book (the first twenty months of your life), you brought me and your mother as much joy as two people can experience. Your frequent smiles and continual laughter became wind in the sails of this authorship endeavor. Your presence is an ever-present display of "the most beautiful kind of masterpiece" and my reminder that I want every person to know the poem that God penned deep in their soul.

ACKNOWLEDGMENTS

The greatest joy of all things Younique is a God-given, Olympic-quality core team.

I'm especially grateful to Younique cofounder Dave Rhodes, who is the best disciple-making thinker and toolmaker I know. He is the chief master trainer at Younique and a true friend. The whole of the Younique Life Plan is our deep collaborative work. But where his original thought, leadership, and biblical insight are showcased, I indicate with special attribution.

My collaborative writer, Cory Hartman, has been indispensable. He is a stellar thinker with a special gift for developing and expressing the key ideas of the Younique Life Plan in written form. He brought great encouragement as a friend, enthusiasm as a practitioner, and excellence as a fellow idea-artist.

As an organization, Younique would not exist without a very special person—Kelly Kannwischer. As our first and our current CEO, she is one of the best leaders I know, bringing excellence, discipline, strategic thinking, and personal sacrifice to make our organization a reality. If she was not leading, I could not be writing.

I will be forever grateful to Kandi Pfeiffer who, before Kelly, was instrumental in leading day to day in our start-up mode as Younique's executive director.

Many thanks go to the wonderfully supportive team who provided amazing coordination and thoughtful feedback. Tessy McDaniel and Stefanie Drawdy always have my back with daily workflow. And a passionate team of volunteers made the final form of this book so much better. This group includes many initial readers from our first fifty certified coaches, with special contributions from Kelly Kannwischer, Kimber Liu, Luke Francis, David Bowman, and David Loveless.

I am grateful for the team at B&H Publishing, especially the leadership of Jennifer Lyell and the editorial work of Taylor Combs.

Finally, I am grateful to my wife Romy who graciously supports me when I take the tons of time required to put ideas on paper, giving me the love and freedom to live out my Younique. (Thank you, Darling. I couldn't be me without you!)

Romy, along with my central circle, will forever be the guinea pigs of Younique tool development. Thank you, Romy, for expressing compassion; Jacob, for activating growth; Joel, for animating truth; Abby, for simplifying connection; and Poema, for giving smiles. (I can't wait to know your *real* Two Words!)

CONTENTS

Part Three: Your Identity

How to Declare Who You Are Today
Vision Frame

Part Four: Your Direction

How to Develop a Simple Plan for Tomorrow
Horizon Storyline

Part Five: Your Renewal
How to Live with Clarity Every Day
Life-Making Cycle

Part Six: Your Destiny
How to Fulfill God's Dream of You and for You
The Younique Vision Journey

The Younique Vision Journey

Clarity Spiral	Sweet Spot	Vision Frame	Horizon Storyline	Life-Making Cycle
Start the Journey and Never Stop (Part 1)	Name Your One Thing (Part 2)	Declare Who You Are Today (Part 3)	Develop a Simple Plan for Tomorrow (Part 4)	Live with Clarity Every Day (Part 5)

Figure 0.1

PREFACE

Welcome to *Younique*, a journey of learning to find your calling in life and live it out God's way—what we call gospel-centered life design.

Are you the kind of person who doesn't read a book from front to back, or who reads a book like a jungle safari, hunting here and there for answers to specific questions? If you like to jump around a bit, I have good news for you. Below are some focused reading plans centered on different aspects of your special calling from God.

If the twenty-seven chapters of this book make up a full-course meal, think of this as your healthy snacker's guide.

The Case for Personal Calling: The reasons I'm convinced that knowing and naming your special call from God is wildly important:

- Chapter 1: Backstory
- Chapter 2: You
- Chapter 8: Bull's-Eye
- Chapter 26: Destiny

The Essentials: The absolute, bare-minimum, rock-bottom tools and practices:

- Chapter 8: Bull's-Eye
- Chapter 10: Mission
- Chapter 17: Ninety Days from Now
- Chapter 22: Sabbath

What Makes You, You: Revealing tools to help you look in the mirror, see who you are, and put it into words:

- Chapter 5: Passion
- Chapter 6: Ability

- Chapter 7: Context
- Chapter 8: Bull's-Eye
- Chapter 10: Mission
- Chapter 11: Values

Dream Bigger: A mega-encouraging jolt to your imagination to run wild with the possibilities of what your life can be:

- Chapter 2: You
- Chapter 14: Dream
- Chapter 15: Three Years from Now
- Chapter 25: Bucket List
- Chapter 26: Destiny

Execute Better: Best practices for taming your time and putting it to work toward your goals:

- Chapter 13: Strategy
- Chapter 17: Ninety Days from Now
- Chapter 18: Now
- Chapter 20: Calendar
- Chapter 21: Energy
- Chapter 22: Sabbath
- Chapter 23: Priority

Thrive in Your 9-to-5: The knowledge anyone can gain and the steps anyone can take to love their job more every year:

- Chapter 3: Climb
- Chapter 6: Ability
- Chapter 7: Context
- Free bonus content: *Clarity Spiral: The 4 Break-Thru Practices to Find the One Thing You're Called to Do*, an e-book available at WillMancini.com/clarityspiral

Barriers and Pitfalls: The most common obstacles that prevent people from designing and living out the life God dreamed for them:

- Introduction: Difference
- Chapter 3: Climb
- Chapter 4: Break-Thru

- Chapter 20: Calendar
- Chapter 22: Sabbath

General Calling: *Younique* is about your unique, individual calling from God. But I've still packed in some serious substance about the universal calling that God has issued to all believers:

- Chapter 3: Climb
- Chapter 5: Passion
- Chapter 12: Measures
- Chapter 14: Dream
- Chapter 27: Death

DIFFERENCE

The Two Missing Ingredients in
Most Intentional Living Books

*"To achieve success in any art the artist must know his tools and for what
purposes they are designed. Furthermore, to achieve the highest success, he
must know what he cannot do as well as what he can do with them."*

—Brett Page

This book is all about a journey I'm inviting you to take—the journey to know, name, and live out your personal calling. I myself am still walking this journey; I haven't arrived yet. As I'll explain in part 1, I will be making this trek for the rest of my life. We all will. Yet I wrote this book now, incomplete though I am, because the ideas in it have dramatically changed the trajectory of my life, and I simply couldn't keep my learning to myself any longer.

Along my journey I've devoured every book I could get my hands on that purported to teach me how to live with more clarity, focus, and impact. I learned much from these books that I want to share with you, but I also stumbled into gaps that I longed to close. Above all, I discovered that there are tons of books about the gospel and there are countless books about how to live your life. But I dare you to find more than a few on gospel-centered life design! That's what I wrote *Younique* to be.

This book wants to deliver something that's missing. Admittedly, that's hard to do when the library of "intentional living" books could fill the solar system. Yet in the virtual ocean of books on personal purpose and fulfilling your dreams, I have charted a trip for uninhabited land.

As you will learn in this book, it is fantastically freeing to have clarity not only about what to do but also about what *not* to do. So at the start, let's cover what this book is not:

1. *Younique* **is not about growing your relationship with God.** For that, I could recommend a truckload of books, starting with J. I. Packer's classic *Knowing God.*

2. *Younique* **is not about biblical principles taken from characters of the Bible.** If you want amazing stuff on Nehemiah, then Visioneering, by Andy Stanley, is hard to beat.[1]

3. *Younique* **is not a sequence of stories, quotes, and Bible verses to pump you up.** For inspiration, pick up *Soulprint*, by Mark Batterson.[2]

4. *Younique* **is not a workbook to grow in one area of your life.** To be taught about your talents, grab *StrengthsFinder 2.0*.[3]

5. *Younique* **does not use the term "purpose" or "vision" in a general way—** that is, defining the common call of God to all people. That topic is covered in brilliant books like Rick Warren's *The Purpose Driven Life*.[4]

6. Finally, *Younique* **is not a theology of guidance.** For great biblical material I recommend Ramesh Richard's *Soul Vision*.[5]

While these books bring basketfuls of blessing, my job is to show you the missing fruit. The truths that books in the purposeful-life category teach rarely make a lasting difference in people's lives because the books lack two essential ingredients that *Younique* provides:

1. *Younique* **starts with special calling, not common calling.** I'm not going to let you get stuck in the "unoriginal sin" of neglecting your uniqueness. You have a one-of-a-kind calling that will be our focus.

2. *Younique* **provides a real pathway to walk on so you're not just walking around.** Good intentions have a way of evaporating by the time you're ten feet away from your favorite reading nook. (I know that's true for me.) So we'll lay the stepping stones to get you somewhere new in your life.

Let's consider these two distinctive features a bit more.

Special Calling versus Common Calling

While Christian books on purpose readily acknowledge that every person is unique, over 95 percent of the content is aimed at the common call of discipleship. This is understandable. Most of the authors are pastors who are helping diverse people access the general invitation to follow Jesus. They are dealing with themes of salvation and sanctification (that is, how to grow in holiness and walk with God). They are opening up God's world and God's Word and encouraging people toward character development. But at the end of the day, very little content is aimed toward uncovering and applying your uniqueness.

You may be surprised to know that 50 percent of your DNA is the same as a banana's. That's right—all living things share a huge amount of DNA. Believe it or not, a chimpanzee shares 96 percent of its life code with you and me. But what about two random human beings? The difference of identity between any two people in the world is found in less than 1 percent of their DNA. Yet embedded in that 1 percent is jaw-dropping potential for different personalities, beautiful relationships, and bountiful dreams. That 1 percent, together with the peculiar combination of finely detailed surroundings that only you have ever experienced, ushers in the meaning of being uniquely you. This book is a 1-percent book. And that 1 percent changes everything.

A Pathway to Walk On versus Just Walking Around

While many books offer reflection questions at the end of chapters, most books about intentional living offer no real "how-to's." If they do they are usually disconnected exercises with no pathway or system that leads you somewhere specific. They don't include tools, process steps, assessments, integrated questions, or compatible coaching experiences.

In addition, there are few, if any, life examples. There are always plenty of life *stories*, but that is not the same as specific examples of a life-planning exercise or a life-design deliverable. For instance, it's not uncommon for a Christian author to talk about the importance of life values without illustrating any. In fact, if you were to read a hundred books on life mission, you'd be lucky to find five where the author actually shares his or her own life mission!

Why is this the case? The answer is simple. These writers, many of whom happen to be pastors, do not spend their days trying to help others work through the process of life design. It's not their fault. It's just not their specialty and not what most of them do day to day, which is largely consumed with preparing to preach and teach, managing the programmatic ministry of a church, and caring for people as they walk through the struggles of life.

Younique does much more than sprinkle a few questions at the end of each chapter. This book will guide you through an entire set of tools and experiences to utilize on life's journey. In fact, I have named the transforming trip that I want you to take the Younique Life Plan Journey (or, "The Journey" for short). Page xvi shows the five movements of The Journey, each represented by a single master tool. Think of these as the signposts of your personal vision adventure! The first five parts of this book will each cover one master tool in sequential fashion. The sixth part returns to the overall arc of your life's impact with closing teaching and insight on achieving your destiny.

As you read the book, the Younique team has created free resources to get going on The Younique Life Plan (LifeYounique.com/starterkit) and online courses to give you additional coaching on specific topics (LifeYounique.com/courses). That means I am giving you something to do, not just to read. The Starter Kit includes the Life Discovery Grid tool covered in chapter 5—the launching pad for The Journey. If you want to engage an experience with a small group or larger discipleship class, we've created the *Younique 6-Week Primer*; find it at LifeYounique.com/primer.

Finally, this book reflects an actual coaching experience that you can pursue in any of three ways. The first is a four-day accelerator in cities near you. The second way enables people to attend from anywhere in the world. We call it a "virtual cohort" consisting of five to eight people who meet online weekly over twenty-four weeks. Finally, you can work with a certified coach for a one-on-one retreat that usually lasts two days. (Learn more about these options at LifeYounique.com.)

Our biggest dream, however, is for your local church to become the main provider of the Younique Life Plan. We can picture every church attender enjoying the Younique Life Plan Journey with local leaders they know and trust. Our vision is to see life planning and life design as a regular part of what the local church offers. The goal is not just to slot people into a volunteer position for an hour a week but to slingshot them into their life calling every moment of every day.

The Art of Break-thru

Younique's two distinctives—its total focus on your special calling and its proven pathway for real progress—add up to break-thru: a new, accessible point of view that powerfully changes the trajectory of your life.

As we grow as a life designer, we will find inspiration from many others. But as we do, we must beware of "voices from the balcony." These voices call out, "You are special!" and "Find your purpose!" and "Discover your destiny!" Then we spend time daydreaming about how good that balcony must be. We take pictures of people smiling in the balcony. We listen to podcasts from people enjoying the balcony. We go from one inspirational "balcony moment" to the next, buying another book from a "balcony author." We even tell our friends how wonderful it looks up there in the balcony.

But there is one problem: none of this inspiration alone will actually take you to the balcony.

The screaming need today is not for more voices from the balcony, but for someone to show you the staircase. You need ladder-makers and escalators. You need people throwing you ropes, not false hopes. You need access points to the upper level. Unfortunately, inspirational glimpses into next-level living don't take you there; only steps do.

That's where I come in. The book you're holding is the staircase. Many are climbing it; now it's your turn!

> Inspirational glimpses into next-level living don't take you there; only steps do.

Top Ten Panel: 10 Things to Anticipate Because *Younique* Is Distinct

1. *Younique* **offers a bird's-eye view of life design.** The book is made up of many short chapters that link together to provide a panoramic snapshot of life vision and personal calling.

2. *Younique* **offers a God's-eye view of life design.** Its simple yet comprehensive approach to designing your life is centered in the gospel. It takes seriously the beautiful biblical paradox that God is sovereignly shaping your life according to his dream for you *and* that he designed you to design it with him.

3. *Younique* **is both a full-course meal and a tasty snack.** Either way it will nourish your life. Read it straight through, all the way through, or pick and choose one chapter that motivates you today. Each part of the book will stand alone as snackable treats, and you can go back to the preface at any time to review the healthy snacker's guide.

4. *Younique* **gets you unstuck and driving again.** Sometimes we need a tune-up and sometimes we need a tow truck. You will find easy diagnostic tools and a helpful mechanic standing by as you look under life's hood. Before you're finished, you will probably fall in love with the feeling of the road again.

5. *Younique* puts the frame around the jigsaw puzzle pieces. The "intentional life" genre throws a lot of stuff at you because there's complexity to being human and figuring out how to live. This book gives you clear and helpful categories that simplify the complexity. For example, what's the difference between having a core value (an identity thing) and setting a goal (a direction thing)? This book will clarify how far to think into the future, keep you from trying to do too much this week, and provide many more practical principles.

6. *Younique* slingshots you into your life's next chapter. Are you a millennial needing a break-thru at work, or a sixty-something seeking convergence for the next decade? This book will help you discern what God has been preparing you to do next. And God is always preparing you for something next!

7. *Younique* gives you laser-beam focus. A typical flashlight might shine twenty feet away, but a penlight laser can shine to the moon. This book will show you how finding your "one thing" is one of the most neglected disciplines of personal clarity. You don't need another list of "can do's." You need to know the one thing you "must do" for God—what we call your LifeCall.

8. *Younique*'s got groove. I have included a playlist of songs for a read-along experience on Spotify and Apple Music. Go to WillMancini.com/playlist to catch the backstory. (Warning: It's mostly '70s and '80s classic rock.)

9. *Younique* is more fun to share than popcorn. Each part of the book comes with visual "master tools" for two reasons. First, since we are all visual thinkers, creating a picture of our big concepts makes them easier to understand. Second, I want you to have a blast sharing your break-thrus. The drawings give you an excuse to turn a napkin or whiteboard or party hat into a mini-session on life. You'll be surprised how much fun it is to draw your Younique Life Plan for your friends.

10. *Younique* is more than a book. It's a toolbox used by thousands of people in local churches everywhere. And it's a community of passionate life designers you could run into anywhere.

PART ONE

YOUR JOURNEY
How to Start the Journey and Never Stop

CLARITY
SPIRAL

"Grace brings man a task, opens up for him a field of activity, bestows upon him the joy of accomplishment, so that he can identify himself with his mission and discover in it the true meaning of his existence. Grace gives man a center of gravity that, like a magnet, draws all the forces of his nature into a clear and definite pattern that is neither foreign nor cumbersome to the patterns already formed in his nature, but engages them, like idle laborers, in a task that is both pleasant and rewarding. . . . For man's mission in life is not something general and impersonal like a ready-made coat; it has been designed specifically for him and given into his possession as the most personal of all gifts. By it he becomes, in the fullest sense of the word, a person."

—Hans Urs von Balthasar

Once upon a time—but not that long ago—ordinary Americans wore suits and dresses whenever they went out in public. Today we live in a drastically more casual age, especially as to our clothing. As a society, we place a higher premium on feeling good than looking good.

It's interesting that we tend to view feeling good and looking good as a one-or-the-other trade-off. Maybe it stems from childhood memories of having to dress up for church or for a family portrait. Formal clothes for kids are ill-fitting, itchy, uncomfortable, inflexible, and worst of all, your mom won't let you run around and play in them!

But as an adult, were you ever fitted for a suit or dress that was perfectly tailored to your body's exact shape and size? When the measurements are just right, clothes feel fantastic. They don't feel like a child's polyester semi-straitjacket; they feel like pajamas. Yet when you wear them you look like a million bucks! Why? Because those dazzling clothes are *made for you.*

Nevertheless, when you stepped up to the tailor to be measured for your one-of-a-kind outfit, she probably didn't eye you up and down with pursed lips and then say, "Well, I'm going to have to invent an entirely new tailoring technique for you." That would be odd and even ridiculous. Every customer has different measurements, but the method of tailoring remains the same.

The same can be said of life design. God dreamed an entirely unique life for each one of us. However, the fundamentals of how to discover and design that unique life—the perfect-fitting suit—remain consistent from person to person.

The Younique Life Plan is built on that principle, and we're going to explore its dimensions especially broadly in part 1.

To begin, I'm going to share with you my own personal story of how and why the quest for personal calling became so important to me. Then I'm going to pivot to why it's so important to God and why it should be so important to *you*.

In chapter 3 we're going to explore the first of the Younique master tools, the Clarity Spiral. It contains four essential steps that everyone must learn to practice through their whole life to keep climbing up the mountain of personal clarity. Finally, I'm going to let you in on the missing link whose absence explains why so many people who take the journey of self-discovery don't get anywhere with what they've learned. (Spoiler alert: *Younique* has it.)

Ready to start? Let's learn the universal truths of finding your special calling.

Chapter 1

BACKSTORY

A Terrible Way to Learn the Incredible Value of Personal Calling

"Calling is the truth that God calls us to himself so decisively that everything we are, everything we do, and everything we have is invested with a special devotion, dynamism, and direction lived out as a response to his summons and service."

—Os Guinness

Welcome to your guidebook for gospel-centered life-design.[1] This book is about taking in the breathtaking vistas of audacious dreams. But I want to start at an unexpected place—the dark and narrow gorge of my life's greatest failure. After all, we all have high points and hard times on the journey.

One of my hardest was the first Christmas after the unraveling of my decade-long marriage. I was thirty-three years old with three kids—Jacob, Joel, and Abby—who were nine, six, and three respectively. I moved out of my home and rented a two-bedroom apartment for the four of us. The second bedroom was really more of a big closet where the kids slept during their 50-percent time with Dad. All three kids managed to fit into a bargain bunkbed—the kind made with flimsy, white metal tubing.

While walking this deep valley with my bewildered kids, the Christmas season heralded a "different kind of holiday" for my now-broken family. But I still wanted to make it memorable, so I started from scratch with decorations for the apartment. Sadly, my bank account was as empty as a Christmas tree bulb.

I found an artificial tree at Walmart with cool fiber-optic lights. The clearance section price was appealing, but I noticed that after five minutes of glittering fun, the high-tech tannenbaum would overheat and shut off. I convinced myself that it was no big deal: the kids could just blow on it until it cooled down and then hit the little reset switch.

I can still see the cash register that day ringing up the $72.56 price tag for the additional holiday paraphernalia. *Another purchase that I don't have the money for*, I thought, swiping the credit card with one hand and brushing the tears off my cheek with the other so my kids wouldn't see. I think they had a decent Christmas that year, but I had never felt more lonely. I'm sure I devoured plenty of sweet holiday treats, but the taste I remember most is failure.

You and I have both experienced different levels of failure. But why would I start a book on personal vision with a snapshot from a deep valley of personal pain?

First, I want to testify to God's goodness. Although people let us down, the Lord has a knack for sticking around. He is always faithful, and a book on how to design your life would be a waste of time if I didn't start and end by giving all glory to him.

Second, I am so optimistic about your life's call—even though we've never met—that as this book goes on you will be tempted to think I am a pie-in-the-sky guy. I want to blow your mind with your own potential, the capabilities you've not tuned into yet, but I can assure you that I don't have rose-colored glasses strapped to my face. I'm not afraid to call out unfounded optimism. Unlike many writers and speakers in this category, I use words like *dream* and *destiny* with precision; I approach life design as an engineer—my profession before entering ministry—not as an ice cream man.

But third and most urgently, I don't want you to have to go through what I went through to learn what I learned about the power of your life's call.

How the Lesson of Calling Changed Me Forever

Before my deep valley experience, I was an ordained pastor enjoying ministry in a rapidly growing church. You could say I was a "called" man, but I was not living from "calling." How do I know? Looking back, I see a man who always had something to prove and something to lose.

I maneuvered people to make things happen. I sought the visible and vocal affirmation of the people I taught. I grew jealous when coworkers thrived. Something is driving our vocational motivations. For me it was *not* a deepening awareness of my special assignment from God. It was a soul drift that sought approval and used a local church ministry context to find it.

I like the definition of "idol" that goes, "the thing you add to Jesus to make life work." Of course, the very nature of idolatry makes it hard to spot. Before my marital crisis, I didn't see my idolatry problem. I didn't know how heavily I was relying on being an all-American guy with a beautiful wife and picture-perfect kids as an up-and-coming pastor to make *my* life work.

> Looking back, I see a man who always had something to prove and something to lose.

But failure is an effective teacher. And the classroom of life's challenge schooled me in two ways.

First, the failure deepened my emotional connection to the gospel. I needed to know the person Jesus beyond the Sunday school categories and seminary-speak. "Savior and Lord" he had been. "Alpha and Omega" I had preached. But he would become more—a Friend. A delightful kind of friend who profoundly *liked* me and wanted to be *with* me just as he *made* me. Jesus came through—he stayed close to me and his love grew even sweeter.

Second, the failure challenged me to pursue what he put me on earth to do. Now that I was more secure as a human *being* and not just a human *doing*, I was free to find my calling. I was now prepared to get the *doing* part of life right. After all, God does makes humans to *do*; he commissioned us from the beginning to be fruitful, to multiply, to fill, to rule, to name, to serve, to generate life. I was ready to grab hold of that "commissioned sensibility." Some days, the raw, dry hope that God had made me to do *something*—even though it wasn't totally clear yet—was the only thing that got me out of bed in the morning.

Today I can testify to the awesome power of life calling. Despite a chapter in my life that included a subplot I didn't choose—bringing hurt, failure, and shame—the unfolding story of my life was being written. How so? It was being guided by God's dream for my life from before time. Yet at the same time, it was also being shaped by my proactive design. Each day through the mountains and valleys and even from the pit, a calling from God was present. The calling always starts with his initiative, as he alone is Maker and Caller; he alone is the ultimate Guide. Yet, that call moves from response to response and from grace to grace until it is known truly.

Eventually, if we pursue it, the reason that God put us on earth works its way into our life each day. For me, that calling over time became clear, specific, and articulated. It rooted me in very practical ways. It yielded a wonderful variety of fruit marking my life with optimism, hope, and vision. It grew *out of* disciplined self-awareness and *into* vocational risk-taking. It became vastly more precious to me than any artificial, manu-factured image, including the one I had lost. My calling strengthened my identity, cultivated my confidence, powered my passion, and directed my dreaming. It kept me going and it kept me growing even through one of my deepest valleys.

That was then. Now add fifteen years.

Each month gets better as a calling-conscious follower of Jesus. Today I live out my one life call through six different vocational "vehicles." I enjoy the autonomy, mastery, and euphoria of working in my sweet spot almost every minute of my day. I have a beautiful, supportive wife and four amazing children. Although I'm occasionally distracted by material things, I can honestly say that after my first job decision at twenty-one, I've never made a vocational decision based primarily on money. Yet I have earned more than I ever planned for or even imagined.

Top Ten Panel: Why You Should Keep Reading Because of My Backstory

1. I read practically everything else in the category so you don't have to, and I'll give you the most important of the most important stuff.

2. I've lived the principles of this book with dramatic failure and pretty decent success. I won't hold back in revealing those stories; I want to maximize your benefit.

3. I don't just like break-thru—I am fanatical about it. I am a freak about it. If something promises to make a difference and doesn't, I detest it. I am only interested in the stuff that leads to a lasting trajectory change.

4. I have personally walked with hundreds of teams and thousands of leaders through a break-thru process face-to-face, every week for fifteen years. I didn't write this book for superstar leaders, but for the "rest of us."

5. In addition to my love of God and clarity, I love adventure sports, Mexican food, traveling, '70s music, and of course, my family. These may influence my writing without me knowing it.

6. I have a secret: I'm not that disciplined and I keep people fooled. I really don't do hard work, I do focused work. I'll show you how to do focused work too.

7. I'll show you how to "arrive" with your Younique Life Plan. Very, very few people who write on this subject actually give you a blueprint. I'll give you something that you can actually design your life with.

8. I'm not rehashing the *basics* of spiritual life or discipleship or maturity in Christ. I assume you're already oriented in these topics, and if not, you have literally a thousand books in that category to every one like *Younique*.

9. I have a secret weapon that changes everything. I call it "singularity with specificity." It's the portal to maximum meaning and profound progress in your life.

10. If you actually read this book and convince me in an email, I'll meet you for breakfast, lunch, or dinner to talk about your "One Thing." You're buying.

Four Ways to Live

The benefits of living from a "Called Self" are enormous. But keep in mind that there is another way to live: living from a "False Self." As we'll see later, there are many influences that lead us away from being the persons God made us to be. In truth, it's easier to live from a False Self, but it doesn't *feel* easier. It comes naturally to live from a False Self, but it doesn't *feel* natural. When we're not living from our Called Self, we know deep down that something isn't right—we know there's something more for us.

Given the slice of strife in my own backstory I want to speak hope into who you are today and where you are today. That's because the life calling that I discovered in and through my successes and failures is to make a life of more meaningful progress more accessible to every believer. God put me on earth to honor him and serve others by "applying essence"—articulating what a person, team, or organization is made for at its core and putting that "One Thing" into action. You can think of this book as a manual for applying the essence of you: your Called Self, your Life Younique.

> The life calling that I discovered is to make a life of more meaningful progress more accessible to every believer.

You *can* discover the dream God has for *you*. And you can proactively design a powerful life; one that releases all of the potential God put inside of you.

You have too much talent to settle for a False Self. You can seize the substance of who God made you to be.

The world is too broken to live from a False Self. You can bring amazing value to the people around you.

Life is too enjoyable to endure a False Self. You can experience more meaning and blessing every day.

In the pages ahead, I'll show you how.

Chapter 2

YOU

Why We Should All Stop Trying to Be Just like Jesus

"Every person born into this world represents something new, something that never existed before, something original and unique. . . . Every man's foremost task is the actualization of his unique, unprecedented and never-recurring potentialities, and not the repetition of something that another, and be it even the greatest, has already achieved."

—Martin Buber

Let me tell you about a Scripture passage that changed my life. Twice.

Ephesians 2 begins with solemn tones of doom that ought to make any sensible person shudder:

> And you were dead in your trespasses and sins in which you previously lived according to the ways of this world, according to the ruler of the power of the air, the spirit now working in the disobedient. We too all previously lived among them in our fleshly desires, carrying out the inclinations of our flesh and thoughts, and we were by nature children under wrath as the others were also. (vv. 1–3)

After this terrible news for all of us comes magnificent news—the ringing tones of the gospel:

But God, who is rich in mercy, because of his great love that he had for us, made us alive with Christ even though we were dead in trespasses. You are saved by grace! He also raised us up with him and seated us with him in the heavens in Christ Jesus, so that in the coming ages he might display the immeasurable riches of his grace through his kindness to us in Christ Jesus. For you are saved by grace through faith, and this is not from yourselves; it is God's gift—not from works, so that no one can boast. (vv. 4–9)

The truth of this Scripture changed my life because the truth it contains changed my life. Ephesians 2:1–9 is a majestic description of the story of God and the human race. It is a story of general calling, the sweeping invitation to salvation and eternal life issued to all people on the face of the earth.

Yet the following verse is just as awe-inspiring, but in a strikingly different sense: "For we are his workmanship, created in Christ Jesus for good works, which God prepared ahead of time for us to do" (v. 10).

Now, you can look at this verse and see it as an extension of general calling as well. After all, God did make all of us. And in one sense he created all of us to do the same good works: to love him and to love our neighbor, to glorify him and to make disciples. It's not complicated.

But let's look again at that word *workmanship*—a word that makes all the difference in the world.

"Workmanship" is a translation of the Greek word *poíema*, from which we get the English word poem. A *poíema* is something made, something crafted, even a work of art. God is the Maker. My question to you is, "Are you ready for that conversation?" Few people are. I wrote this book to address this problem: *even though each believer has a special calling from God, the vast majority never name it and so miss a huge opportunity to make a more meaningful contribution with their entire life.*

The weight of evidence is that he does not. A bit of travel reveals that no landscape on this planet is quite like the rest. A look into the heavens reveals that no planet or moon is like the others either. And most important, a quick glance at every person you've ever met reveals that no two people are alike—not even close.

God doesn't make generic art. He crafts each individual as one of a kind, utterly and irreducibly unique.

So let's look at Ephesians 2:10 again in this light. If each of us is God's one-of-a-kind handiwork, then isn't each of us created in Christ Jesus to do *one-of-a-kind good works?*

To me, the conclusion is inescapable. God prepared in advance—before he even made the world!—specific good things that you, and only you, can do. *No one else.*

This earth-shaking truth changed my life a second time. I came to realize that God sent his One and Only Son to die on the cross to put me in the position to do something that he made only me to do. I cannot overstate or overestimate how invested God is in my special calling; he gave everything for it! So if it matters that much to God to make me for a specific contribution in his kingdom, I had better get on the ball with living it out.

Ephesians 2:10 taught me that God had a dream for me before I was even born, and no matter how badly I was lost, he would do anything to make that dream come true. And God did the very same thing for you.

Preparing for Your First Face-to-Face with God

Imagine that super-duper selfie that God saw in his mind's eye when he thought you up in his image and likeness. How are you progressing toward that God-inspired version of yourself?

Let's imagine it from heaven's point of view when your life on earth is finished. When you stand before God far above the stratosphere someday, what do you think he will ask you? How will your life be measured?

He might ask the question, "Why weren't you more like Jesus?" That would certainly be good biblical question. After all, the apostle Paul did write, "Imitate me, as I also imitate Christ" (1 Cor. 11:1).

But what if God were to ask a different question. What if he asked, "Why weren't you more like *you*?"

This book is written to prepare you for *the latter* question. And it's a wonderful question. It's just as playful as it is profound. Have you ever given yourself permission to ponder this idea?

Every part of you was made by God according to very detailed specifications. So you better believe he's going take your one-of-kind design into consideration in that first meet-up. If you planned a special dinner party for out-of town friends, would you spend time talking about it when it was over? Of course you would. So then, imagine that God has prepared your entire life. He designed you for a special assignment. He dreamed up your every day. He set into motion your every notion. Don't you think he is going to want to talk about *you*?

Remember, he is the God who taught us to call him Father, the one to whom David reflected, "I will praise you because I have been remarkably and wondrously made. . . . Your eyes saw me when I was formless; all my days were written in your book and planned before a single one of them began" (Ps. 139:14, 16). David's own life is a telling example of this. A thousand years after he died, Paul was making the case that David's psalms foretold a Messiah to come who would rise from the dead. Along the way, Paul made a comment pregnant with significance: "For David, after serving God's purpose in his own generation . . ." (Acts 13:36). The remark sounds almost offhand, but the Holy Spirit doesn't put anything in Scripture by accident. It points to a deep truth that David exemplifies—that God has a purpose for each of us to serve in our own generation. God will someday talk to you about the special assignment for which he made you.

No Cloning in Heaven or Earth

Younique is not a book about "What would Jesus do?" (WWJD). We need to upgrade our four-letter acronym. We are going to get a little more specific in these pages and ask, "How would Jesus live if he were you?" (HWJL).[1] How would Jesus live if he:

- worked at your job?
- sat next to your classmates?
- drove your car?
- married your spouse?
- put on your pair of pants in the morning?
- invested your money?
- disciplined your kids?
- spent time at your hobby?

Scripture clearly teaches that God is shaping us into the image of Christ. "For those whom he foreknew he also predestined to be conformed to the image of his Son" (Rom. 8:29). But that doesn't mean God wants you to train as a carpenter, preach in temples, and die on a cross. That call of Jesus is the life of an unprecedented and never-recurring human being. Likewise, you were born an original, not a carbon copy.

So how are we being conformed to the image of Christ without becoming a carpenter-savior clone? When we become more like Jesus, the process of transformation does not reduce our personality but redeems it. It does not box the real you in but unlocks you out. To become Christlike is not to be forced into some prefabbed mold of perfection. Rather, it's the life of Jesus—the only perfect human—working in and through your story, working out and through your gifting. "I am sure of this, that he who started a good work in you will carry it on to completion until the day of Christ Jesus" (Phil. 1:6).

Eugene Peterson spikes the ball on this very point when he writes:

In the life of faith each person discovers all the elements of a unique and original adventure. We are prevented from following in one another's footsteps and are called to an incomparable association with Christ. The Bible makes it clear that every time there is a story of faith, it is completely original. God's creative genius is endless. He never, fatigued and unable to maintain the rigors of creativity, resorts to mass-producing copies.[2]

To put it another way, heaven's yearbook isn't thousands of pictures of Jesus. It's thousands of pictures of real saints—redheads and brunettes, introverts and extroverts. One day in the future, Paul writes, "In a moment, in the twinkling of an eye, at the last trumpet . . . the dead will be raised incorruptible, and we will be changed. For this corruptible body must be clothed with incorruptibility, and this mortal body must be clothed with immortality" (1 Cor. 15:52–53). In that glorious moment, at the dawn of your immortality, you retain your identity. You don't lose it. Or maybe we should say you regain your glorious identity, becoming the finest version of you, a sin-free self, in the undiluted presence of God.

How are you doing with this mind-blowing reality of your one-of-a-kind personality? I find that Christians struggle with this point. It sounds too good to be true. We don't give ourselves permission to like ourselves that much. We don't imagine that God is so good that we actually get to become more like ourselves as we become more like Christ. Do you believe that your uniqueness is not lost in holiness but illuminated by it all the more?

Consider the snowflake as a case study. Imagine the infinite amount of random ice crystals blowing in one winter storm on one winter day in just one northern city. Now multiply that across every city and every snowstorm on every winter day since creation. Did you know that no two snowflakes that fall on earth are exactly alike? No two "cells" in Frosty's frozen figure are precisely the same. That's right. Slide any microscopic flake under a microscope and you will discover a never-repeated, intricately beautiful, crystalline pattern.

As every snowflake is formed, its micro-climate impacts its development. Endlessly swirling, each snowflake is built in the clouds by crystal chemistry and unique forces: turbulent winds, fluctuating temperatures, shifting altitudes, and colliding dust particles.

And so are you. As each human being is formed, the micro-context impacts his or her development. Carefully woven in the womb, each baby lands in a new home with a turbulent heritage, fluctuating parents, shifting influences, and colliding emotions. God is the author of your story, storms included.

Thirteen years after Thomas Merton began pursuing a monastic life as a Trappist monk in Kentucky, an old friend visited who knew of his life before his dramatic vocational change. The friend was surprised that Merton's personality hadn't changed that much. Finally he commented, laughing, "Tom, you haven't changed at all!"

"Why should I?" Merton replied. "Here our duty is to be more ourselves, not less."[3]

There Is Only One You

You are created by God the Father with a one-of-a-kind assignment. You are redeemed by God through the death, burial, and resurrection of Jesus Christ. You are filled by God with the Holy Spirit. That means you are empowered to grow in the resemblance of God's family. And just as with sons and daughters, you see hints of Dad's attributes in his children, not a mirror image. Being washed in the blood of Jesus doesn't change the color of your eyes. Jesus-followers are not Jesus-photocopies.

The fruit of the Spirit grows on every kind of tree—males and females, short and tall, artists and accountants. The characteristics of godliness, by God's grace, are continually being worked out in all believers. The Spirit of God is growing more patient plumbers *and* pilots. God the Father wants more joyful jockeys *and* janitors. Jesus today is making more kind cosmetologists *and* cardiologists.

While believers everywhere are growing up to be more like our Savior-Leader Jesus, there is still only one you. Your greatest opportunity in the Holy Spirit's transforming work is to become your true self, to be a powerfully productive disciple in your particular way. So we never stop asking, "How would Jesus live if he were you?"

Chapter 3

CLIMB

How the Worst Meeting with My Boss
Became the Best Day for My Career

"Life is either a daring adventure or it is nothing at all."
—Helen Keller

Have you ever hiked up a steep mountain? You can't sprint in a straight line to the summit. You have to take a more indirect approach, walking by switchbacks or spiraling up until you reach the peak. The hike is longer that way, but it is less steep and more accessible.

When you picture the Clarity Spiral, that's what I want you to capture in your mind's eye: a journey up your own personal Everest. Grasping your "One Thing"—your unique assignment from God—is not something you can do immediately or directly. It takes years of spiraling—hiking slowly up the mountain of your life. At every turn around the mountain you see the same features on the landscape of your life, but you see them from a different altitude. Your perspective stretches wider the higher you climb.

And here's a hint: as long as you are breathing there is always more perspective. That's why I encourage you to start and *never stop* discovering your personal vision. While I have enjoyed fantastic views on the way up my personal Everest, there is still a lot I can't see. And I can't wait to learn what's next. I like the way Maria Popova captured this idea when she said that life is a continual process of arrival into who we are.

But making the climb isn't automatic. To reach the summit, you have to attend to four steps that guide the work of life design. These are essential. Leave one behind and the journey stops. Without a commitment to these four imperatives, every life planning tool under the sun is a waste of time. But build them into your life and you will discover the daring adventure of living your special assignment from God.[1]

Most of all, keep in mind that these essential steps are the continual on-ramps to your life design journey. We must never lose the sense of journey. As Os Guinness proclaims, "Journeying is the most apt metaphor for human life itself . . . the human odyssey at its highest is life with a quest for purpose, meaning, destination, and home."[2]

Step 1: Courage to Know

I had finally completed my second four-year degree, a master of theology in pastoral leadership, and I was hungry to get started in a full-time ministry position in a church. By that, I meant "preach," but I knew I had to "pay my dues" to earn the right to pulpit time. So I was ready to endure ministry grunt-work on the way to fulfilling my dream of becoming a legendary communicator.

There was no doubt I was going to be the next John Ortberg, by the way. If you don't know that name, he was the teaching pastor at America's largest church during my seminary days—Willow Creek Community Church in Greater Chicago. He preached like a sage on stage. His eloquence flowed with casual and relatable ease and the perfect dash of humor. It was *obviously* just my style.

So as seminary was winding up, I looked only for pastoral positions in churches that religiously followed the Willow Creek way of "doing church." Clear Creek Community Church in Greater Houston fit the bill perfectly. Unfortunately for my tastes, the only position that Senior Pastor Bruce Wesley had open was children's pastor. *I did NOT torture myself learning Greek and Hebrew for this*, I thought. But I saw the role as my path to the platform, so I took the job.

The good news was that Clear Creek was growing by leaps and bounds and would be hiring a teaching pastor soon. I vividly remember the day that Bruce was going to promote me to John Ortberg—I mean, Teaching Pastor. I strolled into his office and took my seat, eager for my job review. After ten minutes of small talk, Bruce dropped a bomb. "We are going to look *outside* the church to hire a teaching pastor," he revealed.

Shock. Disbelief. Betrayal.

Clearly Bruce had failed to consider God's plan for my life. While my face revealed utter disappointment, my mind was rehearsing my immediate resignation. I was ready to pack my entire life into a U-Haul and abandon Bruce and everyone else at Clear Creek Community Church.

But I didn't. Little did I know it would become the best day of my career, because I learned the importance of a new kind of courage—the courage to know myself.

It's a logical place to begin, is it not? The problem is that most people are not fully aware of their greatest abilities and deepest passions. When it comes to our limitations, we prefer blind spots to brutal facts. When it comes to our strengths, we position the abilities we like over the strengths we live. Ben Franklin once said there are three hard things: diamonds, steel, and knowing oneself.[3] Physicist Richard Feynman wrote, "The first principle is that you must not fool yourself, and you are the easiest person to fool."[4]

Many kinds of distractions make it easy for us to fool ourselves and keep us from grasping our True Self. First there's the *expectation of others*, or "the Me Others Want Me to Be." From birth, people praise us for doing some things and disapprove of us for doing others. Our self-awareness can be hopelessly and undetectably obscured by deep layers of people-pleasing.

Then there's the *imitation of success*, or "the Me That's Sexiest to See." Every field of human endeavor has its rock stars and its assumed metrics of achievement. When we think we're looking in the mirror of self-awareness, we might be looking out the window at a statue on a pedestal.

Third is the *captivation of money*, or "the Me I'm Paid to Be." Some people convince themselves that they are made to do certain work because they can make a lot of money doing it. Others don't care about the size of the paycheck but demand that it be steady. Self-awareness becomes masked by the allure of gain or fear of loss.

A fourth distraction is the *preoccupation with busyness*, or "the Me I'm Too Busy Not to Be." On the assumption that more is better or that the world will collapse if we don't hold it up, we pack our lives and race from one thing to the next without time to reflect on what we ought to be doing. Self-awareness is crushed under the load of opportunities and responsibilities.

Last but not least is the *projection of self*. While all of the distractions I have described here have swayed me at one time or another, the projection of self had an especially strong influence around the time of my unforgettable meeting with Bruce. In those days I would have been described well by something Parker Palmer wrote: "There is a great gulf between the way my ego wants to identify me, with its protective masks and self-serving fictions, and my true self."[5]

Picture a projector in my heart that's running virtually all the time, casting its image on the surface that you see and hear when you encounter me. It isn't the real me; it's "the Me I Want to Be." It shines so bright that not only does it keep you from seeing the real me—it keeps me from seeing it too.

When I was a young pastor, a counselor named Bill kept telling me that I wasn't okay with myself. At the time I just could not see what he was talking about. After a while I grumbled to a friend how the whole counseling exercise seemed like a total waste of time, and with one sentence from him the scales fell off my eyes. "Will," he said, "you *are* 100 percent okay with yourself: *the self you are trying to project.*"

There it was; it was so obvious. I was okay with my affinity for the teaching pastor career in a growing church. I was okay with the image of an up-and-coming, go-getting, charismatic ministry dynamo. I was okay with being the head of an idyllic household. But the Me I Wanted to Be was holding me back from seeing the Me God Made Me to Be.

The day I sat down with Bruce, he told me I was a leader first and a teacher second—I was a solid-B communicator but an A-plus leader. He was correct in his evaluation, but I couldn't see it yet, because I was operating out of a self-projection that needed to be confronted.

Bruce's declaration that I would not be the next John Ortberg was brutal. It sent me into a tailspin for months. But it was also beautiful—or, as I like to call it, "brutiful"—because he was helping me to see who God made me to be. It still stands as the worst meeting I have ever had with a boss. But it started the adventure of a lifetime.

Because you're human, I suspect that the same may be true for you: *you* are your biggest barrier to knowing you. But with a bit of courage, you can set aside that false self-projection and find yourself for the first time.

Imagine for a moment two versions of you standing side by side. The first version is the you that you wish you were. The second version is the you that God dreamed you to be. If you could actually see both versions of you, I have no doubt that you would pick God's dream of you and for you every single time.

Step 2: Experience to Grow

The second essential step of the Clarity Spiral is experience, but not just any experience. It's the experience which enables growth. It's experience that accelerates how you make your best contribution to the world. While "courage to know" gets you started, it's "experience to grow" that keeps it sustained. Working hand in hand, these two commitments make you an unstoppable learner as you pursue your life vision.

Another way to think of it is this: once you truly have the courage to know yourself, every experience becomes a gift. Everything speaks. Your successes develop your confidence and your failures deepen your convictions. As it's said, "When the student is ready, the teacher will appear."

Please note that experience is not the best teacher; *evaluated* experience is. (If experience by itself was the best teacher, we would all be equally wise.) The key is to refuse to let your work experiences go by unexamined. With the simple commitment of reflecting on seasons of your work past and present, each month of your life becomes a step on a ladder, taking you up, up, up to a clearer vantage point.

There's good news and bad news in this. The bad news is that you can't microwave the process. You don't get break-thru in the drive-thru.[6] Finding your groove takes time—as in, years or decades. "Experience to grow" asks us to embrace experimentation with how we use our time. Do you work better with people, things, or ideas? Do you excel at persuasion, painting, or planning? Do you prefer quiet one-on-one settings or highly charged team dynamics? Do it and you will know. There is no shortcut around the time it will take to find out.

Now for the good news: the longer you have lived and worked, the more experience you have to revisit and evaluate. And even better: you can benefit from your bad experiences as much as the good ones. How so? Work tasks that you hated bring great clarity—it's clear that you weren't standing in your sweet spot while doing them. So don't worry about that job that grew tired or that boss that got you fired. Pay close attention and you'll find the work that keeps you wired.

The great thing about experience is that it just keeps coming, which means that as long as you evaluate it, you keep growing. This runs counter to the discouraging mental model that contemporary Americans have of how life works. Biologically, most human functions peak in people's early twenties. However, at age forty we still retain most of our youthful vigor but have gained a great deal of wisdom and skill through experience. Unless you're a professional athlete, age forty might be your performance peak.

But then we face a crisis. Our physical strength, stamina, health, and looks are going to continue to deteriorate. We have a shrinking number of days in this body before us—soon fewer than the days behind us. Are we where we thought we'd be by now? Is there any reason to dream anymore, or is this all there is? In our youth-enamored culture, is it all downhill from here?

Fortunately, the Bible doesn't view the trajectory of a person's life as a ballistic arc to a pathetic crash. Rather, Psalm 92 promises, "The righteous thrive like a palm tree and grow like a cedar tree in Lebanon. Planted in the house of the LORD, they thrive in the courts of our God. *They will still bear fruit in old age, healthy and green*" (vv. 12–14, emphasis added).

Picture life not as an arc or a bell curve but as a series of rising stairsteps (figure 3.1). At about age twenty you reach a crisis about what to do with your life, about whether to live for spinning-in-place pleasures for yourself or whether to accept the challenge of being responsible to others on the adventure of life. Some people don't pass that test; their impact plateaus or declines. Yet others overcome and move on to the midlife crisis of whether to pursue their calling or play it safe. Again, some stay stuck, but others navigate it and move up higher.

At around age sixty people face one more crisis, this one having to do with their remaining years. It's about whether their productivity is based on their *activity* or on their *generativity*—that is, how they're preparing the next generation to carry on their legacy. The brilliant truth is that those who overcome this crisis *impact more* just as they begin to *work less*. They "bear fruit in old age, healthy and green" in the form of the work being done by all those they have nurtured and guided over time. Their impact in retirement and even after death becomes greater than in all their working years. Peak performance may be long gone, but peak impact is one step away.

 By the way, if you want some free bonus content that expands on the ideas in this chapter, you can find it at WillMancini.com/clarityspiral.

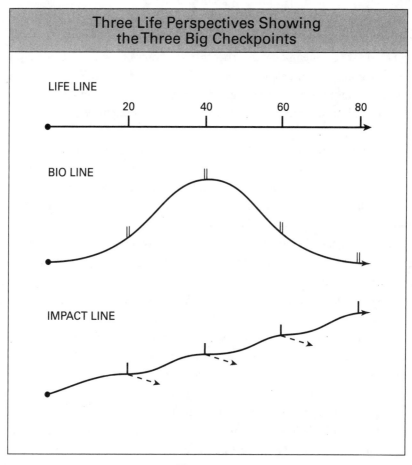

Figure 3.1

At each stage, the watershed difference between expanding impact and shrinking impact is whether you seize the opportunities to grow from your experiences. You get the opportunity each day to practice the trial-and-error lifestyle and learn along the way. And you get the opportunity at the three big checkpoints to gain insight from your journey and design your life afresh. Will you see increased life contribution through each stage of your life from your "experience to grow"?

Step 3: Value to Show

As you get to know yourself ("courage to know") and learn from your experiences ("experience to grow") you will soon make yourself more valuable. The third essential step to life design is all about value, but not just any value: it's "value to show" your employer for the sake of advancing your calling.

Value to show means striving for the continual refinement of your role description in your current vocation or place of employment. It means that you proactively broker a great exchange—you bring more contribution *to* your work and you get more vitality *at* your work. That's aligning your 9-to-5 time with your divine design.

The "value to show" imperative introduces a way of approaching life that is frankly quite rare. Most people settle for the slots that employers provide. Most people haven't given themselves permission to negotiate with their supervisor. Work begins to feel like life on a conveyor belt. You feel intimidated by your boss. Your treadmill job continues rolling day after day after day. It's amazing to me how many people don't second-guess the best way to invest their talents and time on behalf of their employer—even when their employer is themselves.

If you are doing the same job the same way you did last year, you are not growing. This is an unacceptable condition if you are walking the Clarity Spiral. By contrast, when you show your value at work, you are moving toward the highest and best use of your time. What is the specific use of your experiences, passions, skills, and abilities that is the highest and best use not just for you but for your organization?

In the end, every employer wants a return on investment. Whatever your role description or job expectation, your employer is making a financial investment into you in the form of your paycheck. You, Inc. is responsible to provide your share-holder—that is, your employer—with a valuable return. You can do this in four ways: by *making money*, by *advancing vision*, by *increasing capability*, and by *solving problems*.

In addition, you can look at each one of these kinds of value through the lens of bringing *progress* or bringing *order* to your employer. Progress has to do with attaining what the company wants but doesn't have yet; it's future-oriented. Order has to do with managing what the company already has; it's present-oriented.

By applying the progress-and-order "lens" to the four kinds of value, we arrive at a total of eight ways of adding value at work, as summarized in table 3.1. Then all you have to do is *add* something to, *increase* something in, *delete* something from, or *decrease* something in your daily work role so as to add value.

Eight Ways to Add Value at Work		
The Four Kinds of Value	**Order Orientation** *Managing what presently exists*	**Progress Orientation** *Attaining what is hoped for*
Make Money	**Reduce Expense** *"Find a cheaper supplier"* *"Negotiate lower rent"*	**Increase Revenue** *"Sell more widgets"* *"Preach on generosity"*
Advance Vision	**Strengthen Culture** *"Foster healthy unity"* *"Celebrate core values"*	**Innovate Mission** *"Design a new product"* *"Reach a new people group"*
Increase Capability	**Improve Efficiency** *"Streamline how to order"* *"Check kids in faster"*	**Expand Capacity** *"Add another product line"* *"Launch a new campus"*
Create Solutions	**Solve Problems Now** *"Answer the support line"* *"Fix the copy machine"*	**Prevent Problems Tomorrow** *"Install better firewall"* *"Diversify leadership teams"*

Table 3.1

The point is, in every work experience, you are the one responsible to increase your value. Your boss is not responsible to wring every drop of potential out of you. If he or she is forward-thinking enough to devote some of their time, energy, and money to invest in your development, that's great, but it ultimately isn't their obligation. It's yours.

You are also responsible to demonstrate your "value to show" your employer. Yes, if your boss is an attentive manager he or she will recognize what you're doing, but unfortunately many aren't. And even if your boss is attentive, they may not automatically connect the dots between your initiative and the valuable outcome. It's up to you to enable them to see the value of what their subordinate is doing just as you would want to see it if you were in their shoes.

Remember, "value to show" is in the eye of the beholder. When you consider how you can add value at work, realize that you must add what is valuable *to your boss* and *to your organization*. In fact, just as a GPS device plots your location by communicating with three satellites, you can identify your best way to show value by triangulating the intersection of (1) what you can do well, (2) what your organization requires, and (3) what makes your boss look good. Are you trying to solve your boss's problems—as *your boss* sees them, not what *you* think your boss's problems are? And are you contributing the highest and best use of your time to your organization's mission, vision, and values? When you can answer "yes" to these questions, you're truly showing value.

As you show greater value to your employer over time, pay attention to what energizes you. Every time you do something well, or you like what you're doing, take notice. You'll start to see patterns that clarify each next vocational step up the mountain of personal calling.

Step 4: Risk to Go

The fourth essential practice to walking the Clarity Spiral is about risk, but not just any risk. I call it "risk to go," because it's the risk to leave one place for another. It's the big leap into a new vocational direction or a change in vocational "vehicles." Think of your company, non-profit, freelance role, or ministry as a vehicle for your calling. For those who find their special assignment from God, the need to make a move to a new vehicle will inevitably come.

But the kind of vocational risk I'm talking about is not a random leap. It's not even doing something new that you merely think you'd *like* to do. As a practice of the Clarity Spiral, "risk to go" is a strict discipline.

The problem with success is that it multiplies the things you *can* do. The more success you achieve, the more people you meet, resources you gain, and skills you learn, the more opportunities line up like paper clips to a magnet. The problem is that, as more "can-dos" fill the top of the funnel, it makes it harder to see and focus on the one thing you *must* do for God (figure 3.2). The truth is that most opportunities are distractions in disguise, distractions from the "must-do" that God has been preparing you for your entire life. When I was a seminary student, Professor Howard Hendricks would pronounce to the class with haunting precision, "My greatest fear for you is not failure with your life work but success at the wrong thing." The key to life is not being distracted from your one "must-do" no matter how many "can-dos" come along.

> The truth is that most opportunities are distractions in disguise.

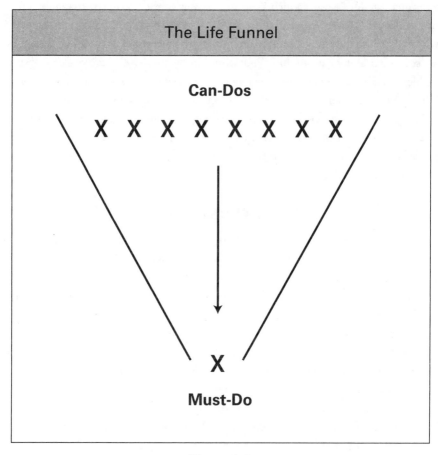

Figure 3.2

To clarify, I am not suggesting that there is only one project or job or occupation or even career that you're supposed to stick with your whole life. To the contrary, remaining rigorously fixed on your one "must-do" is actually what launches the best leaps in your career. The absoluteness of your One Thing enables you to see how relative your life is right now. When you know the One Thing about your calling that never changes, you awaken to how changeable everything else is. You take the "risk to go" because doing your One Thing more often, more purely, and more effectively matters more than whatever you're doing now.

The extravagant richness of a life's calling fully expressed is available to everyone. So why do so few take it?

Over the last twenty years I've sat across a table from hundreds of people who flash a sparkle in their eye when they talk about a "must-do" that is waiting to be named and pursued. But that suppressed flame is barely flickering, almost smothered by one word: *fear.*

It's not just any fear—the fear I'm talking about usually has a specific shape. It is the fear of *what might happen if I walk away from something good.* Maybe it is a job that I do very well. Maybe it is a place where I am greatly loved. Maybe it is a cushy retirement if I finish my career with the same organization. Maybe it is my mortgage payment or my neighborhood or my standard of living. Maybe it is the comfort—I might call it "health"—of my children or my spouse. Maybe it is the silent inflation my ego gets from a job title or occupational field.

The fear of what might happen if you expose any of these things to risk can be extreme. But you will never find God's greater good if you settle for your lesser good. I agree emphatically with Robert Brault: "We miss our goal not because of obstacles but because of a clear path to a lesser goal." For so many people, the biggest barrier to clarity is that thing—that lesser goal—that they are gripping with white knuckles. It's that thing they already possess. When God's better calling comes along they can't reach out and grab it.

But here's what I've found:

- When someone knows that God is calling them . . .
- When they see risk as an act of worship . . .
- When they give the burden of risk back to God . . .
- When they cut fear down to size . . .
- And when they fear regret more than failure . . .

. . . that person will take the risk to go.

As I look back on each of my own big "risk to go" moments, I shiver with delight. The memory is one of euphoria—stepping off the cliff to walk on the wind. In my case—and this is by no means true of all people who "risk to go"—at each point I was leaving a proven record of success when I stepped into the unknown. I had thought I was already flying, but until I took the risk I never knew what flight was.

Your "can-dos" are the big house you live in. You might not spend time in every room, but you've seen them, and they're familiar; you know they're there. But taking the "risk to go" is, as with Lucy Pevensie of *The Lion, the Witch, and the Wardrobe,* to enter the wardrobe into a fantastic new world.

Your must-do is behind the wardrobe door. Your housemates may not believe you, and they may not understand—not at first. But a glorious reality awaits you on the other side.

A Warning

Now that you've learned the fundamentals of the Clarity Spiral, I hope you're chomping at the bit to design your life. So it probably comes as a surprise that I'm going to pull back hard on the reins for a moment.

The Younique Life Plan Journey isn't merely about life design. It's about *gospel-centered* life design. That's why this is an especially sensitive juncture in our journey together, because a person stubbornly rebelling against God or neglecting him can get away with going their own way—for a while. The result, however, is a climb up a very different mountain than the one God has prepared for those who love him—or falling off the cliff just as they reach the summit.

Even Jesus-followers, who have come to new life by the Holy Spirit, are liable to be tempted to strive for clarity in a fleshly, self-centered way. While personal fulfill-ment is a real outcome of life design, it is never to be the primary motivation of a believer. "Seek first the kingdom of God and his righteousness," Jesus said, "and all these things"—including personal fulfillment in one's special calling—"will be pro-vided for you" (Matt. 6:33).

The main point isn't our fulfillment. The main point is God's glory. The subsidiary point is the benefit of the world around us. The point for *us* is to find our satisfac-tion when God's glory and the world's welfare are amplified through us. In short, the point is love—love of God and love of neighbor. That is the law of life design as God designed it.

So the climb up the mountain is a climb not only to a superior level of clarity but also to superior breadth, depth, comprehensiveness, intensity, and effectiveness of our love. This is what God is up to. Therefore, we can never let our work of stewarding our calling eclipse God's work in forming our "character to glow."

Character formation inevitably involves difficult situations, unwanted pain, and challenging people from time to time. That bad boss, stubborn coworker, wearisome assignment, or ugly office might be genuinely repugnant to God's ideal, but then again, you aren't yet up to God's ideal either. Those painful things might be a chisel in his hand to sculpt you into the image of Christ.

God uses work—especially unpleasant work—to teach us *spiritual contentment, submission, servanthood, sacrifice,* and *suffering well.* These five marks of godly character make for a useful checklist against which to examine your motives for taking your next step at work.

I'm convinced that when you are living out the lessons those five marks teach, you become even freer in your calling. Calling isn't opposed to these virtues; it is defined by them. When they are embedded deep down in your life, they aren't a brake to the fulfillment of living your life's call; they are jet fuel.

There's nothing inherently wrong with hoping that a role adjustment or a new job will bring you more joy or will release you from a bad situation. All I'm saying is, those aren't big enough reasons to go for it. In the end, your "value to show" and your "risk to go" mustn't be for the sake of your pain or pleasure. They must be for the sake of love—how you can best love God and your neighbors. When love is your motive, you'll know what to show and when to go.

 (If you are ready to make some "value to show" or "risk to go" moves, I have created an online course just for you entitled *Your Dream Job Guide*. Check it out at LifeYounique.com/courses.)

Chapter 4

BREAK-THRU

One Powerful Secret Most People Miss When Attempting Great Things

"As a believer you need to recognize and actively claim with faith the fact that the Holy Spirit desires to help you think at the highest possible levels. The Holy Spirit has been made available to you to achieve breakthroughs in understanding. The Holy Spirit is capable of entering the reasoning process and desires to do so. Your desire should be that the Lord's desire is at the top of your mind, continually viewed in living color and in three dimensions."

—Tom Paterson

Mia loves to read about intentional living. As a teacher she has been thinking about starting her own online nutrition business for some time. In addition, one of the student pastors at her church has encouraged her to pursue ministry—she has a real heart for middle-school girls. Yet despite everything she has learned about developing a vision for her life, nothing has really stuck.

She took the Myers-Briggs Type Indicator three years ago—she's an ESFJ. Last November she learned her top five strengths according to Clifton StrengthsFinder. As a church volunteer she took a DiSC personality assessment when she signed up. Mia has been studying hard to be a straight-A student at UU (the "University of You").

But the principal at her high school never talked with her about her personality assessments. She was surprised that her husband wasn't too interested in a conversation about her "SC" profile on the DiSC. Even the pastor who administered the DiSC didn't seem to care too much beyond getting a few laughs at the volunteer training.

Year after year she has not taken any significant new steps in her life. She has not acted on her hunches to start a business or her gleaning about going into ministry. Her role description as a teacher hasn't changed in the slightest.

Three months ago she finally decided to make a life plan following a popular guidebook. She followed the book's steps even though the process felt a little too complicated: develop eight "life accounts" and create a vision statement, a purpose statement, and four goals for each. Mia took an entire weekend getaway in the mountains to complete the plan. But two months later she looked again at what she had written down and it all seemed like a blur. She hadn't reviewed it regularly because it felt too laborious with thirty-two goals, eight different purpose statements, and eight different vision statements. With so many "moving parts," the life plan didn't energize Mia or focus her life.

Mia's experience is common. On the journey of building your dream life, it's easy to sketch out some exciting blueprints, but few ever start the construction process. Why is it so difficult to get traction when setting new goals?

Identity: the Missing Ingredient

Let's drill down and answer the important question: *What keeps break-thru from happening when people plan their life?*

On the surface there are many possible reasons, but they share a common root problem. Specifically, the desired change in activity is not rooted in a break-thru understanding of identity that is named in a specific, personal, and powerful way.

There are two critical steps for this break-thru to be understood and named. But before we cover them, let's explore why identity is so important.

God wants us all to excel both in God-awareness and in self-awareness. The trouble is that people tend to make these kinds of awareness compete instead of cooperate. The default posture for many people is to strive for high self-awareness but to neglect God-awareness. They go to great lengths to understand their strengths and maximize their skills, but it is for the narcissistic pursuit of self—it's all about whether *they* find meaning or not.

Some godly believers see people living this way and react by swinging the opposite way. They make life all about God—or at least that's how they talk. They prize learning about God, but they think that learning about themselves is a worldly waste of time. They attribute everything to God's will, but they do it in a fatalistic sort of way. They are suspicious that dreaming about the future and desiring to do something about it is sinful, so they settle into passive resignation to whatever comes next.

But God wants us to have high God-awareness *and* high self-awareness. He wants us to know him deeply *and* to know how he made us to reflect him. He wants us to recognize his sovereign presence in all things *and* to take action. He wants us to grasp the identity he dreamed for us *and* to design the life it implies. He is the Creator who formed us in his image to create like him. "We are God's coworkers" in everything (1 Cor. 3:9), including in the task of making a life. As the saying goes, you can only give as much as you know about yourself to as much as you know about God.

Knowing your identity is essential to making progress in your life with Christ because all behavior is rooted in belief. Someone invests in a stock because they believe it will go up. Someone buys an electric car because they believe it will save them money or help the environment. Likewise, we could say that all activity flows from our identity—what we believe about ourselves. If you want to change your habits, actions, or behaviors, it works best to root those changes in the soil of identity. Identity is like the rudder on a giant barge that carries everything else in your life. One small turn of the rudder—a relatively tiny piece of metal—and the one-thousand-ton ship adjusts its course to a new bearing.

The pattern of teaching in Scripture reveals that transformation must happen in our identity before it happens in our activity. When Paul writes to the church at Ephesus, the first three chapters are all about who they are in Christ. Only after establishing what is true about their spiritual identity does Paul coach them on how to live. Chapters 1 through 3 are filled with indicative statements of fact such as, "You were chosen before the foundation of the world" (Eph. 1:4, paraphrase). It's as if Paul is repeating over and over, "This is who you are . . . this is who you are."

Then in chapters 4 through 6 he opens a floodgate of imperatives. How they live *for* Christ is first anchored in who they are *in* Christ. The first command in chapter 4 is like a giant pivot in this six-part epistle. Paul writes, "*Therefore* I, the prisoner in the Lord, urge you to *live worthy of the calling you have received*, with all humility and gentleness, with patience, bearing with one another in love, making every effort to keep the unity of the Spirit through the bond of peace" (4:1–3, emphasis added). The very structure of Paul's teaching reveals that lasting behavior change flows *from* identity *to* activity just like water flows from mountaintops to ocean shores.

I will never forget a vivid example of this truth from my life as a young father. Joel, my second son, was three years older than his sister Abby. One day he was picking on her as big brothers often do. My consistent pattern was to yell something like, "Joel, stop slapping your sister!" I wasn't getting very far. But one day, I changed my approach. As he was pestering Abby, I interrupted, looked right into his eyes, and gently said, "Joel, the way you are treating your sister is not who you are called to be."

Filled with the desire to influence my son's behavior, I stopped trying to force his behavior a certain way. Rather, I aimed for identity. He stopped bullying his sister that very day. Almost magically his behavior improved permanently from that point forward.

How to Build the Identity Bridge

Let's now describe Mia's problem a different way. Remember, we have said that her new goals were not rooted in a break-thru perspective rooted in identity.

While her getaway weekend was inspiring, it didn't turn into daily follow-through. We might say that she tried to jump from *inventory* to *implementation. Inventory* is taking assessment of your life—your personality, gifts, strengths, and so forth. It asks the question, "Where am I today?" *Implementation* is setting some new goals for yourself. It asks the question, "Where do I want to go?"

There are two logical and important steps between inventory and implementation. If you try to jump from one to another, it's like trying to jump the Grand Canyon on a motorbike. Unfortunately, Mia couldn't jump the inventory-implementation gap. Instead, she fell to the bottom and got stuck. (See figure 4.1.)

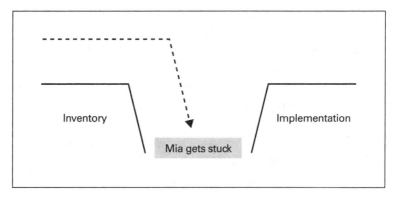

Figure 4.1

What is the bridge that she needs? It's *identity!* Without understanding her inventory on a deeper level, her implementation will be shallow or short-lived.

The identity bridge is made up of two important steps. The first step is *interpretation*. Interpretation asks the question "Why?" The second step is *inscription*. Inscription is the step of articulating or naming things in our lives that celebrate and encode the work of interpretation for the future. Let's picture these two steps as pillars of the identity bridge (figure 4.2).

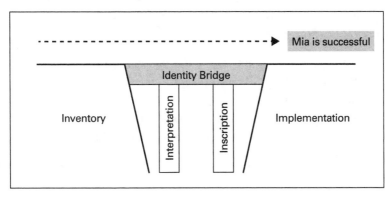

Figure 4.2

The first step of creating an identity break-thru is taking time to interpret. Interpretation is asking deeper questions of why the inventory says what it says. Here are a few of the questions that illustrate what interpretation looks like:

- Why do I have these strengths?
- Why do I have these weaknesses?
- Why did God allow these experiences to happen to me?
- Why do I get a sense of accomplishment doing this?
- What are the natural limitations of my personality type preferences?
- Where did this passion come from?
- What has God been preparing me for next?

These questions and many more are covered in part 2 where I show you how to uncover what I call your "One Thing."

The second step is translating learning into articulation. One of the biggest ideas of this entire book is that your identity and your dreams can be named. Naming is absolutely basic to experiencing meaning as a human being. Naming is also how power and authority are discharged in God's universe. When God creates, he calls or names reality into existence. In the second chapter of Genesis, when Adam begins exercising the power given to him by God at creation, his first tool isn't a flint, a hammer, or a wheel. It's a word: he names the animals.

You learned this in Mrs. Smith's third-grade class. You don't understand the storybook until you can put it into your own words. The same is true with your story of your life.

What exactly will you name? We have part 3 to answer that question more thoroughly. But to introduce you to the concept now, ultimate clarity comes from naming the answers to five questions:

- What I am called to do? (*LifeCall* as personal mission)
- Why do I do it? (*LifeCore* as personal values)
- How do I do it? (*LifeSteps* as personal strategy)
- When am I successful? (*LifeScore* as personal measures)
- Where is God taking me? (*LifeMap* as personal vision)

When you answer these questions with words that are *thought through*, you experience *break-thru*.

Perhaps you're thinking, *I'm not going public with my life plan. Is it really so important that I nail down the perfect wording if it's just for me?* It certainly is! Words create worlds. How you think and how you live is guided by the words (and related images) you use for self-identification, reflection, and communication. The language you use really does matter. When it comes to life design, you are your most important audience.

> Words create worlds.

I call this step "inscription" because that's when people etch, engrave, or write very important words in a book, monument, trophy, or other important gift. Inscriptions are the few words that pour out a heart-full of meaning, as when a lover opens a locket to read and reread, "I will love you forever." When you inscribe something in the Younique Life Plan, you are etching new words of identity on your mind and heart.

Why is articulation and naming things so important? There are many reasons. When we take the time to write down and speak aloud important ideas, we experience:

- More concentrated thinking
- A thorough reflection process
- The power that comes from a single idea
- A reward for a journey of reflection
- The ability to share our ideas with others
- A declaration of faith in the future God has prepared for us

I could list even more beneficial outcomes of inscription. But boiled down, inscription is valuable because it moves you past the sloppiness of generic thinking. You will never realize the amazing future God has in store for you with merely a general sense of where you are going. Generic is the enemy. Generic is vague, nondescript, commonplace, bland, and boring.

But getting dynamically specific and naming the truth about you is a wake-up call. The language you inscribe becomes the alarm clock to an energized day. It becomes the soul food that powers your way.

Every morning I arise and see an oil painting I purchased from the picturesque Greek island of Santorini. It is the beautiful artifact of one of my favorite places on planet Earth. That Mediterranean landscape is the constant reminder of a once-in-a-lifetime journey. Likewise, when you write down your LifeCall or figure out one of your core values with fantastic words, you have an artifact of perhaps life's most valuable journey—the journey to know yourself. You can celebrate God's authorship in a powerful way. You can hang a new portrait of your identity and a new landscape of your future and see it every day.

In the following pages I will show you how to bridge the inventory-implementation gap with an identity bridge that rests on interpretation and inscription. I hope this imbues these words from Habakkuk with new meaning:

> The LORD gave me this answer: "Write down clearly on tablets what I reveal to you, so that it can be read at a glance. Put it in writing, because it is not yet time for it to come true. But the time is coming quickly, and what I show you will come true. It may seem slow in coming, but wait for it; it will certainly take place, and it will not be delayed." (2:2–3 GNT)

PART TWO

YOUR ONE THING
How to Name What Only You Can Do

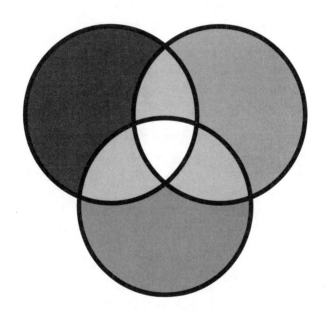

SWEET
SPOT

John Venn was a philosopher and mathematician born in England in 1824. In addition to his career as an academic, he was a pastor in the Anglican church and an inventor of unique devices. One popular invention was an automatic bowling machine for cricket balls, the analog of a pitching machine for baseballs.

But he gave us something else that we use a good deal more often, unaware of the genius behind it: a peculiar way of drawing three circles to explain a wide variety of subjects and how things or ideas relate. John Venn is known for those three overlapping circles called the "Venn diagram."

This three-circle picture is the visual guide for part 2. It's as simple as it is powerful. You no doubt have seen this little device used before in biology, mathematics, and yes, even in books on intentional living.

Here is how it works in the Younique Life Plan. The circles represent careful inventories of your passions, your abilities, and your ideal context.

- **Circle #1: Passion**—*What fuels me the most?*
- **Circle #2: Ability**—*What can I do the best?*
- **Circle #3: Context**—*Where is my impact the greatest?*

But the real secret of this chapter isn't these three inventories. In fact, they're easy to do, and you probably already have some good data on yourself about those three topics. The secret is all about finding break-thru in the overlap. You don't want to stand in only *one* or even two of these circles; you want to stand in the place where all three come together. That's your Sweet Spot.

A sweet spot on a tennis racket, a golf club, or a baseball bat is where you make the maximum impact for a given amount of effort. If you hit the ball just slightly off the sweet spot, it won't go as fast and as far as it could have given the energy in your swing. But if you connect exactly on the sweet spot—if you've ever smashed a perfect ground stroke, blasted a drive down the middle of the fairway, or hammered a base hit into center field—you know the oh-so-glorious sensation of the sweet spot like a wave of liquid power rippling up your arms.

Think about that idea and relate it to your life. Every day you are exerting energy where you live, work, and play. Are you getting the maximum response from your swing?

In part 2, after we talk through each inventory circle, I will reveal the tool that helps you find the Sweet Spot of your life. I call it the "one tool to rule them all," just like Frodo's ring in *The Lord of the Rings*, because it's a powerful template that pulls all of your perspective and learning together in a concise yet comprehensive way— what I call "singularity with specificity." It encapsulates your *One Thing*—your unique assignment from God—to illuminate all the insights you have ever gained and assessments you have ever taken.

Max Lucado describes what hitting the Sweet Spot feels like in your day-to-day life:

> Connect with these prime inches of real estate and *kapow!* The collective technologies of the universe afterburn the ball into orbit, leaving you Frisbee eyed and strutting. Your arm doesn't tingle, and the ball doesn't ricochet. Your boyfriend remembers birthdays, the tax refund comes early, and the flight attendant bumps you up to first class. Life in the sweet spot rolls like the downhill side of a downwind bike ride.[1]

Are you ready to live a life like that? I'm not talking about a "Zip-A-Dee-Doo-Dah" life where everything breaks your way. I'm talking about a life where you *know* your way, and knowing it propels you down the path God laid out for you from before the foundation of the world.

Chapter 5

PASSION

Five Tools to Unlock and Unleash Your Inner Motives

"It is a coal from God's altar that must kindle our fire; and without fire, true fire, no acceptable sacrifice."
—William Penn

To get you standing smack in the middle of your personal Sweet Spot we begin with passion. We start with spark. What fuels your emotion and stokes your devotion? Blaise Pascal said, "Nothing is so intolerable to man as being fully at rest, without a passion, without business, without entertainment, without care."[1]

The subject of passion is a bit tricky, however. On the one hand we are bombarded with a thousand different "follow your passion" mantras, from "Successories" posters to Instagram quotes. On the other hand, figuring out your passion can feel like walking through a maze. *What exactly am I passionate about? If I don't feel it, how do I find it? Can I really expect to harness my passion to make a living?*

Passion means having a strong desire for an activity, object, concept, or cause. It's as important to your life as the wind is to a sailor. As eighteenth-century poet Alexander Pope wrote in his masterwork *An Essay on Man*, "On life's vast ocean diversely we sail. Reason the card, but passion is the gale." I love this quote. Pope uses the word *card* to refer to a compass. He is saying that our mind sets a direction, but our heart fuels the motion. Everyone needs a compass in their head and a fire in their belly.

> Our mind sets a direction, but our heart fuels the motion.

Holy Passion

Before we open the toolbox for discovering your passion, let's consider the biblical perspective. If you were to do a short Bible study on the word *passion*, you would find the word used negatively. When our English Bibles warn us to avoid lust, inordinate affection, and a lack of self-control, they often describe these as "passions." Consider the verse that follows the famous list of the Spirit's fruit: "Now those who belong to Christ Jesus have crucified the flesh with its *passions* and desires" (Gal. 5:24, emphasis added).

When we promote the discovery of passion, we must be clear that we are not talking about the range of controlling emotions that arise from the flesh. In the Scriptures, "the flesh" often refers to the residual power of sin in our physical bodies. Flesh is the bad fuel inherited from Adam and augmented by a lifetime of sin-stained emotion and decision-making habits before our salvation. Even though we are spiritually born again, our ungodly affections can still grow like weeds in a brand-new garden.

To embrace the idea of positive passion used in The Journey, we have to remember the command Paul delivers immediately after his warning about the flesh: "If we live by the Spirit, let us also keep in step with the Spirit" (v. 25 ESV). The words for *Spirit* in both of the primary original languages of the Bible, Hebrew and Greek, also mean "breath" or "wind." The Holy Spirit is like the wind of God, powerful yet unseen. He indwells the believer, sealing our inheritance in heaven. He leads the disciple of Jesus into all truth. Whether a summer breeze or a raging hurricane, his effects are deep and powerful. His guiding presence aligns our heart, mind, and will to God's. His power keeps renovating us, weeding out the passions of the flesh and fleshing out the compassion of God in us.

So what, in the name of Jesus, do you care deeply about? How does the Holy Spirit within you cultivate a passionate spirit in you? *On life's vast ocean diversely we sail. Reason the card, but passion is the gale.* In the believer's life, passion is the power of Holy Spirit-force winds blowing in our lives to motivate our day. He helps us sail a few more miles. As we live in our Christ-identity, the Spirit himself not only marks us and makes us—he moves us.

Passion is redeemed when your strong desire for an activity, object, concept, or cause dovetails with his greater purposes. It's stuff you love to do that God loves to work through. So how do you turn a gentle breeze into a full gust of good in your life?

The Five Passion Tools for The Journey

When a Younique Coach walks someone through the Sweet Spot, they take a look at five different tools: the Life Discovery Grid, Life Lies and Truths, the Passion Funnel, Offenders, and the Passion 360 (figure 5.1). Each one provides a unique insight into your motivational makeup.

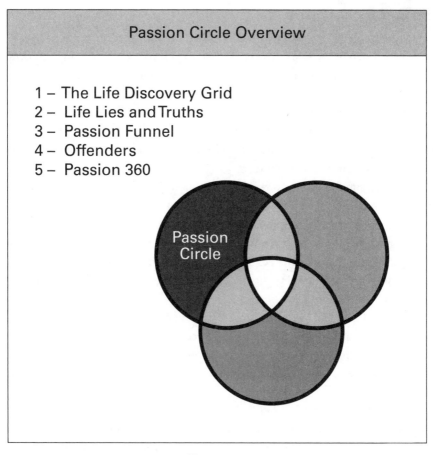

Figure 5.1

The Life Discovery Grid

The single most powerful tool I have used for spiritual formation and life planning is the Life Discovery Grid, an adaptation of a tool I encountered at the Center for Christian Leadership at Dallas Theological Seminary.

 (You can use the Life Discovery Grid tool yourself for free at LifeYounique. com/StarterKit.)

The first step of the Life Discovery Grid is to plot your top ten "hinge moments," or turning points, on a time line of your life. Then you rate each event on a scale from +10 (extremely positive experience) to –10 (extremely negative experience). This first step, taught by Donald Miller, is relatively simple, but by itself it can bring significant break-thru.[2] I can remember one woman who, within fifteen minutes, recounted in tears her gratitude for God's grace: "I can't believe how God has preserved me through the many crisis points," she recalled.

Using the simple "ups and downs" plot, the next step is to divide your life into four or five chapters, creating a tentative chapter title for each. The chapter titles become your creative labeling of God's authorship of the story of your life.

The next step is to evaluate the first chapter of your life through five lenses: Heritage, High Points, Hard Times, Hand-of-God moments, and Heroes. Record two to five key observations and insights for each lens. Then repeat for the other chapters of your life.

A finished Life Discovery Grid may have fifty to one hundred biographic bullet points that show an amazing panoramic perspective on your life like never before. The learnings always blow people away. Why? When you view your life from this vantage point, you can see connections and patterns with ease. You begin interpreting why you are the way you are.

For example, as a kid I found it challenging when we moved every two to three years. Yet when I later looked back on that chapter of my life from the vantage point of a thirty-something, I could better understand both my frustration and how God was using those moves to prepare me.

How was moving difficult? First, even though I am an extraverted people-person, I always felt like an outsider wherever we went. That dynamic amplified my insecurity and sense of loneliness. Second, while Mom and Dad always provided a wonderful home, I remember the feeling of not having a hometown. As a young adult when people would ask me where I was from, there was no crisp answer. Third, as I became an active Christ-follower, I was slightly embarrassed by my denomination-hopping.

I felt like a spiritual mutt—as we moved we attended different kinds of churches. As faith become more important to me, I wondered what faith-tribe I really belonged to.

But when I stepped back and examined the big picture of my life, I saw how God used it to prepare me for my calling. As a perpetual outsider, I developed an active thought life. I learned to feel at home when I am on the road, which reflects my life now as an itinerant church consultant. And my early exposure to different kinds of churches helps me to relate to the wide variety that I now serve. In fact, I love creating tools that any kind of church can use.

Furthermore, it was our relocating that ensured I would encounter the gospel. To this day I am forever grateful to First Presbyterian Church of Augusta and the teachers at Westminster Day School, whose evangelical faithfulness demonstrated to my mom, then me, then my entire family what it means to follow Jesus.

These transformative insights came from one observation of what was written on my Life Discovery Grid. It's not uncommon to have five to ten major insights your first time through. With extended reflection you will mine even more gold with this tool.

Life Lies and Truths

Once you finish the panoramic perspective, you can experience unprecedented break-thru in applying the gospel to your life. The goal is to identify lies from the devil that you have believed unknowingly at different stages of your life—lies about God, about yourself, and about life in general—and then to recall and rehearse the truth of the gospel that sets you free. In other words, Life Lies and Life Truths are the two-part tool you use to connect your story to the story of God that arches over the whole Bible.

In Luke 4:1–15, Satan used three temptations, each attacking Jesus from a different angle, to try to get him to forfeit his calling. The first temptation, to turn a rock into bread, is all about the desire of *appetite*, the temptation to *have* more—possessions, money, experiences, food, alcohol, sex, and so on. In this case Satan was tempting Jesus to become his own provider, rather than trusting in his Father's provision. The second temptation was to gain power over all the kingdoms of the world by bowing to Satan and conveniently side-stepping the path of suffering. This desire is all about *ambition*, the temptation to *accomplish* more and to use whatever means necessary to do so. Here Satan tempts Jesus with a legitimate end but with a means that sidesteps his call to be a suffering servant as Messiah. The third temptation—to jump from the pinnacle of the temple—is all about the desire for *approval*, the temptation to be more, to be liked and acknowledged by others by showing the world that you are somebody.

The temptations of appetite, ambition, and approval become a powerful lens by which to evaluate mistakes and sin patterns in each chapter in your Life Discovery Grid. We call these Life Drifts.[3]

Look at your life's story one chapter at a time. In the first chapter, was there a besetting behavior pattern that you often lapsed into that caused trouble in your life? See if you can classify it under the heading of appetite, ambition, or approval.

Now dig one level deeper. When you were prone to that persistent sin-pattern, was there a stubborn, sensitive hurt that you were trying to compensate for? Was it *fear* that you didn't *have* enough (appetite)? Or *guilt* that you didn't *do* enough (ambition)? Or *shame* that you *weren't good* enough (approval)? Very often, the "Life Lies" of the primary Life Drift come from an area that's different from the more obvious compulsive behavior that covers it up (the secondary Life Drift).

The break-thru comes when individuals discern with greater clarity the lies they believed in each life chapter. Looking at the Life Lie from God's point of view takes the power out of the deception. Then, you can recall and explicitly record the beautiful promise of the gospel that subverts and overcomes the lie. We call that your "Life Truth."

When I was in elementary school, my dad was climbing the corporate ladder at DuPont, starting businesses, and flying C-130s in the Air National Guard. He was always a hero, but there were seasons we didn't spend much time together. I began believing a series of Life Lies about God (God doesn't have time to care about me), about myself (Little Willy isn't that likable), and about life (people in general don't want to be with me).

In my early twenties, my primary Life Drift toward approval that started in childhood manifested itself in a secondary Life Drift toward ambition. I worked obsessively to hear supervisors say good things about my performance. I hoped that would fill the approval vacuum and make me feel worthy.

The Life Truth I desperately needed—and eventually found in the gospel—is that on the cross Jesus experienced the ultimate rejection so that I might have the ultimate acceptance. As my good friend and Younique cofounder Dave Rhodes likes to say, "What Jesus resisted in the desert personally, he defeated at the cross permanently. The cross takes the stinger out of my need for approval." The Life Truth is that, in Christ, I am God's beloved Son in whom he is well-pleased. My heavenly Father not only loves me—he *likes* me just the way he made me and is remaking me. He wants to be with me always. That's the ultimate good news to me. (And by the way, my dad today is my greatest hero and a model Christ-follower. We continue to enjoy the best times a father and son can have!)

Passion Funnel

The Passion Funnel is a simple but important tool to think about "lighter" and "heavier" passions in your life. One practical problem with the idea of passion is that there are so many things to be passionate about along such a broad spectrum of importance. One can have passion for pizza or Porsches on the one hand and a passion for eliminating homelessness on the other.

The Passion Funnel is a simple funnel diagram where you sift between "lighter" and "heavier" passions:

- List five or so things you are *interested in*. These include activities you enjoy, things you do for fun, and what you check out when you get a free moment.
- List four things you are *excited about*. These are the sort of things in work or play that you plan for in advance and look forward to. You get filled with energy doing them and even preparing to do them.
- List three things you are *driven by*. These are the things you are bound to do or address—you can't stop yourself. They get you up in the morning; engaging with them makes you feel alive. You will instinctively find a way to live them out even when there is no obvious way.
- List one or two things you are *burdened for*. These are the things that keep you up at night. They are places of pain or imperfection in the world that you can't let go of—you can't live without doing something about it.

Let me give you an example from my own life. I am *interested in* really good chicken enchiladas with mole sauce. I am also interested in real estate and snowboarding. I am *excited* about adventure travel and unforgettable experiences. I am *driven by* learning opportunities and precious, intimate moments with my family. Yet I am *burdened for* churches not experiencing redemptive movement. That is, I am undone in my gut when I encounter a church that is not producing disciples as everyday missionaries. As agonizing a burden as that is, I would never willingly give it up. As we say in The Journey, passion is a conviction that becomes contagious because it withstands the test of pain.

This burden is so helpful in bringing practical focus to my life. Consultants and authors who follow Jesus can sometimes wrestle with how much time they are spending in the "Christian space." Do they utilize a faith-based platform and then cross over into the business world? Do they charge a high billable rate in their industry so that they can do pro bono work at their church? The discernment gets sticky.

Ultimately, of course, the answer for each person is found in calling. For me, the possibility for increased influence or income in "crossing over" doesn't register on my radar. It would even feel like death to me because it would fall outside of my burden. As a minister of the gospel, I know I am called to the church. I strictly discipline all of my best thoughts and energy to help the church accomplish its mission.

When you live passion before profit, your passion becomes profit. And when you know what activity would "feel like death" to you if you lost it, you are close to knowing the passion at the core of your life.

Offenders

A helpful perspective on your passion is the question: "What offends you the most?" People present a broad range of answers: for some it's unbalanced budgets and for others it's schoolyard bullies. Maybe it's something seemingly superficial like a ball coming over the fence into your yard. I encourage you to know your top three. For example, I can't stand it when religious leaders use legalism to abuse or manipulate people. Another one: it drives me crazy if people are busy-busy-busy without a view of the big picture.

Don't dismiss the things that feel like a pet peeve; rather, look for the deeper meaning behind them. For example, I always want to talk to the manager if I see crumbs on the table of a sit-down restaurant. It's like those little crumbs are screaming at me, *We shouldn't be here!* Why do I care so much? It's actually not that I'm a clean-freak; it's because I have strengths of maximizing and activation. A dirty table tells me that I did not maximize my investment of a night out by getting the best experience possible. I also immediately sense that restaurant employees are not activated to excellence by their manager. Finally, it's a clear sign that the restaurant is off-mission in its execution, and that goes against the grain of my brain.

The point isn't to find fuel to complain but to ascertain clues to your Spirit-given bent. Naming your offenses helps "play offense" with your life to honor God and help others.

Passion 360

The Passion 360 tool is super-simple, super-revealing, and super-fun. Send a text message to four family members, four coworkers, and four friends that simply says, "Crazy question: What three things do you think I am most passionate about? Three words only, please." My friend Todd Wilson, who runs the Exponential Conference for church planters, heard back from his son; "Church multiplication. Family. Guns." So Todd's son wrote four words, but the three-point sermon still came across loud and clear.

Will you get some expected answers from the people who know you? Absolutely. But everyone who does this simple exercise with at least twelve people will be enlightened by something—perhaps even some unexpected and revealing insights.

Putting Passion Together

People today usually describe me as a passionate guy—they sense intensity or a tone of tenacity in my being. But I can guarantee that I was not always this way. As a teenager and young adult I was relatively shy, more aware of the confidence that I lacked than any fervor that I had. Later, when Aubrey Malphurs invited me to coauthor a book with him entitled *Building Leaders*, I began to reflect on the leader I had become. I came to the conclusion that passion can be developed and even practiced.

The starting point to practicing passion is awareness; we simply must become more conscious of those deeper motives and inner convictions. Then something beautiful is unlocked. Conscious passion becomes practiced passion, and practiced passion become more passionate passion. It's the best kind of virtuous cycle in life. The more you are conscious, the more you practice. And the more you practice, the more you are conscious. It's a snowball effect that brings greater momentum to your work and life. Over time people see a divine spark in your eye. You live with a God-glow. You work with wind at your back and a gale in your sail.

> Conscious passion becomes practiced passion, and practiced passion become more passionate passion.

Perhaps the greatest reason to know your passion is to know the thing for which you are willing to suffer. It's getting out of bed with a motivation to run through brick walls or to rise up from the ashes of failure. It's the ultimate fuel for the day. That's why we call the suffering of Jesus' last week on earth his Passion. Living with passion is being able to endure anything because of the "joy set before you." As it is written of Jesus in Hebrews, "For the joy that lay before him, he endured the cross, despising the shame, and sat down at the right hand of the throne of God" (12:2).

It's important to complete these inventories and let them work together and soak in your soul. Remember our imperatives of "courage to know" and "experience to grow." As you mine the treasures of your passion circle, you are one-third of the way toward naming the "One Thing" at the center of your Sweet Spot. Now let's explore the next circle on the Sweet Spot: your ability.

 (If you would like additional coaching on the tools in this chapter, the Younique team has put together an amazing course entitled *Your Story Matters*. Find it at LifeYounique.com/courses.)

Chapter 6

ABILITY

Five Tools to Discover and Deploy Your Greatest Strengths

"Serve one another with the particular gifts God has given each of you, as faithful dispensers of the magnificently varied grace of God . . . so that God may be glorified in everything through Jesus Christ."

—The Apostle Peter

Every human being is endowed with greater potential than most have ever begun to realize. Thomas Edison once said that if we did the things we were capable of we would astound ourselves.

It's not hard to find incredible human feats. Just Google it or turn on the news. Several years ago, a forty-one-year-old Danish woman decided to take up running in response to the diagnosis of multiple sclerosis. Eventually Annette Fredskov would run a full marathon every day for 365 days straight. She burned through twenty pairs of running shoes along the way! Or how about Felix Baumgartner, the first human to break the speed of sound? He completed a 24-mile-high skydive from outer space and hit a top speed of 800 miles per hour.

Whether it's wacky feats or it's extreme athletes, award-wining artists, or business innovators, the media keeps superhumans in plain sight.

Although we witness types of greatness "out there," most of us never come face-to-face with greatness within. Do you know today what makes you astounding? I believe you have some amazing feats inside of you, but they don't show up automatically or grow up accidentally. They are cultivated deliberately.

The first step is identification. You can't build very well with the Legos of your life if you don't know the size and color of the bricks God has given you. And this has a serious effect on how you look at your life. Tom Paterson proclaims, "Show me a person who doesn't know his gifts or hasn't developed them for service to others, and I will show you a person who has little sense of purpose, meaning, motivation and value."[1]

This chapter is all about consciously capturing your capability. It would be a crime of ingratitude against God—and of neglect against yourself—to leave the gifts he's given you unwrapped. This chapter contains the five best methods to see the specific kind of super-ness you have inside.

The Abilities God Gave You

Scripture is explicit that God gives us abilities. One fabulous snapshot of this truth comes from Exodus when God gives Moses instructions for the tabernacle—a mobile temple for God pitched in the middle of his people. Like an extravagant, custom-built home, God wanted nothing less than the best; every detail of this magnificent portable building shone with symbolic significance.

God not only provided the blueprints for the tabernacle, he provided the skilled labor too. In fact, the very first time the Bible records that someone is "filled with the Spirit," it is not a priest, prophet, or king; it's a highly skilled tradesman named Bezalel. God "filled him with God's Spirit, with wisdom, understanding, and ability in every craft to design artistic works in gold, silver, and bronze, to cut gemstones for mounting, and to carve wood for work in every craft" (Exod. 31:3–5). The term for "craft" here is the same Hebrew word for "work" in the Ten Commandments: "You are to labor six days and do all your work" (Exod. 20:9). God is linking the power of being "filled with the Spirit" with a believer's vocational calling.

The principle that our abilities are gifts of God is a strong thread throughout Scripture, but it is especially prominent in Paul's letter to the Roman church: "According to the grace given to us, we have different gifts: If prophecy, use it according to the proportion of one's faith; if service, use it in service; if teaching, in teaching; if exhorting, in exhortation; giving, with generosity; leading, with diligence; showing mercy, with cheerfulness" (Rom. 12:6–8). Paul emphasizes that our abilities are deposited in us by God and that we should expect to see colorful variety like a jumbo box of crayons. The question is, how do you know exactly what colors you received in your box?

The Five Ability Tools for The Journey

Now let's take a look at the five tools that make up the Ability Circle: Name Meaning, Personality, APEST, Strengths, and Sense of Accomplishment (figure 6.1).

Each tool provides a distinct perspective to create a high-definition, multidimensional view of what you can do.

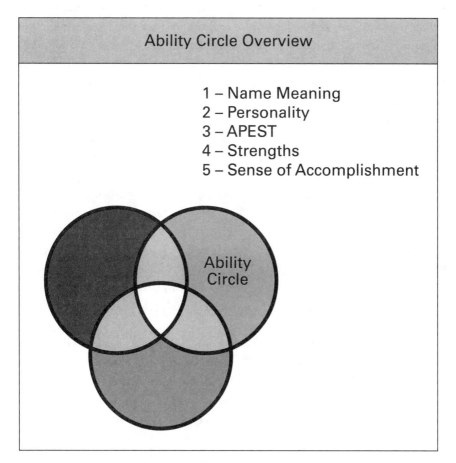

Ability Circle Overview

1 – Name Meaning
2 – Personality
3 – APEST
4 – Strengths
5 – Sense of Accomplishment

Ability Circle

Figure 6.1

What's in a Name?

A spiritual reality that is underappreciated in the modern world is the power of a name. In God's universe, what is spoken is important. "Kind words bring life, but cruel words crush your spirit," Solomon said (Prov. 15:4 GNT).

Words may not break my bones like sticks and stones, but they do mold my soul. Nicknames shape. Family names take root. First names are heard every day of our lives. Have you ever wondered how many thousands of times you have heard your own name? Is it possible that a child's very name spoken over them day after day after day actually informs or reflects their abilities?

What if God meant to say something to you through those letters on your name tag?

Frankly, I was very skeptical when someone first mentioned that idea. I thought it was childish at best and reckless at worst to think that someone's name has any real meaning when it comes to their ability. After all, a parent hasn't really watched their child do anything yet when a name is given, right? Besides, most names today aren't recognizable words in modern English, and many parents don't look up a name's ancient meaning before bestowing it. Many names are chosen simply because they sound nice. Some are even given as a joke!

But after a twelve-month journey prompted by Younique cofounder Dave Rhodes, I experienced a change of heart. I am now the world's biggest proponent of the descriptive power of your names.

First, I studied the Bible. Over and over again we find people being encouraged to live up to the meaning of their name. Take Gideon, for example. When we encounter this character in the book of Judges, he is hiding from the enemy in a winepress. But an angel from God comes and greets him, "The LORD is with you, valiant warrior" (Judg. 6:12). "Valiant warrior" is what "Gideon" means! Gideon needed a supernatural messenger to remind him who he was to get his life in gear. Despite struggling with self-confidence, God empowered him to defeat the impressive Midianite horde with only three hundred men.

Or consider the many familiar faces of the Bible whose names were changed. Jesus' disciple Simon ("one who hears") heard through God's supernatural revelation that Jesus was the Messiah and then said it out loud—the first of the apostles to do so. In response, Jesus called him Peter ("bedrock"), because "on this rock I will build my church" (Matt. 16:18). This was prophetic, as Peter exerted the most influence and spiritual power in the early years of the church.

One of the most wondrous truths in the book of Revelation is that, after the triumph of the resurrection, we will each be given a new name engraved on a white stone, "that no one knows except the one who receives it" (2:17). If God cares that much about a new name in the new heavens and earth, is it possible that he was paying attention to your name in the current ones?

Dave then challenged me to study my own name. The truth is, I was never a fan of my middle name, which happens to be my mom's maiden name. But when I studied the meaning, I fell in love with it for the first time. All three of my names together mean: a resolute protector (William) of the narrow inlet (Firth) who uses both hands (Mancini).

Say what? When you study your name, it might take a little creative interpretation. Here's how it works for me:

Everyone knows me as the "mission statement guy." What is a mission? It's your One Thing. It's your narrow way, like a key that finds one narrow keyhole to unlock the entire mansion, or like an airplane that finds one narrow runway for passengers to enjoy the entire destination city. Everything an organization does should come though the "narrow inlet" of its mission.

I found significant meaning in my last name as well. As a process designer I have aspired to engage both sides of the brain when facilitating and tool-making. I am 100 percent engineer and 100 percent marketing guy at the same time. I love the fusion of art and science in everything I do; it's a different kind of ambidextrous.

So I interpret my name to mean, "I am the resolute protector of mission (narrow inlet) who uses logic and art (ambidextrous brain skills)." I now believe that God gave me a name in his own mysterious way that reflects what he called me to do.

Even nicknames can be filled with meaning as words that others have spoken over you. When I was on staff at Clear Creek Community Church, we all had nicknames for each other. The two that I got were "Builder," reflecting my role on the team, and "Machini," a play on my last name that reflected how I went at the work I was passionate about as relentlessly as a machine.

But the power of naming still needed some testing. I remember trying it out on my brother one Thanksgiving. John Gregory Mancini is a urologist who spends a lot of time in surgery. His name meaning: "a gift of God who 'watches over' using both hands." We all sat shocked unable to eat our gravy-soaked turkey for a few minutes. Did my mom and dad know he was going to be a surgeon when he was born? Certainly not. But God did.

With one test after another my doubt faded. The first six times we personally walked people (about eighty of them) through The Journey, I was nervous, thinking that most people would find zero meaning in their names. But to my surprise, most of them encountered something rich and beautiful in the process.

I'll never forget a church planter whose last name is "Cravens," which means "cowardly." An immediate disaster, right? Not at all. His One Thing is all about "catalyzing starts" and his first and middle name together mean "to cunningly oversee." He simply interpreted his entire name to mean "to cunningly oversee the cowardly" to start the next step of faith. After all, people are most afraid when they are starting new things!

Before we leave the importance of name meaning, be sure you analyze the nicknames you have picked up along the way as well. What people call us over the years will reflect our capabilities, whether they know it or not.

Personality

For decades, businesses and ministries have used assessments to help people identify behavioral preferences. These tools reveal the hidden circuitry of your default wiring and psyche styling. Your charisma has a complexion. The purpose is not only to know yourself better, but to adapt your communication style to the preferences of others.

Many of these assessments find their roots in the work of Carl Jung, a Swiss psychiatrist who is considered to be the founder of analytical psychology. Three well-known instruments based on his work include the Insights Discovery assessment, the DiSC Personality Profile, and the Myers-Briggs Type Indicator (MBTI). In addition, many spin-off assessments using animals or observable traits in children can be linked back to these tools. Even an ancient four-temperament prototype used by Hippocrates in the fifth century BC follows a similar pattern as Jung's thinking.

Along the same lines, I strongly prefer the Insights Discovery tool, which you can take through the Younique Life Plan Journey. I've found it to be the most comprehensive, detailed, subtle, and useful instrument of this kind, and it delivers a highly readable twenty-page report. I'll never forget watching successful author Max Lucado read his report for the first time and hearing him blurt out, "How did this thing know that I love liver!"

Here's a quick and practical way to grasp the first principles of Jung's personality typology. Upon entering a room full of people who know you or are expecting you, observe which ones walk toward you and which ones wait for you to walk toward them. Extroverts—the first group—are primarily oriented toward the world outside their own minds. They tend to initiate and express themselves directly, making eye contact and exhibiting greater ranges of nonverbal expression like smiling, scowling, and gesturing. Introverts—the second group—are primarily oriented toward the world inside their own minds. They tend to be more responsive in social situations (waiting for you to come to them), more indirect in their communication style, and more subdued in their nonverbal expression.

The second thing to look for is "task"- versus "people"-orientation. Task-oriented people tend to "think with their head." They process logic first before they calculate the emotional stuff. People-oriented people, on the other hand, tend to "think with their heart." They intuitively process emotion first before considering the situation from a logical point of view.

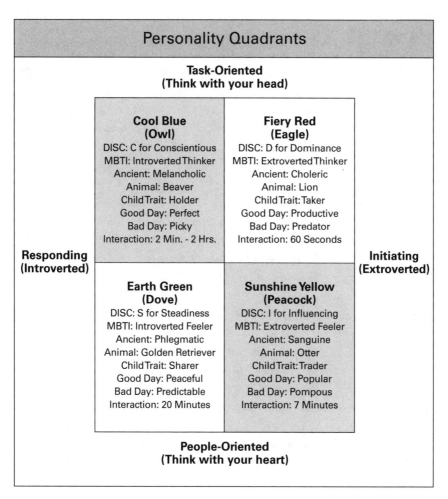

Personality Quadrants

Task-Oriented
(Think with your head)

Cool Blue
(Owl)
DISC: C for Conscientious
MBTI: Introverted Thinker
Ancient: Melancholic
Animal: Beaver
Child Trait: Holder
Good Day: Perfect
Bad Day: Picky
Interaction: 2 Min. - 2 Hrs.

Fiery Red
(Eagle)
DISC: D for Dominance
MBTI: Extroverted Thinker
Ancient: Choleric
Animal: Lion
Child Trait: Taker
Good Day: Productive
Bad Day: Predator
Interaction: 60 Seconds

Responding
(Introverted)

Initiating
(Extroverted)

Earth Green
(Dove)
DISC: S for Steadiness
MBTI: Introverted Feeler
Ancient: Phlegmatic
Animal: Golden Retriever
Child Trait: Sharer
Good Day: Peaceful
Bad Day: Predictable
Interaction: 20 Minutes

Sunshine Yellow
(Peacock)
DISC: I for Influencing
MBTI: Extroverted Feeler
Ancient: Sanguine
Animal: Otter
Child Trait: Trader
Good Day: Popular
Bad Day: Pompous
Interaction: 7 Minutes

People-Oriented
(Think with your heart)

Figure 6.2

A clue to this difference is found in the first phrases spoken in your interaction with someone. Is the subject of the conversation about people, or is it about ideas or things? For example, a people-person is much more likely to ask about my wife and kids or mention a mutual friend. A task-person will ask me about a book, my travel schedule, or something on the agenda for the day.

By combining the two questions of initiating/responding and task/people, we create four personality quadrants. The main type for each quadrant in figure 6.2 is labeled with the colors used by Insights Discovery. The bird typology under that label is my own addition. Can you guess which quadrant is most like how you operate? Which is second-most?

I function most naturally in a "Red-Yellow" style. That means my top two preferences are both oriented toward taking initiative with the world around me. You could say I "double up" on the extroversion side. But I enjoy a more "balanced" approach to the task and relationship side of work, with a tilt toward tasks. By the way, most people "double up" on the side of one of these lines. For example, someone who expresses "Green-Yellow" preferences tends to double up on the relationship side (thinking with their heart first). It's important to know how you "double up" and how you are "balanced."

It's also important to note that no one is pigeonholed into these categories every moment of every day. Each person can and does act like any of the quadrants (some more easily and often than others). At Younique we refer to these as Red, Yellow, Green, and Blue "energy." Anyone can work from these energies or styles of behavior. The issue is, where are you most comfortable? Where do you naturally spend most of your day?

It's important to know what we prefer as a clue to our calling. That said, though, I have also come to believe that growth in spiritual maturity involves stretching ourselves in the behavioral preferences that we do not prefer. For example, since I operate with "Red-Yellow" energies, growing in my love of others often looks like practicing "Green" behaviors. Therefore, while I want people to appreciate their more prevalent or natural personality styles, I don't want them to be "stuck" or too rigid in them. In fact, I believe that adapting your style to those preferences of others is a practical way to serve them. It is a way to "wash one another's feet," to use a powerful image that Jesus left for his followers (see John 3:14–16).

One way to wash each other's feet is to adapt your communication style using awareness of different personalities. On the summary in figure 6.2 is an interaction time-window that is the ideally desired amount of interaction time for each of the personality colors. For example, people operating with a lot of Red energy, especially in a setting that requires productivity, prefer a sixty-second window of interaction that you can summarize as "be brief, be bright, be gone!" When people operate from the Yellow quadrant, they prefer a seven-minute interaction. It's enough to make a connection over kids and sports and still have time left to talk to everyone else. A Green kind of interaction is best experienced with at least twenty minutes of interaction. This kind of energy needs the time to express genuine care and meaningful harmony that can't be rushed. Finally, the Blue quadrant represents interaction driven by intellectual interest and factual accuracy. A satisfying interaction lasts exactly as long as all the details are covered and the topic hasn't become mentally boring, whether that takes two minutes or two hours (or more!).

APEST

The acronym APEST is our next ability tool. It is based on Ephesians 4:1–16, especially verses 11–13:

> And [Christ] himself gave some to be apostles, some prophets, some evange-lists, some pastors [literally, "shepherds"] and teachers, equipping the saints for the work of ministry, to build up the body of Christ, until we all reach unity in the faith and in the knowledge of God's Son, growing into maturity with a stature measured by Christ's fullness.

Here we find the clearest picture of abilities that Jesus gives to his followers to continue his ministry on earth as "the body of Christ." It is noteworthy that the pages of Scripture present Jesus as the ideal exemplary **A**postle, **P**rophet, **E**vangelist, **S**hepherd, and **T**eacher. Today, Christ works through his church vibrantly and effectively through the interdependent activity of individual church members who fulfill the APEST functions. Alan Hirsch explains that "the APEST functions and callings are no less than the modes of Jesus' presence in the church."[2]

In addition to the explicit application to ministry, Hirsch has persuasively argued that these functions are expressed through creation generally before they are exercised by Christ specifically in redemptive history. In his words, "APEST is a meta-idea that continues to shape, not just the church, but *all human culture* . . . the five patterns are indeed primal *archetypes*—universal patterns of human behavior and thinking."[3]

But before we look at Hirsch's expanded definitions of these functions, a word of explanation is in order. When I attended Dallas Theological Seminary in the 1990s, I was formed in an educational community where I was taught that the era of the apostles and prophets was over. No doubt, if by *prophet* or *apostle* we mean an infallibly inspired author of the Old Testament or New Testament, respectively, then it is certainly true we no longer have apostles or prophets today. No one is currently receiving revelations from God that deserve to be added to the canon of Scripture. But that is not what I mean by referencing these terms. In what follows, when I use the words "apostle" and "prophet," I am referring to *functions* that follow examples we see in the New Testament church. I am not talking about apostolic or prophetic authority to dispense new revelation; I'm talking about apostolic and prophetic ministry styles that build up the body of Christ in similar ways as the apostles and prophets did in the first generation of Christians.

The *apostle* in Scripture is literally the "sent one." This role refers to the pioneering functions of the church: designing and deploying new manifestations of mission (principally churches) and protecting their gospel-DNA along the way. In creation generally, apostolic ability includes entrepreneurial, innovative, business-extension, and leadership abilities (table 6.1).

Apostolic Roles	Examples of Apostolic Functions
Founder	Extending the organization
Designer	Maintaining focus on mission
Cultural architect	Championing a paradigm or vision
General	Designing scalable organizations
Agent-envoy	Nurturing the core culture
Visionary	Planting the new ideas (gospel)
Pioneer	Developing start up teams (new churches)
Adventurer	Cultivating entrepreneurship
Strategist	Creating trans-local networks
Innovator	Mobilizing people and initiatives

Table 6.1

The *prophet* is the "guardian of the covenant relationship with God,"[4] helping a community to stay faithful to God above any other allegiance. In the performing of this role, truth must be spoken forth at times with urgency and boldness. Prophets call for justice and reform. Broadly applied, prophetic ability spans roles from activist to artist (table 6.2).

Prophetic Roles	Examples of Prophetic Functions
Activist	Maintain a God-orientation
Politician	Create encounters with God
Advocate	Highlight covenant obligations
Aid worker	Promote holiness
Poet	Call to repentance
Reformer	Speak truth to power
Iconoclast	Awaken people to spiritual warfare
Hacker	Distinguish true and false worship
Liberator	Champion justice
Environmentalist	Communicate urgency

Table 6.2

The *evangelist* proclaims the good news of Jesus Christ by promoting the faith and inviting others into the family of God. Evangelistic ability broadly applied includes the functions of sales, storytelling, and recruiting (table 6.3).

Evangelistic Roles	Examples of Evangelistic Functions
Messenger	Communicate
Salesman	Elicit response
Negotiator	Create invitational culture
Journalist	Seize the movement message
Recruiter	Ensure cultural relevance
Promoter	Develop sticky messaging
Achiever	Present the value proposition
Believer	Create branding
Champion	Value the individual
Storyteller	Demonstrate catalytic witness
Marketer	Recruit to the cause

Table 6.3

The *shepherd* represents the dominant role of church leadership as we're traditionally familiar with it—we call our leaders "pastors," which comes from the Latin word for "shepherd." Shepherding roles ensure healthy relationships for faith formation in a local community. Broadly applied, the role can be expanded to various forms of counseling, caregiving, and coaching (table 6.4).

Shepherding Roles	Examples of Shepherding Functions
Caregiver	Enrich communal experience
Defender	Develop social bonding
Peacemaker	Demonstrate credible witness
Helper	Protect the community (congregation)
First responder	Promote and facilitate healing
Servant	Encourage wholeness
Healer	Champion inclusion
Coach	Cultivate rich and loving community
Counselor	Enable human flourishing
Human resource	Model daily formation

Table 6.4

The *teacher* is the one who transfers knowledge, wisdom, understanding, and skill. Teachers keep the saints learning and growing in all areas of faith by keeping people rooted in God's Word. Broadly applied, the teacher's role includes disciplines of specialized knowledge such as scientific, legal, and engineering roles, as well as others (table 6.5).

Teaching Roles	Examples of Teaching Functions
Sage	Bring wisdom and understanding
Professor	Develop worldview formation
Philosopher	Cultivate a love of truth (Scripture)
Scientist	Ensure ideological discourse (Theology)
Guide	Develop learning resources
Debater	Integrate life and thinking
Engineer	Transmit ideas
Reseacher	Develop traditions
Legal worker	Create a culture for lifelong learning
Accountants	Translate languages

Table 6.5

I have found APEST to be incredibly helpful at uncovering the driving instinct that God built into people. For me, the expanded definition of the apostolic calling has greatly informed my clarity journey and enriched my daily work at Auxano and Denominee. Like the apostle Peter, I am a "sent one" to the existing church, helping re-found the mission of Jesus. It requires the design of new meaningful and missional strategies in the ever-shifting dynamic of church teams, cultural change, and the tendency to over-program. I help churches remake and reset a "core team" of staff, leaders, volunteers and attenders around clear vision—God's dream for their future.

Because of APEST's simplicity and flexibility, I prefer using it over traditional lists of spiritual gifts. Which function most characterizes your instinct as a follower of Jesus? Which function do you perform most evidently in your local church? Are you utilizing this capability in your vocation as well? You can take the APEST test in the Younique Life Plan Journey or learn more at 5Qcentral.com.

Strengths

With APEST providing a broad, five-component summary of human functioning, it's helpful to have a tool that can break your abilities down into more detail. We need a rainbow of possibilities to illustrate the nuances of your capability. Strengths will give us that palette, or better yet that pot o' gold at the end of the rainbow. Strengths are your developed talents—skills that bring thrills to bosses, team members, and customers. What kind of reproducible results do you create everywhere you go?

A helpful showcase of human ability comes from one of the most-read vocational planning books of all time: *What Color Is Your Parachute?* by Richard Nelson Bolles. Originally published almost fifty years ago, Bolles lists forty human skills: fourteen for working with people, fifteen for working with ideas, and eleven for working with things.[5] Another team has generated an even more helpful list. In 1998 Donald Clifton and Tom Rath with a team of Gallup scientists created an online assessment based on a list of thirty-four strength themes known as CliftonStrengths.

CliftonStrengths is one of the standard tools of the Younique Life Plan. The strengths are arranged into four big categories (table 6.6):

- *Executing*—making things happen
- *Influencing*—speaking up, taking charge, and influencing people to move forward
- *Relationship Building*—building stronger teams, groups, and relationships
- *Strategic Thinking*—gathering data and information to make better decisions

(For more information, go to GallupStrengthsCenter.com.)

CliftonStrengths Themes

Executing Themes	Influencing Themes	Relationship Building Themes	Strategic Thinking Themes
Achiever	Activator	Adapability	Analytical
Arranger	Command	Developer	Context
Belief	Communication	Connectedness	Futuristic
Consistency	Competition	Empathy	Ideation
Deliberative	Maximizer	Harmony	Input
Discipline	Self-Assurance	Includer	Intellection
Focus	Significance	Individualization	Learner
Responsibility	Woo	Positivity	Strategic
Restorative		Relator	

Table 6.6

As you read the list, be aware of how these interrelate to name, personality, and APEST, at the same time augmenting them with detail. For example, my top five themes are Activator, Self-Assurance, Individualization, Maximizer, and Strategic.

These both correlate with and nuance my name meaning, my "red-yellow" personality, and my apostolic APEST gifting.

Sense of Accomplishment

The fifth assessment of ability is your internal Sense of Accomplishment. The first time I began to appreciate this viewpoint is when I read the work of Arthur F. Miller on giftedness and motivated ability. Rather than assessing skills or strengths, the Sense of Accomplishment tool looks at the vital component of inherent satisfaction. What kinds of activities make you feel more alive? What do you "like to do and do well"?[6]

A few important qualities distinguish your Sense of Accomplishment:

- It has nothing to do with your education.
- It's very different than your personality type.
- It's not a talent you develop.
- It's not an ability that you acquire.
- It's probably not something that a teacher or boss awarded you for.

In fact, the last bullet point is very important. Most people are more aware of the external awards—like raises, bonuses, ribbons, and trophies—than they are of internal awe. When mining your Sense of Accomplishment, you don't want to be distracted by what your school teachers, parents, or bosses thought was an accomplishment. It's not about what made them proud, but what made you feel as though you had done something significant, and done it well. What really turned your crank on the inside that was invisible to the world? When were you walking on cloud nine when others only saw you walking down the sidewalk?

> Most people are more aware of the external awards—like raises, bonuses, ribbons, and trophies—than they are of internal awe.

For example, I was conducting a Sense of Accomplishment interview with Karen, and two experiences immediately arose. The first was what she did when she volunteered at retirement centers as a high school student. Evidently she was initially given things to do that didn't really help the elderly that much. Then, one day she took the glasses off of an older woman who was reading and cleaned them for her. The woman beamed with thanksgiving. She knew she had uncovered a secret strategy to add value to the old folks that no one else had figured out. It was literally right in front of everyone's face: glasses need to be cleaned.

The second experience was thrift shopping. Karen loved to spend time buying clothes that others had dismissed as too old and not worth keeping. Her favorite place on earth is a second-hand store. It created a deep sense of internal satisfaction for her to discover something usable and put it back into circulation.

When I connected the dots of these two events, Karen named her first Sense of Accomplishment: restoring value in a way that people easily miss. She restored value to the elderly by cleaning their glasses. She restored value to the act of volunteering by creating something practical to do in retirement homes. She restored value by fixing up or cleaning up shirts and skirts to be happily used again.

These activities pass the test. They aren't related to education, personality, talents, or external rewards. Restoring value is an intrinsically motivated activity for Karen. No one gives her accolades for these things. In fact, she could have easily listed ten career achievements. But they would not rank at the top of her Sense of Accomplishment list. You simply can't discover it on a test; you must listen to your soul.

Questions to help you discover your Sense of Accomplishment include:

- For each stage of growing up, what event, project, initiative, team, or thing gave you a deep sense of satisfaction? Keep in mind that no one else probably noticed.
- For each stage in your job history, what activities, roles, seasons, moments, or kinds of relationships did you enjoy the most?
- For jobs, what specific tasks or situations energized you the most?
- In your history of work, when did the right conditions really come together? What did that look like?
- What was the real payday for your work, not defined with money but with sense of happiness deep inside yourself?
- What have you secretly believed you would be really good at but never told anyone?
- Can you remember specific moments where you felt more fully alive? If so, what were you doing? Why did you feel more alive?

One of the greatest acceleration moments in my own Clarity Spiral over the years was coming to understand my own Sense of Accomplishment. After four years of seminary and another year working my way into the ideal vocational fit in my church job, I could still remember a Sense of Accomplishment from non-ministry activities I did well before my journey into ministry. But it was not easy to retrieve those memories at first, because the noise of affirmation and reward coming from outside of me distracted attention from the voice of deep accomplishment and joy inside of me.

When I answered the questions above for my own life after several hours of concentrated reflection, two windows of time beamed with significance.

My biggest Sense of Accomplishment comes when I learn something new when concepts get tested or put to use in real-life application. The first place that revealed this was the organic chemistry lab at Penn State. Organic chemistry has a terrible reputation—most students hate it. But I couldn't wait. There was a literal bounce in my step when I walked from the whiteboard classroom to the black-tabletop laboratory. I got excited handling flasks, Bunsen burners, and flammable chemicals.

The second place was the oil field where I was being trained as a field engineer after college. Every day for three months I would go to a classroom and a workshop; then I would work in a mock-up, life-sized oil field. For example, we would learn the concepts of five different pumps in one area of the building, rebuild the pumps in another, and operate the same kinds of pumps in the test drilling rigs. Those were long eighteen-hour days, but each one felt like Christmas to me.

Here is the list of things that create a Sense of Accomplishment in me. I encourage people to identify six and capture them in a single sentence or phrase:

1. Engaging the learning intersection when concepts get tested in real-life application
2. Seeing a team wrestle through dialogue and then agree on a big idea
3. Orchestrating a team of people who are influencing other people
4. Communicating an idea with a visually compelling design or a tool
5. Reading synoptically in a subject to distill the essence or to solve problems
6. Experiencing a learning curve in the presence of others who exhibit mastery

Other Assessments and Tools

The five tools to discern ability I described in this chapter and the five tools for passion in the previous chapter are by no means an exhaustive set. After years of studying the myriad of tools out there, however, I believe these are the best for a comprehensive and complete *first run* at your One Thing.

So what do you do with other inventories you may run across? Ask three questions of them to discern their use for your lifelong climb up the Clarity Spiral.

First, which ones are looking at the same information about yourself in a different way? At best these tools may give you a more complex and nuanced view. At worst they are 100-percent redundant. If you already know your DiSC profile, then Myers-Briggs will give you more helpful and specific detail about your personality. Insights Discovery, in turn, gives you much more than Myers-Briggs. But if you reverse the order—Insights, then Myers-Briggs, then DiSC—you don't gain much, if anything, from subsequent tools.

Second, which assessments are a bit more complex and require a coach or instrument expert? Explore how to get maximum benefit from working with a skilled practitioner beyond doing it yourself.

Third, where does the instrument fit in the toolbox of your life? As you acquire more self-data—and I certainly hope you do—think of the three circles of the Sweet Spot tool as big drawers in your clarity workbench. For example, does the tool help you zero in closer to your ability? Or does it help you understand a Life Drift in a deeper way?

As an example of what to do with a new tool, last year my executive coach recommended to me an emotional quotient inventory, the EQ-i 2.0. It was an excellent instrument. It helped show me how my default style of communication as a leader and some of my behavior preferences taken to an extreme limit my relationships. Again, I wouldn't recommend this instrument as a *first-run* tool if you have not named your One Thing yet, but I always champion new "courage to know" next steps.

Another instrument deserves special attention: the Enneagram, which is named for the nine-point diagram that classifies a person's predominant personality (figure 6.3). The Enneagram is a unique, multifaceted assessment that has been time-tested across the globe. It has been used for centuries, albeit with various accounts and different opinions about its evolution and influence. It's an open-source tool that isn't owned by any one person but has a community of practice that can testify to its value.

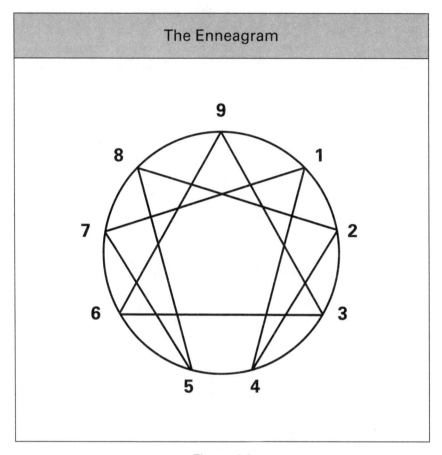

Figure 6.3

Today the Enneagram is experiencing a resurgence of interest among Christians and younger generations, I believe for good reason. Most personality inventories classify a person by how they function in the world, but the Enneagram is different. It classifies a person by their inner drive, by their prime motivation and aspiration. Other personality assessments especially help a group to improve in teamwork and communication, but the Enneagram especially helps an individual to grow in spiritual and emotional health. The model of what full maturity looks like varies for each type.

I believe that this is what appeals most about the Enneagram: it fills an assessment "slot" that no other tool does by looking at aspects of a person that no other tool does. Comparing it to the Younique toolbox, however, it does connect closely with Life Drifts as a deep expansion of where a person is most susceptible to temptation and why. It really is a Swiss Army knife of personal growth.

Yet despite the focus on the individual, the Enneagram also has use for analyzing interpersonal relationships, especially very intimate ones as in a marriage or family. For example, I am a Type 3, which is usually called the "Achiever" or "Performer." My wife Romy is a Type 4, known as the "Individualist" or "Romantic." The Enneagram has been an extraordinary lens to analyze how we function and interact in our relationship; it has brought unique insights to our marriage that we did not gain from any other tool.

Once again, if you haven't already explored the Enneagram, I don't recommend it if you haven't fastened on to your One Thing yet. (We actually had the assessment in an earlier version of the Younique toolbox before replacing it with others that are better for finding your Sweet Spot.) But once you've attained a break-thru grasp of your Life Younique, the Enneagram can be an outstanding tool for tapping more deeply into your passion.

Ability from Every Angle

Let's review our progress through the inventory of ability. We started with the somewhat mystical idea that your name may reflect some aspect of your calling or ability. Then we looked at personality as a way to define the style of communicating and interacting with the world that you prefer the most. From there we walked through APEST as both a biblical calling and a broad pattern of human functioning. To provide even more nuance, StrengthsFinder reveals how you turn talents into demonstrable value to people. And finally, the Sense of Accomplishment looks even deeper into your motivation makeup, clarifying when you feel most fully alive. Take all five together and you have an image of your ability from every angle.

That's the second circle of the Sweet Spot Master Tool. Now let's turn to the final inventory: context. Now that you have a growing self-awareness of passion and ability, let's zero in on where they can be applied best.

Chapter 7

CONTEXT

Five Tools to Find and Design
Your Ideal Environment

"Knowing where one belongs makes ordinary people—hardworking, competent but mediocre otherwise—into outstanding performers."
—Peter Drucker

At the beginning of part 2 we talked about the sweet spot in sports. One of the essentials to getting the maximum return for your effort (hitting it in the sweet spot) is getting the position just right. Take tennis, for example—you could have the best racket in the world, and you can have the smoothest, strongest swing on the court. But if the ball doesn't hit the racket in the right position—location, speed, angle, and rotation—you are going to leave power on the table.

The same is true with your special assignment from God. You can work extremely hard getting crystal-clarity on your passion and abilities but never find the best context to use them in. It's a huge waste of your potential to work in areas that aren't related to your purpose.

Context is everything. Have you heard of the Tanzanian folklore of the monkey and the fish? The rainy season in the African valley was worse than ever and many animals were fleeing the rising floodwaters. The monkeys were safely perched in the tree tops as other animals struggled for survival. One looked down and saw a fish, struggling in the current, apparently trapped by the raging water. So he reached down, grabbed the fish, and placed it safely into a nest of branches. Finally, the fish rested comfortably.

The monkey didn't realize that water is the life-supporting, vitality-creating context for the fish!

Environment matters. You don't want to be a fish out of water. You don't need any helpful monkeys in your life (parents, friends, coworkers) unaware of the kind of air you breathe.

Context as a Car Ride

Unfortunately, the subtleties of workplace context are invisible and go largely unidentified. But before we get into the five tools that bring your ideal context to light, let's look at a metaphor to help us understand context better.

> You can work extremely hard getting crystal-clarity on your passion and abilities but never find the best context to use them in.

Think of a company or organization or ministry team as a "vocational vehicle" that you can "ride" for the sake of your calling. Some vehicles are better than others at enabling you to fulfill and express your calling. Some jobs are like stepping into a 737 and others are like riding a scooter.

There are several reasons I like the metaphor of vocational vehicle. First, just as some vehicles aren't suitable for a particular journey, some contexts don't work at all for your call. You want to know that before getting on board. You can't go off-roading in a Mini Cooper. And you can't cross the ocean on a steam train. Likewise, you can't leverage your passion to play the saxophone while you're at work in a library.

Second, different vocational vehicles aren't good or bad in and of themselves; they are just unique. Some have certain advantages depending on where you want to go. Some give you a distinct kind of ride. Both a Jeep and a Camry can get you to the beach, but the ride is going to be a lot different. Likewise, accounting work in a Fortune 500 company has one vibe; keeping the books at a family donut shop has quite another.

Third, imagining your work as a vehicle helps you separate your identity from the work itself. For example, when I started my consulting company, Auxano, I didn't separate who I was from what I did very well. It was all lumped together in my mind and heart. But by choosing to see Auxano as one particular vehicle for my special assignment from God, I can better understand it and evaluate it as one vehicle among many possible others. It's totally freeing! In fact, without this helpful metaphor, I would not have the benefit of six different vehicles in my "vocational garage" today.

Which brings us to the fourth reason I employ the metaphor of vehicle: you will have multiple vehicles over your lifetime and can have multiple at the same time. My dad handed down to me a 1970 ¾-ton Chevy pickup years ago. The orange beast is a rarity in the world of vehicles. It sits in my garage and sees the road at most one time a month. It's a vehicle I really enjoy, but I don't use it every day. As I write these words as an expression of my vocation, I feel like I am riding in my 1970 Chevy; I thoroughly enjoy writing, but it is not my daily drive. Consulting, training, and toolmaking are.

The Five Context Tools

I want to help you find your perfect ride. To do so, let's walk through five simple yet powerful tools to explore your ideal vocational context—the third circle of the Sweet Spot Master Tool. The tools are: Activator-Advantage, Work Style, Life Stage, Workplace Motivators, and Vehicle Preferences. (See figure 7.1.)

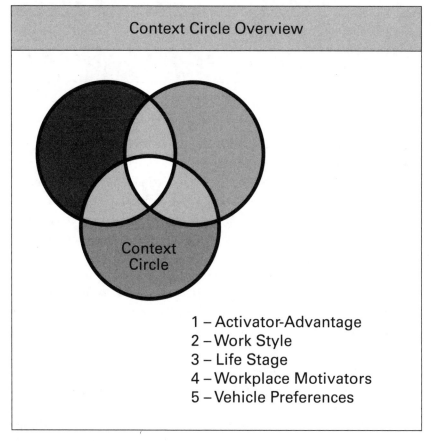

Figure 7.1

Aligning Your Advantage

The first tool looks at what activates you and what your competitive advantage is. It's Younique's adaptation of a life-planning construct by Tom Paterson called "Drivers and Comfort Zones." This tool provides a very broad perspective on basic context alignment— it's like deciding between taking a plane, train, or automobile to get to your destination.

Your "activator" is one of three broad ideas: command, creativity, or contribution. Your "advantage" has three components as well: ideas, things, or people. (See table 7.1.)

Activator-Advantage Alignment Categories

Activator What gets you going the most each day?	Advantage In what area do you excel the most relative to others?
Command	Ideas
Creativity	Things
Contribution	People

Table 7.1

The three areas of activation answer the question: "What gets you going?" Think of it as the spark plug of your day: it's what triggers action for you.

"Command" doesn't have to look as strong as it sounds; it simply means directing, leading, orchestrating, or guiding. It's about being in charge at some level, having a final say, and making things happen. Don't confuse it with being in the limelight, as there are many behind-the-scenes ways to command. Command-activated people want to see change happen and accept the mantle of leadership more quickly than others.

"Creativity" is about speaking up to exert influence in and through a group without being the one to give "marching orders." The group may be as small as a tight-knit collaborative team or as large as an entire industry. The work of creativity often involves aesthetics or image, but it also often involves making discoveries, solving problems, or making plans. Creativity activates people who love doing branding or public relations; designing products or physical structures; writing computer code; performing on stage or on screen; developing a winning strategy; or sharing knowledge by lecturing, preaching, or writing.

"Contribution" is about serving. It can be helping in a one-on-one setting as a counselor or a nurse does. Or it can be working with ideas and things to "make a contribution to the world" as a firefighter or a construction worker does. Tom Paterson explains, "People driven by a desire to serve or make a contribution do not want to be in charge. They may have very little concern about how something looks or is perceived by others. They are driven instead by a desire to see goals reached and people helped."[1]

You can sum up the differences between activators this way: command sets direction; creativity influences direction; contribution supports direction.

Unlike activation, your "advantage" is all about the zone of work where you kill it. People have a predominant affinity with ideas, things, or people. Which one gives you an unfair advantage?

Idea-people excel in the creation, curation, and distribution of all kinds of ideas. A snapshot of idea-people in motion includes writing music, using a spreadsheet, filing documents, writing poetry, or drawing with a whiteboard marker. I'm primarily an idea guy; I liked theological debate in seminary and I love using a flip chart to diagram a new strategy—not to mention, I am writing a book right now! In the realm of ideas I have a competitive advantage.

However, I'm at a serious disadvantage with things. People who are good with things can use, control, fix, manipulate, and manufacture the entire universe of stuff. From wielding a surgeon's scalpel to a plumber's pipe wrench to a cook's colander, these folks are awesome with their hands. The things advantage also includes the vast world of handling and nurturing living things, from plants to animals to the human body.

The third advantage category is people. Some roles require extreme focus in isolation while others demand constant personal interaction. Do you like to talk, inspire, motivate, sing, listen, console, connect, network, or sell? You probably have an advantage with people.

In the Younique Life Plan Journey, people force-rank their three activator and advantage categories. It takes sixty seconds. Then you evaluate your current context. Is your primary vocational vehicle aligned well with your ranking?

When Jack was in his twenties, he inherited the family farm with his wife Stella. He continued to manage the farm while she stayed in law school. When they each turned fifty they evaluated their lives, and both of them wanted a vocational change. Jack's shift was about "advantage," and Stella's change was signaled by her "activation."

Jack stepped from working the farm, which is all about things, to working with ideas. He had always dreamed of being a college professor; he now excels at teaching economics at a local college. Stella was motivated to move from the activator of command to contribution. She left a high-profile role as a corporate attorney that was a perfect fit for someone with command; it required decision-making and directing all of the time. So she became a legal consultant for the environmental industry. Now, rather than exerting herself to "take charge," she strategically supports key decision-makers.

A simple shift of context based on your activation and alignment can feel like putting a fish into water after agonizing minutes in dry air. Alive again!

Defining Your Work Style

Peter Drucker was one of the greatest management mavens of the twentieth century. He asked great questions not only of organizations but of individuals. The Work Style tool is inspired by the questions he poses in his book *Managing Oneself.* When it comes to knowing your work style, Drucker writes, "'How do I perform?' is as important a question as, 'What are my strengths?' In fact, it may be an even more important question. Amazingly few people know how they get things done."[2]

The tool itself is very simple. You simply reflect on a binary option for each of the following work style preferences: decisions, schedule, work pace, receiving information, and reporting information. Your answers to these five questions give you another perspective by which to evaluate your ideal context. Different vocational vehicles expect certain work styles, and you should strive for strong alignment.

The questions are as follows:

- *Decisions:* Do you prefer making decisions or advising on them?
- *Schedule:* Do you prefer flexible or structured schedule week by week?
- *Work Pace:* Do you prefer variable or predictable pace at work?
- *Receiving Information:* Do you prefer reading or listening?
- *Reporting Information:* Do you prefer writing or speaking?

Let me share an example that illustrates the price you pay when you don't have a good awareness of one of your work style preferences—in this case, receiving information. As Drucker explains, Dwight D. Eisenhower commanded the respect and awe of the press corps while he commanded the Allied Forces in Europe. No matter what he was asked, he always had the perfect, concise, brilliant answer. Bafflingly, the same man, as president of the United States, bombed his press conferences, responding to questions by rambling about different subjects altogether.

The problem was that Eisenhower greatly preferred reading to listening, and as a general he had the privilege of receiving questions in writing before he met the press. When he took on ad-libbed press conferences like his predecessors Roosevelt and Truman where he had to respond off the cuff, he was totally out of his element.

Roosevelt and Truman preferred listening as much as Eisenhower did reading. But they differed from him in another way as well: they altered their work situation to accord with their preference. Those presidents demanded oral briefings from their subordinates so they could absorb information and only then followed it up by reading.[3]

Like Roosevelt and Truman, to the degree that you can make adaptations in your current vehicle, do it (value to show!). To the degree that your vehicle is not optimized, you may be ready to explore some different vehicles for your vocation (risk to go!).

Considering Your Life Stage

If you study how all people work over a lifetime, you'll find a common pattern—there appears to be a standard arc to life's vocational journey. While no two people walk the exact same path, the contours of life's "great hike" across decades look similar from one person to the next.

Robert Clinton pioneered the development of life-line tools after studying the lives of influential biblical characters and historic and contemporary Christian leaders. Evaluating your life through a time line perspective can add significant insight with regard to vocational vehicles in general and the importance of transitions between two jobs. Consider these five benefits (adapted from Clinton):[4]

- *Benefit one:* A life-stage perspective *increases sensitivity* to God's leadership at any given time. Identify where you are. Use the life-stage perspective to ask: "What is God saying to me at this time?"
- *Benefit two:* A life-stage perspective *accelerates movement* toward God's next chapter by minimizing delays. Examine your current roles vocationally with your current age. Do you feel ahead, behind, or completely stuck with your vehicle alignment? Use the life-stage perspective to ask: "What is keeping me from advancing to the next stage?"
- *Benefit three:* A life-stage perspective *facilitates better decision-making* for personal development and vocational calling. Based on where you see yourself, what areas of growth are most important? Use the life-stage perspective to ask: "Do I need a better fit in my existing vocational vehicle (i.e., a better seat on the bus) or do I need a new vehicle?"
- *Benefit four:* A life-stage perspective *creates stability* during times of transition, trials, confusion, and complexity. Consider God's work in your life from a panoramic perspective. Practice your faith by saying a prayer of trust and worship. Use the life-stage perspective to ask: "How can I experience more peace and rest by trusting God in my life right now?"
- *Benefit five:* A life-stage perspective *highlights practices and barriers to finishing well* throughout all stages of life. As Neil Cole says, "Finishing well is not something you do at the end of life but through your life."[5] Use the life-stage perspective to ask: "What decisions today will help prepare me for increased contribution at the end of life?"

Since Robert Clinton's life stages are a tad technical and focused toward those in vocational ministry, I have included three others: a simplified version by Jon Acuff, a super-sticky one by Bob Buford, and a fun one for laughs (guess which one; see table 7.2).[6] It's important to note that these stages aren't intended to perfectly align with decades; the age ranges are helpful approximations only.

Four Life Stage Perspectives

Age	Robert Clinton	Jon Acuff	Bob Buford	Santa Claus
0-20	Foundations	Learning	Warrior	You believe in Santa
20s	Provisional Ministry	Learning	Warrior	You don't believe in Santa
30s	Growth Ministry	Editing	Warrior	You are Santa
40s	Competent Ministry	Mastering	King	You are Santa
50s	Unique Ministry	Harvesting	King	You are Santa
60s	Convergent Ministry	Guiding	Sage	You look like Santa
70+	Afterglow	Guiding	Sage	You look like Santa

Table 7.2

For Clinton, the Provisional stage is so labeled because a person may or may not stay in ministry. The Growth stage is all about sorting through your gifts in a self-discovery process. In the Competent Ministry stage, a leader is using his or her abilities and passions from both self-awareness and demonstrated performance. This kicks them into the Unique Ministry stage where the leader begins making their defining contribution. Finally, Clinton describes the Convergent stage and the Afterglow that follows. This season is when leaders have a conscious understanding of their destiny and ultimate contribution to the world. It becomes the time when the leader influences with sage-like wisdom and guidance.

One illustration of the power of a life-stage perspective came when I decided to sell my first business. At two earlier points, I was approached by suitors who wanted to buy Auxano. But I was still in my "Growth" stage. I was in an "Editing" phase reworking our core strategy to include training and certification. I was content to "pound the pavement" as a warrior-like salesman and had no interest to sell the business.

But as I approached age forty I could see the stages of Competent and Unique Ministry rushing toward me. Personally I became hungry to move forward from "Warrior" to "King" stage. I wanted to extend my influence through developing others to consult more than doing the consulting myself. When I was approached by the third person who wanted to buy Auxano, it synced up completely with my life stage. In fact, everything on my Clarity Spiral accelerated at that point. I remained the leader of that nonprofit "vehicle" (until recently stepping into the role of Auxano founder and launching a new company, Denominee), but I ceased to own the brand and the intellectual property. Linking up with LifeWay brought capital that enabled me to ramp up my work mentoring others. Today Auxano has ten full-time consultants and my influence has continued to multiply as a steward rather than an owner. Without the benefit and perspective of the life-stage perspective, I would not have seen or seized the opportunity.

God Himself weighs in on the life-stage perspective. In Numbers 8:23–26 God directs Moses to establish a vocational transition for the Levites who assisted the priests by transporting and administering the tabernacle. At age fifty, Levites were instructed to stop *doing the work* and start *assisting the doers*. That sounds like a beautiful recipe for mentoring and entering the Sage stage of life.

Knowing Your Workplace Motivators

The fourth tool for the Context Circle utilizes a list of features your vocational vehicle may or may not provide. Like the experience of buying a car, you have options—leather seats, the twelve-speaker premium sound upgrade, the towing package. In The Journey we curate a list created by Adrian Gostick and Chester Elton in their book, *What Motivates Me: Put Your Passions to Work.*[7]

By using a simple list, you can fine-tune your fit with your current role and workplace (table 7.3). I encourage you to know your top five. Mine are autonomy, impact, learning, variety, and purpose. Do you think that self-awareness helps as I make vocational decisions and negotiate role descriptions? You better believe it.

Workplace Motivators List by Gostick and Elton		
Autonomy	Friendship	Problem Solving
Challenge	Fun	Purpose
Creativity	Impact	Recognition
Developing Others	Learning	Service
Empathy	Money	Social Responsibility
Excelling	Ownership	Teamwork
Excitement	Variety	Pressure
Family	Prestige	

Table 7.3

For example, in the story of selling my company, I traded the motivator of "owner-ship" for the motivator of "impact." The spreading of my ideas was a greater desire than my ownership of them. One of the motivators is the same as one of my core values: learning. (We will cover the topic of values in chapter 11.) That makes it a mega-moti-vator for me. Any vehicle that did not have built-in opportunities to learn, including time and budget, would feel like riding in a car with no windows!

Seth is a pastor of family ministries. The office hours required of church staff drive him crazy. He finally negotiated the ability to work out of Starbucks on Thursdays—a step in the right direction for someone motivated by autonomy with a work style that prefers flexible structure.

Sandra is motivated by developing people. But she just took a position in upper-level management at a missions agency that doesn't make room for it. So she's pitching the idea of a mentoring track to the board as her first step in building a leadership pipeline.

While motivators give you some practical design features for your vehicle, it quickly runs up against the biblical warning I delivered in chapter 3. We don't want to design work around our motivators if we are selfishly running from the hand of God trying to teach us character formation. Remember, God uses the workplace to teach spiritual contentment, submission to authority, servanthood, sacrifice, and suffering. God had to guide me through many foundational lessons in Christian maturity in my twenties before I could significantly use motivators to design my job in later decades.

Optimizing Your Organizational Preferences

For the last tool of the Context Circle, I want to give you a quick categorization of different kinds of organizations you might work for. The goal is to provide you with key categories that may not automatically come to mind as you evaluate your calling. Think of it as a logical "vehicle checklist."

Preference One: Organizational Size—What organizational size optimizes your calling? Organizations of different sizes create different "size cultures," each with dis-tinct advantages and disadvantages:

- **Solo/Technician (1–2 people).** *Example:* I was an engineering assistant to the owner of a few private oil wells. It was just the two of us. I did abso-lutely everything he didn't want to. But in the junior position, if the mentor-apprentice relationship is strong and desirable, or if you are strongly activated by contribution, this setting can be ideal.
- **Small (3–25 people).** *Example:* For years I led the Auxano team of thirteen full-time people (plus thirty part-time team members who are less involved).

Coordination requires more effort than in a two-person operation, but it's a small enough group that I can not only know everyone but know them well.

- **Medium (25–200 people).** *Example:* I worked for a $200-million paint manufacturing company with about 100 employees. It was not too large or segmented that each of us couldn't know everyone else.
- **Large (200–1,000 people).** *Example:* I work for a division of LifeWay with over 500 people. There are more policies and procedures. I meet new people every time I visit the corporate office. I will never know everyone.
- **Enterprise (1,000+ people).** *Example:* I worked for Schlumberger (NYSE: SLB), the world's largest oil field services company. I was one of 113,000 employees representing 140 different nationalities in 84 countries.

Preference Two: Organizational Life Stage—Which organizational life stage best leverages your calling?

- **The entrepreneurial stage of start-up:** initial launch; much adapting based on the public's response to what the organization offers
- **The growing or rapid scale-up stage:** taking on new customers (or members) and increasing staff and specialization to handle demand
- **The stable or plateaued stage:** well-established organization; opportunities for expansion being considered
- **The stage of decline where turnaround is needed:** losing ground against other alternatives people have to choose from; structures, systems, and routines established in the past no longer delivering the value they once did

Preference Three: Relational Mode—What type of workplace interaction optimizes your calling? This combines the question of whether you prefer working virtually or in a brick-and-mortar workplace with your desire to work around people or not.

- **Independent-Virtual:** *Working not only independently by also by oneself virtually.* Sarah is a virtual accountant and works from home for multiple small companies. She has minimal interaction with her clients every day.
- **Social-Virtual:** *Interacting with people regularly but being by oneself virtually.* Javier works as a virtual executive assistant. He is on the phone constantly with people even through he works by himself from home.
- **Independent-Workplace:** *Working independently but with others physically around you.* Joyce conducts research for a pharmaceutical company. She can go all day without much conversation, but she is around people all day in the lab.

- **Social-Workplace:** *Interacting regularly with people physically around you.* Steven sells cars. Even though he does online sales, he stills works the lot, interacting with dozens of customers and others on his team every day.

Preference Four: Organizational Mix—How many vocational vehicles are required to optimize your calling?

- **One organization**
- **Two organizations**
- **Multiple organizations (3–6)**
- **Freelance (7+)**

Preference Five: Organizational Scope—What geographic scope best optimizes your calling? Are the people or organizations you serve distributed:

- **Locally:** in a town, small metro area, or rural area
- **Regionally:** in a large metro area, state/province, or section of the country
- **Nationally:** in multiple regions of the country
- **Globally:** in multiple countries

Preference Six: Organizational Ministry Type—Given the fact that every vocational calling is a ministry that brings glory to God, which ministry type is the best fit for you? This category is the reminder that a follower of Jesus working in a secular organization is still doing ministry full-time:

- **Church:** a local congregation
- **Parachurch:** a nonprofit extending the reach of the church, or the middle or upper levels of a church (denominational) structure
- **For-profit serving the church:** a business that sells products or services to the church and followers of Jesus to help them in their faith
- **Secular nonprofit:** a nonprofit without an explicitly Christian mission or beliefs
- **Public sector:** government, the military, law enforcement, and other publicly funded organizations
- **For-profit serving the general public:** a business that sells products or services to the public at large
- **Family:** a household

Putting It Together

Let's review the path we've taken to discern your ideal context. The five tools in this chapter give you the most comprehensive yet accessible design palette for finding a better fit at work. First we looked at what work mode activates you and whether you excel working with ideas, people, or things. Then we looked at six paired attributes to describe your work style. After that we considered the present stage of your vocational life. Next we explored your workplace motivators. Lastly, we examined six preferences that describe your ideal organization.

Any one of these perspectives on context is so simple yet so significant that an entire book could be written on it; how much more all of them together! Maybe you can now appreciate why I am so passionate about the Younique Life Plan Journey. Imagine working through each of these ideas with a cohort of others and an experienced coach. Knowing your ideal context makes the difference between having a sense that your work setting does not work for you as it should and knowing exactly *why* it doesn't work . . . and exactly what to look for in the next one.

You now have a three-dimensional set of inventories to discover your Life Younique from the angles of passion, ability, and context. Now it's time to find where they intersect and reveal the One Thing God made you to be.

Chapter 8

BULL'S-EYE

How to Name Your One Thing That Makes Sense of Everything

"Simplicity, clarity, singleness: these are the attributes that give our lives power and vividness and joy."
—Richard Halloway

On a three-hour plane ride, I sat next to a professional archer. As it turned out, he had a quiver full of wisdom to share about aiming and focus.

According to my new friend, when aiming at the colored concentric circles of a typical target, there are actually three ways to focus your eyes. You can aim "large" by looking at the target in its entirety. Or you can aim "small" by looking at the bull's-eye—the smallest circle. Most people understand the difference and appropriately aim for the center of the target. But that's not exactly where Robin Hood would be focusing. An expert marksman aims even "smaller" by focusing on the "center of the center" of the bull's-eye.

That sounded fascinating, but I wasn't quite sure what he meant. Then he demonstrated to me how our eyes can focus *very precisely*.

As an illustration, try it out for yourself: hold a quarter at arms length between your pointer finger and thumb with George Washington's profile facing you. As you look at the quarter notice how your eyes naturally capture the whole thing—your eyes take in the inch-wide metal disc. Now bring the quarter a little closer, just enough to focus on George's ear where it peeks out from under his wig. Focus your powers of observation on just that tiniest point; drill a hole through it with your eyes. Note that you can look at his ear to the neglect of his eye or his chin even while you are still "seeing" the entire quarter. That's the concept of finding the "center of the center" of the bull's-eye. Even though a typical bull's-eye is a plain red circle the size of the quarter at competitive distance, the eye can *arbitrarily* select a center point. It's that needle-point spot smaller than the bull's-eye itself that the archer's eye focuses on.

If you hunt or shoot, or if you just like Mel Gibson movies, you may know the phrase, "Aim small, miss small; aim big, miss big"—a line from *The Patriot*. That's the reason to aim for the center of the center. If a Navy sharpshooter aims for an enemy's shirt, he might miss by two feet. But if he aims for a button of the shirt, he might miss by only two inches.

The Simplicity on the Other Side of Complexity

We use the same principle from the world of target shooting to achieve break-thru in your special assignment from God. When most people think about life calling, they aim too large by being too general. They regurgitate ideas from our common call like "glorifying God" or "serving others." *Every* person was created for these noble pursuits! We have to get far more precise. In this case, the bull's-eye is what we call your Sweet Spot—the overlap of the three circles of your passion, your ability, and your ideal context. We want to "aim small" at this point so you don't miss the greatest discovery of your life's calling.

But right now we have a huge dilemma—you have tons of information from your three inventories that together comprise fifteen self-assessments, each with multiple data points. (StrengthsFinder alone gives you five signature themes.) There is far too much to look at to focus your life's aim; your head is swimming with all kinds of possibilities. We don't want you to drown in all of your learning. So how do we take a lot of *good things* and transform them into your *One Thing*?

Before showing you the powerful break-thru tool we use to answer this question, let's consider what this step actually involves. Technically, it's the process of finding meaningful synthesis to achieve a profound simplicity. That sounds pretty heavy, I know. But in simple terms, we're talking about taking all of the parts, perspectives, and pieces and building it into one thing, one idea.

My son Jacob had a profitable side-job of replacing his friends' broken iPhone screens when he was in high school. The first step—taking the iPhone apart—was fairly easy. But when he had to put the device back together, all of those parts on the kitchen table scared the Siri out of me. In essence, he had to take the little pieces of gadgetry and rediscover what it meant for them to be one thing—an operational iPhone.

With everything in life, it's easier to break stuff down (analyze) than it is to put stuff back together (synthesize). The same thing is true with all of your inventories. We have bits and pieces of your passion, ability, and context spread out on the kitchen table. Now we must build them into a unified idea of your unique productive self.

Notable thinkers in history have testified to the path through complexity to singularity.

"The whole is simpler than its parts." This was a proverb frequently spoken by J. Willard Gibbs, a chemist, physicist, and mathematician of such stature that Einstein called him "the greatest mind in American history."[1] You have heard it said that the whole is *greater* than the sum of its parts. But it is simpler as well. This idea is true of your One Thing—it cuts through all of the complexity to capture the whole of your life in a way that is way more powerful and true than the sum of all of your assessments.

"The main purpose of science is simplicity and as we understand more things, everything is becoming simpler" (physicist Edward Teller).[2] Translated to personal calling, this means that your One Thing becomes clearer—more powerful and more beautiful—the more you learn about the world and about yourself.

"I wouldn't give a fig for simplicity on this side of complexity, but I would give my life for simplicity on the other side." This is a popular paraphrase of the words of Supreme Court justice Oliver Wendell Holmes.[3] What in the world did he mean by this statement? Imagine the role of a judge who has to evaluate sticky situations and weigh all of the facts to keep the scales of justice balanced. He was explaining that before looking at all of the perspectives and testimony and data (complexity) it's easy to come up with simplicity that doesn't have much value. We might say it's *simplistic*. It's childlike, naive, or even foolish. It's only by finding simplicity on the "other side" of complexity that we can harvest immeasurable value. To say it another way, we must journey through what I call a "tunnel of chaos" that involves processing all of the possible options. You have to wander through the jungle to reach the clearing with an expansive view.

> It's simple to make something complex, but it takes a complex process to make something truly simple.

You won't find many books on intentional living that push this point, because it is not easy to do. It's simple to make something complex, but it takes a complex process to make something truly simple.

Enough philosophy. Allow me to share a concrete example.

Susan's Fabulous Break-thru

One of the very first people I coached through Younique came at a friend's request. Chris's wife, Susan, had been working with a life coach and taking various personal assessments. On her journey toward clarity she was lost in the fog, so Chris asked me to help. You could say she was in the middle of her own tunnel of chaos.

I spent two hours interviewing Susan one afternoon by her backyard pool in Orlando. She had manila folders spread out on the glass table with personality reports and personal notes. The entire time we talked I had the secret weapon in my back pocket.

Here are some features of Susan's life that stood out to me from asking her questions and listening to her responses:

- Susan loves to host parties and has a spiritual gift of hospitality.
- Susan is a very optimistic person who is energized by people.
- Susan started her own interior decorating business.
- Susan can spend hours poring over decisions about colors and textures of furnishings and accessories to make a room look just right for her client.
- Susan is motivated not merely by the final design of a home's decor but by how the decor makes the homeowner feel.
- Susan sees her role as a wife and mother in a similar fashion to hosting a party or designing a home, yet it's not an event or a project she's preparing but a lifetime of "designing" life as a family.
- Susan plays a critical supporting and nurturing role to her family by bringing essential ingredients together to catalyze Spirit-inspired joy.

After a few quiet moments while I reflected on all of this, I shared a big idea with Susan over the hum of the pool pumps; I pitched my best thought about her life's One Thing.

"I want you to hear something, Susan," I said gently. "Allow it to sink in for a second and let me know what you think." I paused. "I think God created you to honor Him and help others by *designing enjoyment*."

Tears of joy immediately started streaming down her face. Her countenance changed. Everything in the files, as important as they were, disappeared for a moment. The whole of her life became simpler than the sum of her assessments. Her entire world made more sense. She tasted the simplicity on the other side of complexity. In Richard Halloway's words, Susan experienced "power and vividness and joy" in naming her One Thing.

What did I say to Susan that was so transformative? I spoke one sentence that ended with what participants in The Journey know as the "Two Words": "Susan exists to honor God and help others by *designing enjoyment*." That's it. Two little words captured her One Thing. Don't miss the profound in the simple.

So what did Susan get out of these Two Words? They obviously moved her deeply, but why?

For one, she got a superior launch point for exploring the dimensions of her Life Younique. As you can guess from how much more book there is ahead, there's a lot more to designing the life God dreamed for you than verbalizing Two Words. But discovering your One Thing is finding the *terra firma* from which you cast off on that voyage. It is the fixed point from which the rest of the map of your life can be drawn.

But in the moment by the pool, that was all far ahead of Susan. What was immediately present, however, was *clarity*. Clarity is what bursts forth when singularity meets specificity. Landing on one thing—*her* One Thing—opened Susan's eyes. In that moment she not only saw the center of her center, but through that center she glimpsed her circumference. To borrow a metaphor from C. S. Lewis, the words *"designing enjoyment"* weren't just a *spectacle*—a wonder to be viewed—but a *pair of spectacles* through which Susan could view everything else in her life.

But I think that Susan was most overcome because, for a fleeting moment with everlasting effects, she knew herself. More important, *she knew that she was known*. Susan grasped by experience that the God who made her "fearfully and wonderfully" and who was determined to make "everything new" in her life formed her "inmost being" and knew it intimately (Ps. 139:13–14; Rev. 21:5 NIV). Despite the fact that sin had twisted and corrupted all aspects of her person—as it has in us all—at bottom there lay God's holy intention for her that nothing could erase, the aspect of his image and likeness that he was pursuing in her with a relentless redemptive love. To be known that deeply and loved that much by One that great—and to see him seeing you—is the supreme rapture that humans were invented to enjoy.

The Sweet Spot Master Tool: The One Tool to Rule Them All

The story I just told you was about how I found Susan's One Thing, but how do you find yours?

By sharing with you Susan's Two Words, I actually ran ahead a little bit. Your Sweet Spot—the coalescence of your passions, your abilities, and your ideal context, at which lies your One Thing—can be expressed in three different, complementary ways. I recommend that you start your Sweet Spot swing with a tool called Signature

Scripture if you tend to "feel" your way to the truth, or start with the Big Sentence if you "think" your way there. Then once you've done that, flip to the other one. Finally, wrap up your synthesis by naming your Two Words.

Sweet Spot Tool #1: Signature Scripture

The Signature Scripture is a tool that connects you emotionally to your One Thing. It is nothing more than the answer to one question: *Which Scripture speaks most powerfully to the center of your soul?*

If you've been a Christian for a while, you might have a reflexive answer to this question, and that answer might be the right one. But if one jumps to mind, take a little time to think it over.

First of all, note that the word *Scripture* is elastic. It doesn't have to be one Bible verse. It can be a chapter or a story or a psalm or a parable. Length doesn't matter; connectedness does.

Second, it is not uncommon for a Scripture to capture our attention and describe us well for a period of life, but as we age it no longer serves the same purpose. It's not that we outgrow it (as if we could ever age out of the Word of the Eternal One). It's that our awareness of God and our awareness of ourselves, not to mention our awareness of Scripture itself, increase with time and expand our biblical horizons.

You may well have multiple claimants for your Signature Scripture. Compare them to your Passion, Ability, and Context Circles. Which one best reflects what you see there? More important, which one speaks best to the widest scope of your life and the longest stretch of your life line, including the future? Most important, which one triggers your inner yes?

Why is it called your "Signature Scripture"? Picture yourself on your deathbed. You're putting the finishing touches on a memoir of your whole life. On the bottom of your last page you intend to sign your name, but instead you write a Scripture reference that seals up the whole. Which is it? What one text should be preached at your funeral to encapsulate all you are?

Sweet Spot Tool #2: Big Sentence

The Big Sentence is a tool that connects you cerebrally to your One Thing. It is complex but not complicated; it is one long step from the wealth of information in your inventories to a single statement of your uniqueness.

The Big Sentence is a twelve-point list in one breathless mouthful. You assemble it by deciding on four summary insights from each of your Passion, Ability, and Context Circles. For example, Cory's Big Sentence says:

I am created to honor God and help others by leveraging my abilities to:

- reform,
- gain insight,
- explain, and
- stand up for good

with a deep passion for:

- belonging,
- both-ands,
- justice and righteousness, and
- peace

in the context of:

- synthesizing ideas (mine and others'),
- a small group of friends and companions,
- intellectual seekers and learners, and
- recognized contribution to something important with national reach.

For expressive types, filling in twelve blanks might seem a little stiff. Admittedly, the Big Sentence isn't artful, but it is joyful. Are you familiar with Mad Libs, the goofy game where you pick random words to populate the gaps in a story and then hear it back in full? Think of the Big Sentence as your "Glad Libs." The words that fill in these blanks are anything but random—they are ultra-faithful to the high-fidelity grooves God has etched into your life. They make God glad when you spin the vinyl and he hears his handiwork.

It makes you glad to hear it too, because in Frederick Buechner's words, "The place God calls you to is the place where your deep gladness and the world's deep hunger coincide."[4]

Sweet Spot Tool #3: Two Words

The concept of the Two Words is derived from the "2-word purpose" developed by Kevin McCarthy and expounded in his book, *The On-Purpose Person*.[5] In The Journey they form the concluding words of this sentence: "I exist to honor God and help others by . . ." The format for the last two words is "_____ing _____." In Susan's case it was *designing enjoyment*. In my case it's *applying essence*. Many other wonderful examples are in the panel on page 100.

**Top Ten Panel: 10 Examples of Two
Words from The Journey**

1. "Fostering congruence" (Dave R.)

2. "Shaping solutions" (Tessy M.)

3. "Raising capacity" (Jim R.)

4. "Intentionalizing integration" (Kim R.)

5. "Empowering momentum" (Kelly K.)

6. "Articulating perfection" (Cory H.)

7. "Shepherding significance" (Will H.)

8. "Orchestrating futures" (Brian U.)

9. "Igniting passion" (Chad P.)

10. "Animating truth" (Joel M.)

Those examples are as mysterious as they are wonderful, because the Two Words rest on the razor-thin watershed between interpretation and inscription. They are the narrow keyhole that all understanding of the data of your inventories finally funnel into and also the tiny opening through which words begin pouring forth on the other side of the door. Consequently, they come across as both revealing and obscure when they aren't explained by the person they belong to. I like to think of the Two Words as a little, fragile, practice copy of the "white stone . . . [with] a new name . . . that no one knows except the one who receives it" (Rev. 2:17).

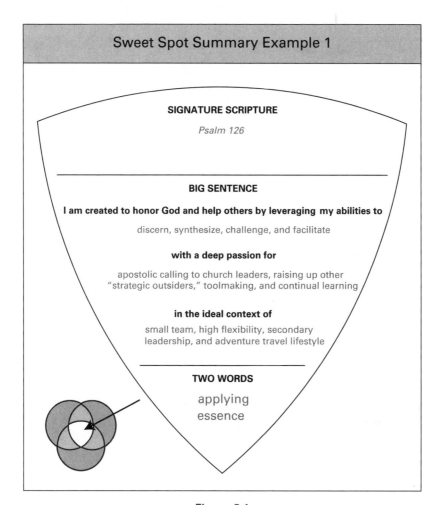

Sweet Spot Summary Example 1

SIGNATURE SCRIPTURE

Psalm 126

BIG SENTENCE

I am created to honor God and help others by leveraging my abilities to

discern, synthesize, challenge, and facilitate

with a deep passion for

apostolic calling to church leaders, raising up other
"strategic outsiders," toolmaking, and continual learning

in the ideal context of

small team, high flexibility, secondary
leadership, and adventure travel lifestyle

TWO WORDS

applying
essence

Figure 8.1

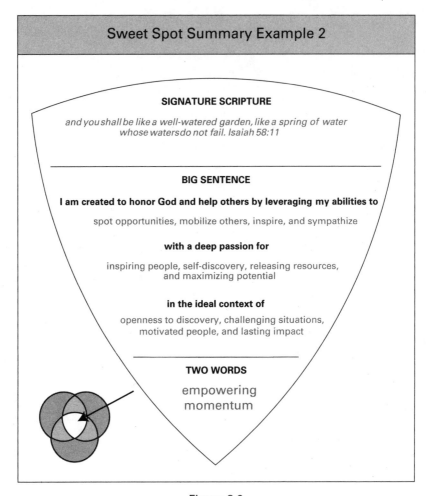

Sweet Spot Summary Example 2

SIGNATURE SCRIPTURE

and you shall be like a well-watered garden, like a spring of water whose waters do not fail. Isaiah 58:11

BIG SENTENCE

I am created to honor God and help others by leveraging my abilities to

spot opportunities, mobilize others, inspire, and sympathize

with a deep passion for

inspiring people, self-discovery, releasing resources, and maximizing potential

in the ideal context of

openness to discovery, challenging situations, motivated people, and lasting impact

TWO WORDS

empowering
momentum

Figure 8.2

Once you've journeyed through fifteen assessments in three inventories, a Signature Scripture, and a Big Sentence, you have the equipment you need to tackle your Two Words. The technique itself is quite simple: just start listing candidates—a lot of them (forty is a good minimum to shoot for). Then look back at your brainstormed list and select three finalists. Then pick a winner. You might manufacture a hybrid—the first word of one pair and the second of another.

How do you know you've found your Two Words? I can think of ten ways.

Top Ten Panel: 10 Things Your Two Words Do for You

1. They excite you when you hear them.

2. They apply to every role in your life.

3. They work in every sphere of influence.

4. They generate almost unlimited energy.

5. They tie together almost all of your assessments.

6. They continue to grow as your life's biggest idea.

7. They make you want to thank God for making you that way.

8. They make you manifest Jesus naturally.

9. They incline you to serve people.

10. They serve as your ultimate must-do/don't-do filter.

 (The contents of this chapter represent a discernment process where it helps to get additional coaching. Consider checking out my online course entitled *Find Your One Thing* at LifeYounique.com/courses.)

The Secret to Life

I hope this chapter and all of part 2 have gotten you raring to know and name your One Thing. But if you need a little more motivation to put you over the top, I can think of no better source than Jack Palance.

Palance won an Oscar in 1992 for his portrayal of Curly, an old, leather-skinned cowboy driving cattle for a dude ranch in the movie *City Slickers*. Over a lifetime, Curly has devoted himself to his vocation single-mindedly, giving up anything that would get in the way, even an opportunity for lasting love and companionship.

Mitch (played by Billy Crystal), a tourist on the cattle drive who is mired in the confusion of a mid-life crisis, is befuddled by Curly's choices because of all Curly missed out on. But as they ride together down the trail, Mitch confesses that he admires the cowboy, because Curly's life makes sense to Curly.

In response, Curly laughs through his cigarette. "Do you know what the secret to life is?" he asks Mitch with effortless cool.

"No. What?" Mitch answers.

Curly stops his horse and holds up one finger. "This," he says. "One thing—just *one thing*. You stick to that and everything else don't mean . . ." well, Paul would say "dung" (Phil. 3:8 KJV).

"That's great," Mitch replies with a touch of sadness, "but what's the one thing?"

Curly's answer is one for the ages: "That's what *you've* got to figure out."

PART THREE

YOUR IDENTITY
How to Declare Who You Are Today

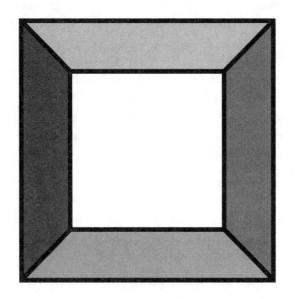

VISION
FRAME

Have you ever put together a jigsaw puzzle?

I'm going to guess that the jigsaw puzzles you've put together had fewer than half a million pieces. Unless, that is, you were one of the 1,600 university students in Vietnam in 2011 who assembled a 551,232-piece behemoth measuring 3,708 square feet—almost as large as a high school basketball court.

Whether you're putting together your very first twelve-piece jigsaw puzzle as a two-year-old, or you're setting a Guinness world record as these Vietnamese puzzlers did, assembling the puzzle has the same first step: frame up the edges. For one, the edge pieces are easier to identify than the others, so assembling them reduces clutter—it reduces the number remaining to sort through. For another, assembling the edges provides the sturdy structure that supports the rest of the picture, the basis for how the rest of the pieces come together and make sense.

Think of your identity as the edge pieces of the direction of your life. Everyone wants to know what they're supposed to do. But you can't get a handle on that until you know who you are. Knowing your Sweet Spot is a huge step toward grasping your identity, but it isn't enough by itself. You need to link together more pieces of the puzzle to frame the picture of where you're going.

Part 3 is where I teach you the secrets of finding and framing the edges of the puzzle through the master tool that I call the Vision Frame. The four sides of the frame—your mission, your values, your strategy, and your measures of success—are the four ways you inscribe your identity and name your Life Younique. In fact, we have a catchy way to remember the four sides:

- Your mission is your *LifeCall*
- Your values are your *LifeCore*
- Your strategy is your *LifeSteps*
- Your measures of success are your *LifeScore*

After you put the identity-edges of your life together, the picture of your future—your LifeMap—will become increasingly clear. When you know who you are, you begin to find out where you're going.

Chapter 9

CLARITY

Five Things That Make the Difference Between the Amateur You and the Professional You

> *"What people don't realize is that professionals are sensational because of the fundamentals."*
>
> —Barry Larkin

John Scolinos coached baseball at Cal State Polytechnic, Pomona for twenty-nine years after fourteen years as the head coach at Pepperdine. If you're not a baseball coach, you've probably never heard of him, but among his peers he was a legend.

In a talk to a gathering of four thousand coaches, Coach Scolinos illustrated a truth about coaching that powerfully applies to the discipline of coaching ourselves.

For starters, Scolinos walked on stage with a home plate tied around his neck and draped across his chest. Not a model of home plate—the actual, genuine, regulation article.

Then Scolinos spoke for twenty-five minutes, never mentioning the piece of equipment bizarrely hanging off of him. Finally, the seventy-eight-year-old coach shared with his audience the secret he learned that governed his entire life.

Scolinos asked, "How many Little League coaches do we have here? Would you raise your hands?" When they dutifully did so, he asked them, "How wide is home plate in Little League?"

"Seventeen inches," they replied.

"Seventeen . . . ," Scolinos echoed. "Very good. Now, are there any junior high baseball coaches here?" They raised their hands too. "How wide is home plate in junior high?"

"Seventeen inches," they said.

"Seventeen," repeated Scolinos. "Now, how about high school? Any high school coaches here?"

And on it went . . . high school, college, minor league, even major league baseball coaches were all in attendance. And as Scolinos asked each group how wide home plate was, each group replied, "Seventeen inches."

"So," Scolinos asked the audience, "*at any level*, if one of your pitchers cannot throw a strike over those seventeen inches, do you widen the plate to make it easier for him to throw a strike?" The coaches shook their heads and murmured dissent. "Of course not," Scolinos continued. "You don't widen the plate. Your pitcher learns to throw over the plate or you send him packing. So why, throughout all society, do we see people widening the plate rather than learning to pitch? We widen the plate by relaxing standards of right and wrong and by lowering standards of excellence. What we ought to be doing is *teaching people how to throw over the plate*."[1]

As you can imagine, Scolinos's illustration has a broad range of applications, but I want to apply it to your Life Younique. I want you to imagine that your One Thing is your strike zone. You won't be successful if you broaden your life's call to make it easier to pitch over it. Rather, you'll succeed by learning to pitch over the plate—that is, by focusing your life precisely on the target that God dreamed up when he designed you.

By knowing your Sweet Spot—expressed in a Signature Scripture, a Big Sentence, and Two Words—you have a stronger grasp than ever before of how to groove a belt-high fastball when you pitch your life. But that's not enough by itself. You need solid dimensions, crisp angles. You need to know not only how to pitch down the middle but also how to paint the corners. You need to know everything your life is and everything it's not. To attain that level of personal clarity, you need a tool that sets your Sweet Spot as your foundation and builds on it. You need a Vision Frame.

The Vision Frame Inside

Do you have a hobby you're passionate about? Something you really love? Something you know well and have gotten good at?

I've asked this question to hundreds of people, and I never cease to be amazed at what people do for fun. I've learned about hobbies I didn't know existed, from making cigar-box guitars to collecting chess sets to hunting wild hogs with dogs and knives.

If I learned that you have a hobby you're passionate about, I would ask you five questions. Based on experience, I bet that no matter how reserved or soft-spoken you are, you would enthusiastically rattle off fascinating answers without batting an eye. (In fact, take a few moments and answer these questions one by one—it's fun!)

First, I'd ask you to tell me in one sentence what your hobby is.

Second, I'd ask you what you love about your hobby.

Third, I'd ask you to tell me the basic steps or phases of doing what you do. What three to six basic activities are involved in your hobby?

Fourth, I'd ask you what makes a really good practitioner of your hobby. If you were grading someone on how good they were at it, what items would be on the scorecard?

Finally, I'd ask you what you'd like to be doing in your hobby in the near-term future and what goal you hope to achieve several years from now.

Go ahead and think about a hobby for a minute and answer these questions.

If you did, you just created a Vision Frame for your hobby. The Vision Frame answers the Five Irreducible Questions of Life (table 9.1). Everything you do has these five questions built into it:

- When I asked you *what* your hobby is, I asked for your hobby's *mission*. In your Life Younique, we call your mission your *LifeCall*.
- When I asked you what you love about your hobby, I was essentially asking you *why* you do it. Your answers are your hobby's *values*. We call your life's values your *LifeCore*.
- When I asked you about the basic activities of your hobby—in other words, *how* you do it—your answers revealed your hobby's *strategy*. We call your life's strategy your *LifeSteps*.
- When I asked you to outline the scorecard to measure a person's mastery at your hobby, I was basically asking you *when* a person can be considered successful at it. Your answers are your hobby's *measures*. We call your life's measures your *LifeScore*.
- And when I asked you about your dreams and goals for your hobby—*where* you want to go with it—I was asking for your hobby's *vision proper*. We call your life's vision your *LifeMap*.

Five Irreducible Questions of Life			
Frame Component	**Icon**	**Irreducible Question of Life**	**Life Orientation**
Mission		What am I doing?	LifeCall
Values		Why am I doing it?	LifeCore
Strategy		How am I doing it?	LifeSteps
Measures		When am I successful?	LifeScore
Vision Proper		Where is God taking me?	LifeMap

Table 9.1

Answers to the first four questions form the four sides of a Vision Frame: a picture frame with your LifeMap in the middle. The Vision Frame inscribes your identity; your LifeMap describes your direction. For the most part, your identity stays the same over time, though your grasp of it may deepen. But your direction changes repeatedly over time as you move from one milestone to the next. We have another master tool called the Horizon Storyline to paint the picture of future vision, and we'll get to that in part 4. In the chapters that follow, however, I'm going to help you build your four-sided Vision Frame one side at a time.

> The Vision Frame inscribes your identity; your LifeMap describes your direction.

But before we do that, here's what I want you to notice. You didn't have to *invent* answers to the questions I asked you about your hobby. The questions simply *uncover* what was already inside you. I have interviewed hundreds of people about their hobbies in front of their peers. Every single time the person has immediate, articulate answers to these questions off the top of their head. When a human being is proficient and passionate about an activity, they exhibit unconscious competence and intuitively master the questions of what, why, how, when, and where. The answers to these questions are always already there.

Now just imagine if you were as passionately proficient at living your life as you are at practicing your hobby. Imagine if you had immediate, articulate answers to all these questions about your life on the tip of your tongue. Imagine capturing the depth, breadth, and richness of your life in a napkin sketch you can show your friends over coffee.

Sound impossible? It's actually within your grasp.

Go Pro at Being You

Remember the story of Mia in chapter 4? She couldn't cross from *inventory* to *implementation* without an *identity* bridge to the other side. The Sweet Spot Master Tool is rich with three inventories comprising fifteen assessments. Implementation comes later in the Younique Life Plan Journey. In between, the Vision Frame is your identity bridge from the one to the other.

Remember that the identity bridge is supported by two pillars: *interpretation* and *inscription*. Each of the tools I'll share with you in part 3 build on your interpretation of your life discovery work as captured in your Sweet Spot. Then the tools require you to inscribe (verbalize and write down) your answers to the Five Irreducible Questions of Life.

That might sound complicated, but it's not. It is, however, *complex*. It would be great if you could answer the five questions about your life as easily as you can about your favorite hobby, but a life is a much more complex and beautiful thing. Moreover, you inhabit your life in a way that makes it difficult to see from the outside.

But the tools of the Vision Frame help you to step outside yourself and see yourself in a new way. As you already experienced if you found your Sweet Spot, each side of the frame leads you through the "tunnel of chaos"—a mental mess—to arrive at the wonderful bliss of simplicity on the other side. When you reach it, the break-thru will change your life.

I recently checked off a bucket list item by spending two weeks in the Outer Banks of North Carolina. In the town of Waves there is a several-mile stretch that beckons some of the best wind in North America for various water sports. (It's not far from Kitty Hawk, where the Wright brothers first successfully tested powered flight.) During that time, a professional kiteboarder named Evan Netsche spent twenty hours coaching me during eight riding sessions.

Evan is a pro. He has ranked in the top ten in some world freestyle competitions. His grace and ease and his effortless forty-foot leaps are wonders to behold. Other than tons of natural talent, Evan has one big advantage over me: he started when he was thirteen years old and has spent more than ten thousand hours flying a power kite with a board between his bare feet and the water.[2]

While I thoroughly enjoy getting better as an amateur, I'll never be professional. I'm too old, even if I wanted to invest the time.

But there is one area of life where I never want to settle for being an amateur. I don't ever want to be an amateur at being Will Mancini. I don't want to be obliviously mediocre or happily average at living my one and only life. And I don't want you to settle either. If I ever get the chance to meet you face-to-face, I want to see you being *you*, making everything look effortless with the grace and ease of my friend Evan.

Now, you don't have to do any of the work in the book to be an amateur at living your life. But what if you could be a professional at being you? You already have the most important advantage you need: an unbelievable amount of hours to practice. In fact, you will probably get ten thousand more hours of practice over merely the next twenty months. You catch my drift? You were made to be a pro.

You were made to be a gold medalist in a special assignment from God. It's not a question of whether you have the talent for it—in fact, you're the only one who does or ever will. All it takes is a bit of coaching and a commitment to work at it until you find home plate in the shape of your personal Vision Frame.

Chapter 10

MISSION

How to Capture the Boldest Idea of Your Life

"Everyone has his own specific vocation or mission in life; everyone must carry out a concrete assignment that demands fulfillment. Therein he cannot be replaced, nor can his life be repeated, thus, everyone's task is unique as his specific opportunity to implement it."
—Victor E. Frankl

Have you ever been lost but didn't know it? Maybe you took a hike in unfamiliar woods or ran an errand in a new town?

During my first year of church consulting, Tom, a pastor in Virginia, brought me in to help grow his church. On my second trip he invited me to arrive twenty-four hours early to experience a day on the best trout stream in the state. Of course I opted in. The river journey was an eight-hour extravaganza of non-stop fly-fishing action.

But we had a little incident that seemed inconsequential at first. Tom had brought a canoe so we could cover plenty of miles of Virginia-stream heaven. Despite our years of fishing experience, we managed to capsize the boat at a twenty-four-inch waterfall drop in the river. (Okay, maybe it was a little less than that, but it's too embarrassing to admit.) Eventually we retrieved all of our gear with the exception of Tom's Coke-bottle-thick eyeglasses. We spent an hour trying to find them walking through the waist-deep current. With no luck, he didn't seem too bothered. So we carried on and enjoyed a banner day of catching trout.

At the journey's end we packed up into Tom's fifteen-year-old, light blue, stick-shift Subaru. We had exactly the two hours we needed to make it back in time for a deacon's meeting at the country church. I noticed that Tom was a little hesitant to get in the driver's seat. He then informed me that he is legally blind without his glasses. No problem. I told him that I would drive. With a dash of jest, I asked him not to glance at the speedometer! Legally blind or not, I wanted him to be totally innocent in case I broke the speed limit.

And that I did. You see, one of Tom's problems was significant angst among his twenty-five rowdy deacons—the last thing he needed was to be bopping in late to his own meeting because he took the consultant fishing! I soon discovered the top speed of that peppy little Subaru. It was a beautiful drive home until a sign flashed by that I never expected to see: "Welcome to West Virginia." In a moment of bewilderment, I double-checked with Tom about our vehicular heading. (He didn't even see the sign, by the way.) It turned out that I had taken a wrong turn—forty-five minutes earlier.

We had to call off the deacons' meeting at the last minute. It became the last straw for that troubled little church. And any help that a young consultant might have brought was henceforth rendered inconsequential. Six months later, Tom left the church.

I learned many lessons that day. First, always steer your canoe head-on into a small waterfall. Second, a hornets' nest can be a safer place than a room of mad deacons. And third, a wrong turn can be quite costly.

The Serious Consequences of the Wrong Direction

My story about Tom is my constant reminder of what happens when energy is spent going in the wrong direction. Many people can relate to a time when they were lost but didn't know it. Yet in my view, the worst problems of misdirection in life are not bad U-turns or turning left when you should have gone right as I did with Tom. As bad as the consequences might be, those errors usually become evident sooner rather than later. Life, however, is more like flying an airplane than driving an automobile. An airplane has three dimensions and 360 degrees of motion and freedom. Your life is not driving down a roadway system of fixed options with 90-degree turns. Rather, you are free to make minor course corrections and altitude adjustments all of the time, every day.

My father was an instructor pilot in the early '70s. He flew the T-38 Talon super-sonic jet out of Williams Air Force Base in Mesa, Arizona, where one-fourth of all Air Force pilots learned to fly. He told me once that when flying the speed of sound, it's easy to get off course. If the pilot is just one degree "off-compass," he will be one mile off-target for every sixty miles moving forward. At the speed of sound, that equates to being a mile off-target every minute.

The speed of sound is appropriate to the speed of life. Time never stops. Every minute you take twenty breaths. Your mind can wander anywhere for those long seconds. You can text a message of love or stew in a moment of bitterness. You choose your groove minute by minute and hour by hour. What, may I ask, is your compass bearing as you fly through life at Mach 1? As Michael Altshuler says, "The bad news is times flies. The good news is you're the pilot."

If you are like most people, you probably don't have a directional heading written down or living in your mind and heart. So if you were lost, how would you know it? And how would you get back on track?

Imagine what's at stake when you are lost and you don't know it:

- You are wasting time.
- You are draining your resources and energy.
- You are moving farther from your destination.
- You are missing important milestones, connections, and people.
- You are potentially guiding others in the wrong direction.

These problems are real and visceral when you are hiking with limited water in your canteen. Or when you are scared to death on a sailboat with no view of shore. Or when you are trying to get a pastor who's already on thin ice back to the church building in time for the deacon's meeting.

But when it comes to the lives we're living, we literally pay the same kind of price but *magnitudes* higher. It's not a silly or scary story that you have fun retelling. It's lost weeks, months, and years of 9-to-5 energy. It's a decade of life missed with your children. It's settling for mediocre when God designed you for meteoric.

How many hundreds of little decisions and dozens of big ones are you making without a life compass? It's a bit uncomfortable to admit, but is it possible that you are living life without a defined, unique sense of purpose? Remember, I am not talking about the general call of following Jesus, but the specific, "for such a time as this" orientation of your life (see Esther 4:14). If you don't know your personal assignment from God, what are you actually spending your time on?

I know what you're thinking: "Enough already, Will; I get the point. Don't you think you're exaggerating a little?" In a word, no—I am not exaggerating as much as I am clarifying how little most people care about the reality of having a meaningful and useful compass for their life.

What about you? Are you ready to get crystal clear and hold a real golden compass in your hand that keeps you pointed in the right direction personally, relationally, and vocationally? Then you're ready for a next-level life mission or purpose statement— what I call your LifeCall.

Personal Mission as LifeCall

Figure 10.1

LifeCall Defined

The LifeCall is the first part of the Vision Frame for you to declare (figure 10.1). To do so, you will go back to the Sweet Spot tool and the Two Words that summarize your One Thing. The focus of that work is precision—*singularity with specificity*. The goal was to use the English language to state as exactly as possible *what only you can do*.

The LifeCall advances that initial work to create a short sentence that is even more meaningful and memorable. We want a statement that is easier to share with others than your Two Words. You may recall my Two Words: I exist to honor God and help others by *applying essence*. While that phrase is very meaningful to me, it is hard to share with folks in a casual way. When I do they give me one of those hollow smiles and an awkward, "I am glad for you" kind of look. My good friend and Younique cofounder, Dave Rhodes, has an even stranger set of Two Words: *fostering congruence*. Weird, right?

> LifeCall is a brief, bold, big idea that best captures today what God made you to do.

Without undermining the importance of the Two Words, we want to build with them. My Two Words of *applying essence* form the blueprint of my LifeCall: *making a life of more meaningful progress more accessible to every believer*.

Your LifeCall is a brief, bold, big idea that best captures today what God made you to do. Think of it as a golden compass pointing the way or a silver thread that weaves through every activity of your life. Ideally, every priority, project, and penny is filtered through, guided by, and championed for your LifeCall.

Your LifeCall is to be soul-stirring and heart-sticky. It's your enduring rally cry, the victory banner waving over everything you do. Imagine every person in your sphere of influence being blessed better, served stronger, and loved longer because you operate from a unique life mission every day.

A man named Brian who went through the Younique Life Plan Journey shared with me months afterward, "I feel different every day. My boss has remarked that I'm different. My coworkers have remarked that I'm different. My wife has remarked that I'm different." Once Brian discovered his LifeCall, his energy level changed, his countenance changed, and everyone around him noticed.

Let's unpack the definition a bit further: *LifeCall is a brief, bold, big idea that best captures today what God made you to do.*

- **It's brief.** Stay between six and twelve words.
- **It's bold.** Declare something that fires you up and makes you confident.
- **It's big.** Account for every relationship, domain, and "compartment" of your life.
- **It's best for today.** Write it down now, even though it may improve over time.
- **It's about God.** Reflect God's goodness and testify to his work of creative genius—you.
- **It's about doing.** Capture a "being-doing fusion" that ultimately clarifies active output.

Why is knowing and naming your LifeCall so important? In a nutshell, your LifeCall guides the trajectory of your life. It enhances every aspect of what it means to be human, to be alive as a follower of Jesus. Ponder these ten benefits:

Top Ten Panel: 10 Benefits of Naming Your LifeCall

1. Your LifeCall solidifies personal identity in a way that nourishes intimacy with the God who created you.

2. Your LifeCall generates internal confidence by revealing how God can use you each day.

3. Your LifeCall unlocks deeper motivation that energizes your tasks and relationships.

4. Your LifeCall refreshes others-centered thinking to build more love into the core of your being.

5. Your LifeCall shapes vocational planning that moves toward increased value to the world.

6. Your LifeCall empowers focused living by fortifying your resolve to say "no."

7. Your LifeCall diagnoses frustrating misalignments in the variety of life's roles at home and work.

8. Your LifeCall provides long-term orientation in the midst of suffering and difficult circumstances.

9. Your LifeCall produces increased passion that leads toward greater mastery and autonomy.

10. Your LifeCall guides lifelong dreaming that fills your days with optimism and hope.

Crafting Your LifeCall

So, how do you build a LifeCall from your previous work on your Sweet Spot? Here are some tips to guide your wordsmithing:

- Start by practicing on someone else. Go to my blog at WillMancini.com/LifeCallPractice and watch the video about Johnny Georges and his "tree T-PEE." Write down a few versions of Johnny's LifeCall in six to twelve words.

- Consider how you would translate the accuracy of your One Thing to a friend in a coffee shop. Give yourself only six to twelve words. I don't want to say, "applying essence" if I don't have time to explain the Sweet Spot tool. But I can talk about "more meaningful progress" very easily. People relate to that. People get that. Making a phrase that makes sense to others actually makes it more stirring and sticky *for you*.

- What words or phrases from your Sweet Spot work deeply resonate with you? Consider including specific content that is meaningful for you without making the statement too long.

- What were your honorable mention Two Words, and how can they impact the final articulation of LifeCall? Maybe there was a two-word combination that wasn't as accurate but is more motivational or conversational.
- Be careful not to make your LifeCall only about your work. What idea helps you narrow your focus yet still enables your LifeCall statement to work for all of your life domains, roles, and relationships? The more you can capture the *singularity with specificity*, the better.
- What words, ideas, or Scriptures have been meaningful for you in your life? How can these impact your final word choice? For example, when I first became a pastor I closed letters with "For His Glory." For about eight years my LifeCall was *to help people experience meaningful progress for God's glory.* I ended my statement with an idea—"God's glory"—that was very motivational to me. Later it would be more meaningful to focus my LifeCall on helping believers, so I changed the articulation.
- What mission statements for people and organizations have you heard before that got your attention? How would you use a similar sentence structure to build your LifeCall? For example, you like your church's mission statement, which reads "loving and leading people toward life change in Christ." You could mirror that structure with this LifeCall statement: "encouraging and inspiring people toward real joy."

**Top Ten List: From Two Words to LifeCall—
Examples from The Journey**

1. From "fostering congruence" to "making the church into a change agent again" (Dave R.)

2. From "shaping solutions" to "helping others organize life with harmony" (Tessy M.)

3. From "raising capacity" to "raising leadership capacity to release God-given potential" (Jim R.)

4. From "intentionalizing integration" to "helping people make every moment matter" (Kim R.)

5. From "empowering momentum" to "converting hidden potential into deployed passion" (Kelly K.)

6. From "articulating perfection" to "speaking the Truth who changes lives that change the world" (Cory H.)

7. From "shepherding significance" to "equipping people and organizations to courageously steward significant transitions" (Will H.)

8. From "orchestrating futures" to "guiding progress by applying biblical wisdom and new insight to current reality" (Brian U.)

9. From "igniting passion" to "coaching people everywhere with the gospel" (Chad P.)

10. From "applying essence" to "making a life of more meaningful progress more accessible to every believer" (Will M.)

Walking the "narrow way" of a specific LifeCall is a strict discipline that opens up into wild freedom. There is a vast range of potential and impact and destiny that you gain when you know the ultimate direction of your life. Your LifeCall is the path that impassions. It is the way back when you drift off-compass. It is the heading that leads you home.

 (The Younique team has additional coaching related to this chapter called *Living on Mission*. Check it out at LifeYounique.com/courses.)

Chapter 11

VALUES

How to Turn Your Life from a Big Puddle into a Whitewater River

"Tell me what you pay attention to and I will tell you who you are."
—José Ortega y Gasset

If I were to offer you a slice of coconut pie and a slice of peach pie, which one would you go for? I think I'd lean toward coconut, but I could really go either way; they're both delicious.

I may not have a strong opinion about which fruit makes a better pie, but I have a firm conviction about which fruit models a better life: the peach, not the coconut.

You might be surprised that the coconuts on display in our grocery stores have already been stripped down before we get a look at them. When you buy a coconut, you're actually buying a coconut *seed*. Coconuts carry their tasty flesh *inside* their seed while peaches carry theirs *around* their seed.

Another way to say it is that coconuts, as we commonly encounter them, are hard on the outside and soft on the inside while peaches are hard on the inside and soft on the outside.

So why do I want you to be like a peach? Because a peach is solid at the center with a firm, fixed core; I want you to have the same in your life.

> LifeCore is composed of your top four values that reveal your character and guide your life decisions.

The second side of the Vision Frame is what I call your LifeCore (figure 11.1), and it's all about your deeply held convictions, or *values*. Specifically, your LifeCore is composed of your top four values that reveal your character and guide your life decisions. When you know your values clearly and hold them strongly, you have a substantial center that you take with you into all of life. Who doesn't want to be rock-solid deep down inside?

Personal Values as LifeCore

Figure 11.1

In contrast to the peach, a coconut is hollow on the inside with a mushy lining and a little liquid sloshing around. A person who lives like a coconut is a person without a core.

Ironically, in the absence of fixed values on the inside, the person's "shell" can get very hard and inflexible. If a person doesn't have a firm grip on who they are internally, they are more likely to cling to people, places, and things externally. So, for instance, a coconut-type person's preferences and routines and physical surroundings are all-important in his or her own eyes, and the person becomes stony and rigid if these come under threat. If you make the dangerous mistake of tinkering with any of this person's things . . . well, how does it feel to head-butt a coconut? *Ouch.*

On the other hand, a person with a solid core like a peach tends to be much more flexible when it comes to externals. The person is more comfortable and pleasant company. When your values give you a strong sense of who you are and what you stand for, you adapt much more easily to change in everything else. You become more willing to release things in your life when the time comes. You become open to new expressions, new paths, new people, new strategies, and new experiences. Gaining clarity on your core values changes you in healthy ways and makes healthy change easier.

How Values Reveal the True You

The first part of our definition of values calls them convictions *that reveal your character*. It's as if values reveal yourself to yourself, like a mirror to your heart. And in the process of this self-revealing you come to know God better and see more clearly his redemptive handiwork in your story.

Values reveal your character *as a character*—that is, as a figure in God's unfolding drama of himself and angels and humans and all things—with unique scenes and situations that he writes in to make your role sparkle. Your values reveal three aspects of your character:

- **Character as personality.** Values reveal your character in the form of your unmistakable "characteristics" on display. What is your distinct style when you are at your best?
- **Character as transformation.** Values reveal the turnaround that the gospel engineered in your story as you went from playing the role of an alienated enemy of God to that of his reconciled child. In what peculiar ways has your mind been renewed by that conversion?
- **Character as integrity.** Values reveal your character by showing how the virtues that you demonstrate today have been formed in you. God takes the combination of characteristics he created in you alone and presses them through the gospel he uses to redeem all believers. What unique concoction of goodness bursts out the other side in your new way of life?

I've been calling values "convictions" because they are firmly held ideals. Yet I don't want to leave a partial impression. Values aren't merely things you know to be *true*; they are also things you know to be *good* and *beautiful* as certainly as you know your own name. There are loads of principles you believe with your whole heart, many of them extremely important, yet that doesn't make them your "values" in the sense I'm describing here. Values are anchored in a much deeper place in your soul than mere beliefs. And as a result, you delight to live from them and act out of them.

If you were to go on an inner safari to catch a glimpse of your values, where would you look? How would you trace the hoofprints that lead to where they live?

Here's one idea. Certain things evoke powerful desire or immense adoration out of your spirit. Crucially, you love what you love *for a reason*. What drives you wild about a person, place, story, activity, or object you love might be different from why someone else loves the very same thing.

If you take the thousands of things that pull that powerful reaction out of you and distill them down to why they grip you, you end up with a few reasons that appear over and over again. I would bet you that these are your values: your ideals of highest importance. You might say that your values are *what you love about what you love.*

These ideals shape what you expect and desire of yourself, of the people around you, even of the whole world. You want to see them come to life everywhere. They are the convictions that suffuse everything about you. Your values aren't what you do; *your values are what characterize everything you do.*[1]

In the end, the richest possible way a person could know you is to know your values. Your unique constellation of values is the core of your unique nature. Your values are the fingerprints of your soul.

Don's Mirror

As I hope you're beginning to imagine, the revelatory nature of your values contains many layers. It's like a rosebud unfolding; each overlapping petal is another layer of revelation that intensifies the brilliance of God's beauty and power shining through you.

Let me show you an example in Don, a Vietnam War veteran who recently attended one of our Younique Accelerators. (By the way, Don proves that it is *never* too late to design the life God dreamed for you!)

Don's articulated core values vividly illustrate the multiple layers of "revealing character." He fought on the front lines in tough times and, as a result, found God in a *literal* foxhole. As a new believer he returned home, physically intact but emotionally beaten up and war-tattered. His marriage didn't survive the dissonance of distance—physical, emotional, and now spiritual. But despite the marital failure, Don didn't give up his faith. In fact, years later, he remarried his original sweetheart and found a wonderful restoration in his Marriage 2.0.

As we worked on "mining out" Don's values, a tender warrior sat before me with tears flowing down his seventy-year-old cheeks. The whiteboard words before him were the mirror to his character that moved him and me and the twelve other men in our cohort. His four core values read:

- Tender Strength: *"Man up!"*
- Responsive Gratitude: *"Blessed and blessing"*
- Maximum Potential: *"Finish well"*
- Unrelenting Responsibility: *"Do the right thing"*

In a subtle way, I will never be the same after watching Don uncover and codify his values. How he fought in war and then battled for redemption in his marriage brilliantly displays his value of "unrelenting responsibility." Observing his significant investment into other men through his church's men's ministry doesn't just reveal a random interest in volunteering. His service incarnates his value of "maximum potential" as he models "tender strength" to other men, hoping that they too might "finish well" in life. His story strengthened the cohort of men that day, because they saw the conviction in his eyes *and* the character of his life wonderfully captured by his four LifeCore phrases.

Nothing gets me more excited than moments like this with Don, seeing people finally uncover their LifeCore. I believe this kind of break-thru is possible for you too.

Whitewater Motion

Water is one of the most powerful components of God's creation. It nourishes all living things, cuts mighty canyons, and even turns turbines to generate electricity. So you would think that the more water you have, the more the water does.

But that's not so. Water doesn't do much if it isn't channeled. A river without banks is a large puddle, even if it's the largest in the world. But a stream with firm banks, no matter how small, is a lively, refreshing cascade. There's a reason that we call water in motion *running* water and why in Jesus' day they called it *living* water (John 4:10–11). The constraints of the banks are what evoke motion and life.

When you know your values by name, they are your banks; they set the boundaries that channel your energy and effort into momentum for your journey. As our definition states, they *guide your life decisions.*

Knowing and owning your values marshals your attention toward what matters most. For example, many years ago I came to recognize my value of *learning*. That awoke my consciousness to seize every opportunity to learn that I possibly could. It changed what I did on an airplane, in a meeting, in my spare time. It escalated the number of books I read each year and shaped how I selected titles. It drove me to do anything to get one-on-one conversations with thinkers and practitioners I admired.

Now you might ask me, "If you valued learning so much, wouldn't you have done those things anyway even if you hadn't named it?" Sure, to some extent . . . but nowhere near as much, as intentionally, and as strategically, and the learning wouldn't have had nearly the impact on my life that compounds on itself year upon year in a steeply sweeping, upward curve.

In addition, as banks of your life's stream, your values help you say "no" for the sake of a greater "yes." They function as filters to evaluate what you're doing and what you might do. When you look at a habit, a commitment, or an opportunity, measure it against your values. If it evokes a green light from each of them, you're on the right track.

That's the genius of knowing and naming your values. Knowing your values helps you *do more* of what you *do best.*

My other values, by the way, are currently inscribed as follows:

- Intimacy *("The Ultimacy of Intimacy")* . . . because friendship is the center of reality
- Focus *("The Secret of Elimination")* . . . because I achieve more by choosing less
- Learning *("The Opportunity of Growth")* . . . because I feel more alive when I am gaining new perspective
- Courage *("The Life of No Regret")* . . . because maximizing life requires risk

Do You Have an Alignment Problem?

When I was in seminary, I spent a couple grand on basic transportation: a used Toyota Cressida with over a hundred thousand miles. Being a savvy buyer, I naturally test-drove it before making the purchase . . . but I neglected to take it out on the highway. It wasn't until I was in the NASCAR-like conditions of I-35 in Dallas that the front end of the car wobbled violently, and my stomach lurched into my throat. My car was no good traveling over forty miles an hour!

If you feel like you're not getting anywhere, you might have an alignment problem. This often shows up in a person's work life when her values don't match up with the values of her organization. She feels like a fish out of water. There's more conflict than seems to be necessary. The more energy she tries to summon to do a good job and improve the situation, the worse things get—like what happened to my car when I gave it more gas.

It's easy to blame your organization for being dysfunctional and your coworkers for being nasty—and certainly there are plenty of examples of that out there. But sometimes the bigger culprit is a values mismatch between you and your organization that isn't doing either any good. This can make for the right reason to take the "risk to go" I talked about in chapter 3.

Values alignment isn't only important when you're in a job that doesn't feel right. It is also critical when you are evaluating a new opportunity. Before a woman named Brooke went through The Journey, she was prone to entertain any job opportunity that came her way as long as it fell in a very broad scope of what seemed to her like an amiable match. But after Younique she had a much tighter filter she could confidently apply to the opportunities she encountered.

Brooke was handed an opportunity to consider after she went through The Journey. When she read the one-page job description she knew immediately that it was not for her even though she would have explored it with interest before. She perceived a mismatch with multiple aspects of her Life Younique, but her LifeCore stands out. One of Brooke's values is "Be Bold," but she didn't see anything in the role that required her to lean on the boldness that comes from the Holy Spirit to make an impact. Another of her values is "Clear the Way," but with this job she would have inherited an established system instead of blazing a trail for something new.

Brooke was able to say no to the job opportunity with clarity and confidence. With a strong grasp of her LifeCore, turning the job down felt lightweight and freeing while previously she would have attached guilt and doubt to that decision.

Top Ten Panel: Benefits of Knowing and Naming Your LifeCore

1. Your LifeCore boosts your energy for life and puts a shot of adrenaline in your relationships.

2. Your LifeCore equips you to have a quicker "yes" and a more gracious "no" in all kinds of decision-making.

3. Your LifeCore generates wiser choices about who you spend time with and how much time you spend with them.

4. Your LifeCore motivates the discovery of ways to express your deepest convictions proactively rather than incidentally.

5. Your LifeCore helps you diagnose conflict with others, including loved-ones. (And you have actual words to express why you are hurt or what you need.)

6. Your LifeCore translates situations from a "right-versus-wrong" perspective into a more precise view of "one value versus another value."

7. Your LifeCore facilitates healthy change in your life by stating securely the things about yourself that will never change.

8. Your LifeCore reminds you of the little slice of the True, the Good, and the Beautiful you were put on earth to call people's attention to.

9. Your LifeCore helps you distinguish between the *many* good opportunities and the *few* great ones over the course of your life.

10. Your LifeCore enables you to do more of what you do best by accelerating your best thoughts, attitudes, and actions.

Mining Your Core

In The Journey, we identify your top four values with a tool called the LifeCore Funnel. It begins by jotting notes in the center of a page to abbreviate much of what you've learned from the journey so far.

Your Ability Circle can yield some useful material for your values—especially the meaning of your names and your APEST gifting. However, you generally get the most and richest substance from your Passion Circle. One of the key elements to pay attention to is your "Offenders," because these are usually manifestations of violated values. That's because our loves are jealous: we react strongly and protectively against anything that threatens or violates what we care about so much.

Another rich source for your values is your Life Lies and Life Truths. That's because values and Life Lies have this curious trait in common: they both are often born out of places of pain in your past. Big hurts frequently result in distortions of reality that get deeply lodged in your heart. They also frequently give birth in your subconscious to powerful principles that say, "If only things were like *this*, I would never get hurt again." The big lie is that we have to do harmful things or act in our own strength to protect ourselves and get what we need. The truth of the gospel is that Christ has done everything to save us and provide us with all we could ever want. A gospel-shaped value is often the hard-won truth on the other side of the hurt-born lie.

> A gospel-shaped value is often the hard-won truth on the other side of the hurt-born lie.

Once you've jotted notes from your Sweet Spot inventories, note the threads or themes that tie together the fragments in the funnel. Don't look for one theme that ties *everything* together; rather, look for any theme that seems to link together a portion of the funnel's contents. In the margin around the funnel, write words and phrases that describe the themes you see. Write your notes about one theme in one corner of the page, another theme in another corner, and so on. The four corners will coalesce into your four values.

To identify the themes, it may help you to consider the following questions, trying to answer them from what you see inside your LifeCore Funnel:

- What motivates you most deeply in life?
- What would people say that you value the most if they watched you make all of your key decisions?
- Which ideals do you want to define your life?
- What convictions do your heroes model and stand for?
- Who are you when you are at your best?

- What convictions appear in all three of the inventories of your Sweet Spot?
- What is always true about you no matter what you are doing, where you are, or who you are with?

A way to test whether a potential value is really at your core is to ask the "3 Whys." Ask yourself why you care about it, and answer your question. Then ask yourself why *that* is so, and answer again. Then ask yourself why *that* is true, one last time.

If you have difficulty, don't be discouraged; for many people this is the most strenuous part of The Journey. For people who are wired to think concretely rather than intuitively, the challenge can overload the mental circuits. (This indicates *nothing* inferior about their intellects!) For other people, digging into their core drives them to face sensitive areas of their lives that require handling with care.

For these reasons, when we lead people through The Journey in a compressed, intensive experience, we provide coaches to draw out themes, show journeyers what they see, and sometimes simply pray for break-thru. I've seen God work miracles in people in these settings! So don't hesitate to share your funnel with a trusted person who is good at "connecting the dots" to help you see yourself with a new set of eyes.

Refining Your Core

You might wonder, "Why four values? Why not three or five?" It's because your Life Younique is worth nothing if you can't remember it. Yes, you could make a list of fifty values or draw out a list of fifteen convictions. It's true that you value more than four. But we want to draw attention to the most important four of your life. As you'll see, each element of your final Life Younique sketch will be composed of either one thing or four things. This creates balance, consistency, even poetry, which makes your Life Younique memorable.

We want poetry in your LifeCore too. Once you have your four value concepts, it's time to shape them into verbal jewels you can't forget:

1. *Select a structure* to mold each of your values into. It could be one word, two words, or a short, patterned phrase.
2. *Work the rhythm.* Get your statements to have the same cadence, the same stress on the same syllables, even the same number of syllables. Make it a chant.
3. *Link with sound.* If you can, start your values with the same letter or consonant sound or prefix. Or end with the same suffix (*-tion, -ness*, etc.). Or make them rhyme.

This isn't frivolous decoration; it is critical to give you instant recall of a top-of-mind LifeCore. (If this sort of work is tough for you, find a wordsmithy friend to give you a hand.)

After you've phrased your values, you enrich them by adding the word "because" followed by a phrase that describes why your value is important. You can enrich a step further by adding the phrase "demonstrated by . . ."; this can help you make your values practical in your own mind.

(For more real-world LifeCore examples, go to WillMancini.com/LifeCore. And why not ride some whitewater with the Younique team in an online course that goes deeper with LifeCore topics? It's called *Living on Mission* and you can check it out at LifeYounique.com/courses.)

Redeeming Your Core

Before we move on from LifeCore, I want you to understand that you have values because God has values. When God looked at the world he created, he called it "very good" (Gen. 1:31)—*he values it.* He was delighted at his own excellencies imprinted in the ingenious universe he made. He created you and the rest of humanity in his own image and likeness (vv. 26–27). So he made you to love *as* he loves and to love *what* he loves—all the varieties of goodness radiated by his glorious beauty.

God's ability to enjoy beauty and goodness is infinite. Yours is not. Yet the few values that you love deeply are an echo of God's vast love for those very same values. You were made to reflect God by valuing a certain combination of ideals that no other person does. When the people around you see you living according to what you love, they see a totally unique glimmer of God's love for his creation. That means they see, from a totally unique angle, the reflection of God himself. Your values reveal your character—that is, his character in you by his design.

The bad news of the Fall is that sin has cracked our character right down to the foundation. Without the work of Jesus in our lives, we pursue what we love to the detriment of all others and makes things in life that are smaller than God to be more important than Him—what the Bible calls idolatry.

But Jesus, the Image of the invisible God, became human in order to renew God's image in us. He purifies our character so that we learn to love what he loves the way he loves it. And this purifying, renewing love goes deep—all the way to the core—to power you with the momentum to do everything he prepared before creation for you to do. Let the world see God in all that you do by all that you value.

Chapter 12

MEASURES

The Biblical Way to Redefine Winning

"Measure what is measurable, and make measurable what is not so."
—Galileo Galilei

Over the years I have enjoyed consulting for Upward Unlimited, a sports program delivered to local communities across the country through church volunteers. When my boys Jacob and Joel were old enough to play, we enthusiastically enrolled in Upward basketball.

As their consultant, I knew the ins and outs of Upward's ministry philosophy, which ultimately is about using sports to introduce Jesus to children. At the time, their mantra was "Every Child Is a Winner," and one of their hallmarks for the younger leagues was not to keep score during games. They have since entered the competitive arena with a much-expanded strategy, but when my boys started playing, the scoreboards were turned off.

I'll never forget the first game. The kids were having a blast without a scoreboard. One kid lost his orientation and the team perfectly executed a "full court miss" with a brilliant bucket at the wrong end of the court. Nevertheless, the kids didn't miss a beat, or should I say, a dribble.

But in stark contrast, the most fascinating observation that day was that no dad could be found who was not keeping score. Some (myself included) constantly updated the math of their private mental scoreboard. Others kept track on a scratch pad. The fathers' embedded sense of competition was not going to settle for both teams being dubbed "winners."

While I type these words, a television in the background is airing the Wimbledon 2019 men's singles championship. Opponents Lucas Pouille and Roger Federer are dueling it out on the Centre Court of the sport's oldest battleground. At all times, the "measurement" of the match is clearly displayed in the lower left side of the screen. At all sporting events, everyone knows who is winning because a scoreboard is continually and instantly updated. Take the scoreboard away and what would happen to the broadcast ratings?

Measuring is not just an athletic discipline; it happens everywhere. When my mom bakes an apple pie, she uses measuring cups and carefully labeled plastic teaspoon devices to get ideal amounts of brown sugar, cinnamon, ginger, and nutmeg. A recipe is nothing more than a set of steps with the proper measurements for each ingredient. (And it just so happens that my mom's recipe is way better than your mom's. Check that—what I meant to say is, "Every Mom Is a Winner.")

What about business? I think back to my five years at the Jones Blair Paint Company in Dallas. While in graduate school I worked as the resin plant manager. We were tasked with shipping more than ten thousand gallons of industrial coatings (think heavy-duty paint) every day. But we couldn't ship that paint without passing the test on eight measurements that defined good paint. Quality Control needed to measure the color, gloss, viscosity, and five other things. (Trust me, you don't want me to type up the rest of the list.)

Whether we're talking sports or stocks, cooking up an apple pie or shipping industrial paint, human beings measure things. And being able to measure means you know when you "get it right." Sometimes measurement provides a true sense of progress; other times it signals that you are winning or losing.

Many things in life are easy to measure. But what about life itself? The greatest irony of life is that in a world that measures everything, the most important thing in the world is the hardest to measure. Ten years from now, how will you measure whether you lived your life well from now until then? How do you measure your life today?

Take a guess: How many times today have you answered the question, "How are you?" At first blush, that common phrase could be the answer to measuring what matters most.

Even though you've heard it a lot, for most of us "How are you?" only means "I acknowledge your presence." Americans usually aren't looking for much meaningful information when they say it. What a shame! The perfect opportunity to really check in on life is reduced to a cultural nice-ism with the auto-human reply, "I'm fine, thank you."

Sure there are exceptions. As a follower of Jesus maybe you've been in a *real* "How are you?" conversation . . . and before you know it twenty minutes have passed and you're sitting in a pile of wadded-up, tear-soaked tissues.

In the discourse of our lives, "How are you?" ranges from the most superficial pleasantry to the most important question you'll ever answer. We all know what the broad range of human conversation feels like. In The Journey, as you might have guessed, we dial into the more meaningful kind of engagement with this question, but with a twist. We want to show you the best way to ask and answer this question with yourself, from God's perspective.

For many reasons many of us don't honestly ask ourselves how we're doing. Being busy often has something to do with it—we're juggling so many balls that we don't have time to look at ourselves. Other times people don't think much about how they are doing because, for a variety of motives, they are acutely concerned about the welfare of others.

But sometimes we hesitate to ask ourselves, "How am I?" because at some level, we don't really want to know. We might be worried about the implications if the honest answer is, "Not very good." Maybe we'll have to face a situation we're in that's been too difficult to look at straight on. Or maybe we'll start comparing ourselves with others, and we're afraid to be embarrassed in the sight of people who are winning at everything. (Of course, we rarely consider the possibility that those who appear to be winning at everything might themselves be as skittish about looking at how they're doing as anyone else!)

But it doesn't have to be this way. Whether things are good, bad, or—as they usually are—a mixed bag, how we're doing in the big picture doesn't have to be tied to our circumstances or to our performance. It *definitely* doesn't have to be tied to a comparison of ourselves with others.

Imagine a new way of answering "How are you?" Imagine that you could:

- look forward to an energizing, weekly moment of reflection on your life calling
- use four simple "dashboard gauges" to assess the four subplots in the story (biopic) you're starring in
- make a powerful and comprehensive self-diagnosis in just thirty seconds
- have confidence that you're winning from God's point of view even when you feel like you're losing

To do this you need a LifeScore. We visually represent LifeScore as the top side of the personal Vision Frame (figure 12.1). I put it on top because the scoreboard is usually the highest and most visible thing in a stadium. I want the same for your life—a highly visible scoreboard "on top" of everything. Our icon for measures is the bull's-eye of the target.

Personal Measures as LifeScore

Figure 12.1

Your LifeScore is a weekly assessment of your life through a biblical perspective that uses flexible storylines, not fixed domains. We'll unpack that loaded definition one chunk at a time, starting with the last word, *domains.*

A Giant Leap Forward in Life Design

Virtually all approaches to life planning use domains. Domains are the various areas that compose all aspects of a person's life.

When I think about growing up in Chadds Ford, Pennsylvania, I can name the domains of my dad's life from where he spent his time. When he drove to the office in the morning, he entered Work domain; when he came home at the end of the day, he entered Family domain; when we drove to church on Sunday morning, he entered Church domain; and so on.

There is no single way to define the domains that make up a life, as illustrated by table 12.1. In the Bible, Luke, the physician-evangelist, described Jesus' natural development according to the four domains of wisdom, stature, favor with God, and favor with men (see Luke 2:52). Since his day many have made other models.

> LifeScore is a weekly assessment of your life through a biblical perspective that uses flexible storylines, not fixed domains.

Examples of Life Domain Categories			
The Bible (Luke 2: 52)	Tom Paterson	Tony Robbins	Burnett and Evans
Wisdom	Personal	Health and Wellness	Health
Stature	Family	Mind and Meaning	Work
Favor with God	Faith	Love and Relationships	Love
Favor with Men	Vocational	Productivity and Performance	Play
	Community	Career and Business	
		Wealth and Lifestyle	
		Leadership and Impact	

Table 12.1

In the Younique Life Plan we pivot from thinking about our lives using domains to using *storylines*. A storyline is a major theme in your life's unfolding narrative. It's a sub-story of your LifeCall. Your storylines are the four big, developing subplots in the movie about your life.

Storylines improve on domains in four ways:

1. **While domains are based in *time and space*, storylines are about a *theme everyplace*.** Following the Industrial Revolution, people ordered their lives like my dad did. Since the Information Revolution, people's work became untethered from the office and their relationships interpenetrated their workday. Add your smartphone to the equation and you can run a Fortune 500 company from your family room or spend all day socializing on Facebook from the office. What domain we are actually in at any given moment is not about our physical location anymore.

2. **While domains evoke *environments as objects*, storylines describe a *person as the subject*.** You get a lot more fired up thinking about an area of your life as *you* than as *it*—especially when the *it* is the same for everyone. Don't focus on whether you are sitting in a cubicle, a couch, or a Camry; instead consider the plotline developing no matter where you are sitting.

3. **While domains are about *activity*, storylines are about *identity*.** A storyline isn't defined as a thing you do so much as a role you play—a role that's totally authentic to you. For example, a domain named "work" tends to conjure up the steps, functions, and assignments of a job to the neglect of the

deeper role and bigger idea of your life. Your trash man is more than a trash man—he is a beauty enabler. A teacher is more than a teacher—she is a truth illuminator.

4. **While domains are *detached from transcendent meaning*, storylines are *attached to God as the Author.*** After you name your storyline, it will highlight God's sovereign goodness in your life more than a generic domain ever could. For example, David Loveless, a master trainer on the Younique team, converted his "work" domain into the "Break-thru Investor" storyline. By naming this storyline, David is capturing a powerful understanding of how God uses him as a pastor and life coach. This understanding transcends the ups and downs of a job and provides more meaning and hope when he looks at his Life Plan Snapshot (the personal plan-on-a-page that participants create at the end of The Journey).

Plotting Your Storylines

In the chapter on LifeCore I said that the balance and symmetry of the Vision Frame is one of the features that makes it memorable. If it's more memorable, it's more actionable. Like the LifeCore's four values, the LifeScore requires exactly four storylines.

So, how do you go about encompassing all that you do in life in fourfold fashion? To start, imagine for a second that favorite show you're guilty of binge-watching—for you it might be *This Is Us*. Like many successful TV franchises, the overarching flow of the show has several subplots or storylines. In an episode of *This Is Us*, three of the storylines involve three adult siblings and their significant relationships, and a fourth is a flashback to an earlier era of the family's history centering on one or both of their parents. Each episode is a four-cord strand of these totally distinct but interrelated storylines weaving their way together into a whole artistic expression.

Now imagine that you had footage of the last three years of your life captured by a top-secret invisible drone. If you binge-watched the last one hundred episodes of the ultimate "You"Tube, what subplots would become apparent? How would you name the four most dominant themes of your life?

Some people can immediately scratch down the name of their life's storylines with this basic TV show illustration and explanation. But others appreciate a little tool we use in The Journey as a helpful place to start: the broad storyline categories of "Health," "Work," "Love," and "Play" as a launchpad to brainstorm one's storylines.

These four life categories are utilized by Bill Burnett and Dave Evans, two professors at Stanford University who help students get intentional about life design. There is something very simple and refreshing about the articulation of these small but punchy words to unveil the storylines of our lives. They are like a scaffolding from which to build, because many people's storylines—mine included—fall roughly into these four broad themes. Think of them as the four-part harmony of the song of human living. It's a helpful place to start, but don't let it limit your art; it shouldn't hinder your uniquely creative capture of your life as a television show.

Here are my storylines and how they connect to this four-part scaffolding:

- "Health" is my *Beloved Son* storyline. Through the most difficult chapter in my life I realized the gospel emotionally through the lens of sonship. I began to integrate my mental assent of the gospel with really feeling like I am God's beloved son in whom he is well pleased. When I consider the subplot of my life where there is no one else but me, with all of the physical, emotional, and spiritual implications of my wholeness, I simply want to remind myself that I am a beloved son of the One True God.

- "Love" is my *Central Circle* storyline. When my children were elementary-aged, we developed a family mission: *building the central circle of love for guiding each generation to courageously follow Jesus.* The idea of family as a central circle is deeply embedded into our family-speak. I can't think of the complexities of nuclear- and extended-family dynamics without calling it the "central circle" of my world—the first place of giving and receiving love.

- "Work" is my *Olympic Contribution* storyline. I am convinced that every person is a gold-medalist-in-the-making at something (which is the driving motive for this book!). When I reflect on my one and only life, I want every day to be executed with the strength, power, and grace of a top Olympic performer.

- "Play" is my *Epic Adventure* storyline. Since I can remember I have continually daydreamed about hiking mountains, fishing remote streams, starting new adventures, and traveling to new places. When I think of recreation, rest, and replenishment, I resonate with this subplot's name as a grand journey filled with adventure sports and far-away escapes.

But as I said, "Health," "Love," "Work," and "Play" make up just one approach to storylines. To illustrate how flexible storylines can be, let me formally introduce you to Cory Hartman, a pastor and good friend who not only went through The Journey but has also mastered the content as a Younique team writer and as my principal collaborator on this book. Cory plotted his four storylines in a different way:

- *Whole Soul* ○ – This rhyming storyline captures Cory's well-being as an individual self—spiritually, emotionally, mentally, and physically.
- *Building a House* ☐ – Everything in his family, from marriage to parenting to home improvement to finances, is represented in this storyline. Its name echoes God's promise in 2 Samuel 7 that he would build David a house: a lineage whose impact in God's kingdom would never end.
- *Disciplefriending* × – Relationships outside the family, all of which have opportunities for discipleship movement, are encoded in this unique term that Cory coined. (See how fun and flexible storylines can be!)
- *Magnum Opus* △ – The Latin term meaning "great work" signifies the storyline of Cory's intellectual output and of his efforts on behalf of organizations as a citizen, as a volunteer, and especially as the owner of his company, Fulcrum Content.

If you compare Cory's storylines to the four life categories I use, it appears that "Health" and "Work" are each represented, and "Love" shows up twice. But that doesn't mean that Cory is all work and no play. Rather, Cory scatters the "Play" category among all four of his storylines, from solitary hobbies (Whole Soul) to fun with his wife and kids (Building a House) to recreation with friends (Disciplefriending) to labors of love as a writer (Magnum Opus).

Also note how Cory uses simple icons to depict the spirit of each of his storylines in a memorable way, from the wholeness of the circle to the floor plan of a house to the intersection of a network (which is also the multiplication symbol) and finally to the pyramids of Egypt. There is no cap on your creativity when it comes to your storylines!

Psalms Spirituality: A Biblical Approach to Life Assessment

So, how do storylines become a LifeScore—a way to measure how you're doing at life? How do they become the biblical way to redefine winning?

You can't define "the win" unless you know what game you're playing. The game of life and its rules are ultimately defined by the gospel.

Historian David Bebbington observes that every ancient civilization that began analyzing history employed the circle as their device to do it. They told the story of the past as a cycle that moved from order to chaos and back. From the pagan point of view, this mythical "story" cycle goes backward in time infinitely, or nearly so. But underlying this ceaseless change was actually the absence of change, because the circular model itself was changeless. So even though the wheel of life turned around and around, it had no traction. The world was like a Ferris wheel; it revolves up and down, yet it doesn't really go anywhere.

Then into ancient humanity broke one tiny people—Israel—that told history in a radically different way that changed the world. Israel described history not as a circle but as a line with a beginning and an end. But it wasn't a straight line; it was more like a checkmark from a good *creation* to a dreadful *fall* to a *redemption*-in-the-making to a *new creation* better than the first.

Does this pattern sound familiar? It should. Christians inherited it, and it transformed Western civilization.[1] It describes the structure of almost all our most beloved novels and movies. Think about them: things start out smooth, then there's a crisis, then the main character struggles to overcome the crisis, and then there's a satisfying conclusion. As William Dean Howells put it, "What the American public wants is a tragedy with a happy ending."

But long before the American public, Israel loved this shape of history so much that it described nearly all of their stories too. Even though the Bible as a whole describes one big story this way, it is chock-full of mini-stories of the nation and micro-stories of individuals that follow the same pattern. The story of redemption is a daisy chain of good-bad-redeemed-better happening over and over. The checkmarks strung together form their own kind of cycle, but not a fixed wheel numbingly revolving yet going nowhere. Instead, Israel's stories form a *spiral*, a turning screw, such that every time through the cycle gets us closer to the final destination of the new heavens and the new earth. In Israel's history, not every revolution through the cycle made the nation better off in the moment, but every one did drive the world closer to the great Happy Ending.

The same pattern is impressed on one magnificent book of the Bible that at first glance appears to be outside the stream of history: the book of Psalms. The Psalms are the prayer book of God's people. They don't tell the story of Israel and the world—not as a narrative chronicle anyway. Yet the shape of Israel's story is baked into this great collection of prayers and songs.

The Psalms, as a prayer book, hold a special key for unlocking life assessment. Understanding this key starts with a simple fact: while all of biblical revelation is God speaking to humanity, only the Psalms, beginning to end, show how humanity should speak back to God. In the Psalms, God is like the father gently instructing his growing two-year-old boy how to address his mother. The parents give the child the correct words to use when addressing the parents.

Now imagine that the way to pray and talk with God has a structure or pattern. That pattern connects with the "checkmark" or "spiral" of creation-fall-redemption-new creation. In seminary, I never understood the power of the Psalms because the technical categories got in the way. Theologians use a technical typology like "lament psalms" or "imprecatory psalms." But the sun broke through the clouds when I read about the Psalms from Walter Brueggeman, a brilliant Old Testament scholar.

Walter Brueggemann maintains that every psalm can be classified as a psalm of *orientation, disorientation,* or *reorientation.*[2] I prefer the more accessible terms *thriving, surviving,* and *reviving* (figure 12.2):

- *Thriving* represents goodness because of creation; it evokes the season of summer. The psalmists sing prayer-songs of thriving when life is going well, when their lives are full of blessing. This category of prayers shows how to speak with God when your spouse surprises you with breakfast in bed or a boss gives you a raise, when you miss all of the red lights on the way home and marvel again at the day's sunset.
- *Surviving* represents brokenness because of sin; it corresponds to the Fall, and it evokes the seasons of autumn and winter. The psalmists sing songs of surviving when life is going badly, when their lives are full of woe. What do you actually say to God when you fail calculus or when layoffs are imminent or when the cancer comes back or when she says she wants to be "just friends"? Most of the Psalms give us the words to say on these uninvited yet inevitable days.
- *Reviving* represents restoration because of grace; it corresponds to redemption, and it evokes the season of spring when flowers are blooming everywhere with a freshness in the air. The psalmists shout prayers of reviving when life is getting better, when their days are full of deliverance. Imagine the prayer of a single mom working two jobs, staring at the bills coming due, who gets an unexpected inheritance check from Uncle Henry. Or imagine the teacher giving you a second chance to write the research paper for a better grade. There's still a lot of work ahead, and you're still dependent on the Lord's help, but he's supplying it as you need it.

Reviving then tips into a new season of *thriving,* only this one is better than before; to borrow from C. S. Lewis, it is "further up and further in."[3] This corresponds to the new creation; therefore, each psalm of thriving speaks both to the goodness that *is* and also to the superlative goodness that *will be.*

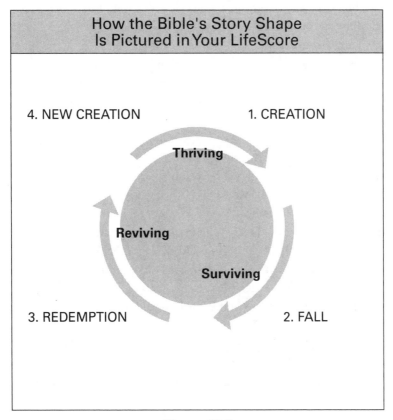

Figure 12.2

The 150 psalms, then, are both a complete gymnasium of prayer and what John Calvin called "the anatomy of the soul."[4] David, the primary author, is exhibited as the model saint—not because of a perfect life but because of the comprehensiveness of his walk with God. David goes to God in every imaginable human experience. He is never at a loss for words with Yahweh. His heart is wide open whether he is bursting with joy or boiling with rage.

Allow me to illustrate how this explodes with practicality and turns the Psalms into a daily go-to tool in your relationship with God. Returning to the technical terms for certain psalms, let's consider the category called the "imprecatory psalms." These are defined as "those that invoke judgment, calamity, or curses upon one's enemies or those perceived as the enemies of God."[5] Operating according to this definition as a younger man, I didn't know how to apply these prayers. I seriously wondered why these psalms were in the Bible. The core problem was that I could not relate to the historical context of this type of psalm and others as well; I just could not relate to David cursing real enemies and dodging actual death threats.

But when I researched Brueggemann and other writers like Eugene Peterson and Thomas Merton, I realized that a better definition for the imprecatory Psalms is "how to pray when you feel like killing someone." I can now connect! In fact, I can connect to *every* psalm, including ones that involve curses, not through David's *situation* but through his *emotion*. Most of us can relate to the *emotions* of deep hatred even though we don't go through the *motions* of violence. In the Psalms, God has already showed you how to talk to him when that time comes.

This insight changed everything for me, including my definition of spiritual success. I used to think Christian maturity was about building a more stoic disposition. Despite the ups and downs of life, I needed to grow more certain, stable, and unmoved in my presence and prayers. But this picture of success was the total opposite of the model life of David in the Psalms. He could dance in the streets like a Super Bowl MVP, *and* he could wail like a newborn baby, grieve like a brand-new widow, or scream like a teenage pop star. Either David was an emotional basket case or my picture of success needed serious correction! In this break-thru I found greater freedom, the story of which could fill another book.

The Psalms, then, provide a sweeping panorama of how to talk *to* God and *with* God in the full range of human emotion and at every stage and season of our lives. As such, they open for us a striking and refreshing way to evaluate the ups and downs of life.

Defining Winning God's Way

Psalms spirituality unlocks your break-thru answer to the question: "How are you doing?" Quite simply, for each of your storylines, assess whether you are thriving, surviving, or reviving.

How do you know where you are in the cycle? By examining your hope:

- When *surviving*, you're looking *for* your hope; you're standing in darkness, with no light in sight.
- When *reviving*, you're looking *toward* your hope; you're walking into the light, a shimmering brightness on the horizon.
- When *thriving*, you're looking *at* your hope; you're standing in the light with blazing noon-day brilliance.

The clarity this gives you is refreshing and profound. In under a minute you can nuance the complexity under the opaque answer, "Okay." You can recognize the good at work in your life when the bad wants to draw all your attention.

Most important, this way of keeping score takes seriously that real spiritual maturity isn't about how well you're doing but about going to God *despite* how you're doing. That's what God is after! The Psalms prove it. They are the infallible, God-inspired record of what it means to engage with him when you're at your best, at your worst, and everywhere in between.

> Real spiritual maturity isn't about how well you're doing but about going to God despite how you're doing.

Here lies the true definition of winning at life: *If you are calling on the name of the Lord and being shaped by him whether you're thriving, surviving, or reviving, you're winning.*

The Benefits of Psalms Spirituality

Let's step back for a moment and consider the great benefits of assessing your Life Younique using these key insights from the Psalms. Keep in mind that you have each of your four storylines to assess independently. Using *thriving-surviving-reviving* as your categories for assessment:

- keeps your pulse-taking God-centered, not self-centered
- reminds you of the hope of the gospel both for now and for eternity
- builds an anticipation of the guaranteed and redemptive goodness of God
- nurtures awareness of yourself and of God
- reminds you that you can be *winning in life* (i.e., going to God in the midst of anything) whether things are good or bad
- provides an epic warning by clarifying what *losing in life* looks like (i.e., choosing not to talk to God at all in the midst of anything; by the way, you are most susceptible to your Life Drifts not only at your lowest moments of pain and failure but also at your highest moments of joy and success)
- accounts for having highs and lows in different areas of life at the same time
- gives permission for the wide range of emotion in life—it's okay not to be okay

So how are you doing at living your LifeCall? The answer is found in an intimacy with God that is reflected in ongoing dialogue and prayer about the four dimensions of your life (storylines). God himself has revealed in ink that his people are either thriving, surviving, or reviving. He has given you the recipe for coming to him in your highest high and lowest low. It is your authenticity both with God and with yourself that determines whether you are winning at life—your LifeScore.

This informs how we depict your LifeScore on your personal Vision Frame (figure 12.3). We place four circles above the frame to symbolize both the gospel-centered story cycle and to represent the four gauges on your life dashboard (think speedometer and RPMs). You can self-assess by marking each storyline as either surviving, reviving, or thriving or by coloring the storyline as red, yellow, or green, respectively.

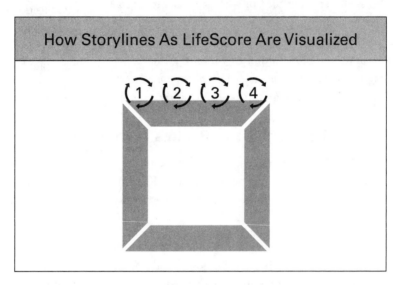

Figure 12.3

As we'll see in later chapters, people who have taken The Journey assess their storylines this way every week and meditate on what the pattern is telling them every three months. There is no better tool for knowing where you are and determining what part of your life needs what kind of work next.

Chapter 13

STRATEGY

Three Secrets to Improving Your Life That Took Me Twenty Years to Uncover

"The essence of strategy is that you must set limits on what you're trying to accomplish."

—Michael Porter

Understanding how to design a great "strategy" for *any* human being to apply was the single hardest nut to crack in the Life Younique toolbox. Despite the "engineer brain" that hums constantly in my mental background, "strategy" was the Rubik's Cube that sat on the desktop of my mind for twenty years before I found the secret sequence of moves that work for me and for thousands of others.

Why the challenge?

If you were to ask people "how" they became successful or "how" they accomplished something significant, you would be overwhelmed with the sheer variety of answers. The result is an ocean of tactics from which people choose:

- Is it a task list of a super-special, "focus" day-planner?
- Is it taking an *x*-minute power nap at *y* o'clock every day?
- Is it that sweet God-time with craft coffee and a leather journal before dawn?

Each of these tactics has been meaningful at different stages in my life, and clearly some tactics work better for certain kinds of people. But I was hunting for the *irreducible essence* of "how." How does *any person* most effectively advance his or her LifeCall?

How can *anyone* confidently identify a next step in his or her four storylines? A life is a heavy load; how does *anyone* know where to apply the power to move it?

Remember those simple machines we learned about in elementary school like levers and pulleys? Most people have experienced the power of the lever from the playground seesaw or teeter-totter. As long as you are sitting on a longer lever you can lift your bigger cousins or even your dad! The ancient Greek scientist Archimedes famously said that, if he had a lever long and strong enough, he could move the earth!

I don't know about you, but I've had many big loads to lift in my life. I have an endless list of things I could do or improve, but I only have so much strength. So I wonder, where can I place the lever in my life to make the biggest difference with the least effort? How can I achieve break-thru as efficiently as possible? What are the few things I should apply myself to right now that will cause a cascade of good to burst into my life?

Another way to ask these questions is: *What is my personal strategy for advancing my special assignment from God?*

The answer in the Younique Life Plan is the fourth side of the Vision Frame, which we call *LifeSteps*. In brief, your **LifeSteps are your one area of focus in each storyline for the next ninety days based on a current assessment of Roles, Resources, and Replenishment.**

That definition is a mouthful, so let's break it down. At Younique we symbolize LifeSteps with a flashlight. (You might have been expecting the symbol of a lever, so hang with me.) A flashlight "shows the way" and illuminates where you are walking, "the how" of getting from point A to point B (figure 13.1).

- *One area of focus.* We are dialing into singularity again! LifeSteps do not create a task list or a set of goals in each storyline but clarify one specific aspect of a storyline to zero in on. A flashlight causes you to focus your sight on one specific area. A flashlight doesn't illuminate your entire house during a power outage but lights up what you need to see to take one step forward. Likewise, your LifeSteps don't illuminate everything you do in a storyline but focus your sight on the one next step.
- *. . . in each storyline.* Since you have four storylines you will have four areas of focus. We draw LifeSteps at the bottom of the Vision Frame in one-through-four sequence to correspond visually to the storylines in the same sequence at the top of the Vision Frame (figure 13.2 and 13.3).
- *. . . for the next ninety days.* The area of focus will last for the duration of ninety days, an important time frame we will discuss more thoroughly in chapter 17.

- *. . . based on a current assessment.* The break-thru of LifeSteps as strategy is the opportunity to assess each storyline with a three-part lens. The assessment takes some effort the first time you work through it, but then it becomes very easy to use for the rest of your life.
- *. . . of Roles, Resources, and Replenishment.* The three Rs are independent but related views of your focus areas. Of the three assessments, the Roles tool is the one most often used to name the LifeStep itself. In other words, it's most common for people to name a LifeStep by the "role they are stepping into" in a storyline for the next ninety days. The square box for each LifeStep is where you can write your area of focus.

Once you grasp how life is defined by your roles, resources, and replenishment, you can identify the locations of leverage to change your life for the better.

Personal Strategy as LifeSteps

Figure 13.1

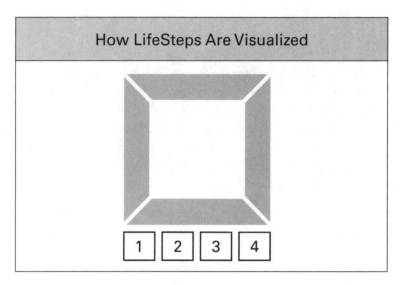

Figure 13.2

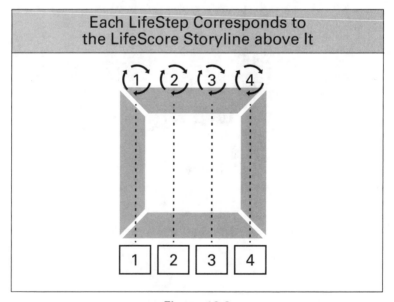

Figure 13.3

The Three Rs that Crack the Strategy Code

I expect you're familiar with the down-home way of naming the fundamentals of education as "the three Rs": Reading, "'Riting," and "'Rithmetic." The fundamentals of how humans live on planet Earth are also three Rs: Roles, Resources, and Replenishment. Most people don't realize it, but all strategies to improve your life involve stepping into a role, increasing a resource, or attending to replenishment, often in combination.

- **A role to step into.** Every human activity has a corresponding role. For example, when I play soccer with my daughter Poema I am fulfilling a Playful Father or Blessing-Giver role. When I am talking to a pastor on a three-way call with an Auxano teammate, I am playing a Networker or Salesman role. When given ample time to reflect, most people can discern the single most important role to emphasize in a given season and area of life. The focus may be a role that's been neglected, or it may be a role to take advantage of the opportunity of the moment. But every human being is always fulfilling some role.

- **A resource to increase.** Every human being has value and resources to invest in their future: most have more than they realize. The secret to increasing a resource area in life—we will identify five of them—is to learn how to identify and invest what you have to gain what you don't. In fact, roles and resources go hand in hand. For example, the roles illustrated above of playing with my daughter and introducing a pastor to a teammate are both forms of trading in "relational capital," one of the five kinds of resources. Every human being is always utilizing five kinds of resources.

- **A replenishment rhythm to practice.** Every human being is like a battery—either discharging energy ("work") or recharging ("rest") at any given moment. By assessing your rhythms of rest and work, you can better steward your energy and output. In addition, it is extremely helpful to look at replenishment rhythms in light of both roles and resources. Playing soccer with my daughter is act of rest for me, but talking with pastors is an act of work. Both roles are relational investments, but they are very different kinds of replenishment rhythms.

Once you understand these fundamentals, you can dig into the fine-tuning of your wiring, and you will never have to stare at a blank page again when you try to develop a plan for activating break-thru in your life. So let's explore the details of how roles, resources, and replenishment rhythms work and how they work together.

Roles

Naming your four storylines brings critical clarity when you're looking down on your life from orbit. But in order to get somewhere on earth we need a much more detailed map drawn much closer to ground level—a Role Map.

Role mapping helps you answer the question of how you do what you do. It's plumbing the depths of each of your storylines to find the different roles you have. Once you name your roles, you can swiftly recognize which ones are working, which ones are broken, and which ones are neglected. This way you can fine-tune the various roles God has called you to and pinpoint his work in a particular place in your life.

Most likely, one of the storylines in your life involves your family, either as a storyline unto itself or bundled together with other relationships or areas of activity. Let's use that storyline as an example. Whatever your family relationships are, how do you "do family"?

Under family, there are different roles for you to live out and step into. Maybe in your family ecosystem you're a son, a father, a husband, and a brother (or a daughter, a mother, a wife, and a sister—we're going to stick with the male example in what follows for simplicity's sake). So your family storyline branches into those four *primary roles*. Naming the plurality of roles you live out clarifies the complexity that is part and parcel of "doing family."

Perhaps you sense that God wants to breathe fresh life into your family storyline. Well, which part of it? Is there a specific relationship that needs to be repaired or reinvigorated? By looking at your Role Map, you can pinpoint the area that needs God's touch—maybe in being a dad. So how do you "dad"?

God has wired you to "dad" in a specific way and to disciple your kids with that wiring. What are three distinct aspects of your fatherhood or three angles by which you approach your kids? God has built certain responsibilities into being a father that apply to all dads, but even two dads with the same basic responsibilities may use different words to describe their roles. In addition, fatherhood changes as we and our children move through different stages of life. A dad with younger children might see himself as an Instructor, a Provider, and a Smile Maker. A dad with grown children might see himself as a Friend, an Encourager, and a Problem Solver. In any case, however you see yourself "doing dad," these are your *secondary roles*.

Primary roles are often obvious and don't require too much reflection, like the family example above. But secondary roles take time to explore and always awaken new perspective. The goal is to "double-click" on each of the primary roles to spell out precisely and ideally how you are fulfilling them.

Take time to name four primary roles for each of your four storylines, then define three secondary roles for each primary role (figure 13.4). In the end, you'll see forty-eight roles that together describe the manifold ways you relate to the world. Some roles you might perform every day, others less often. Some might be dormant, and some might even be roles you aspire to but are not playing yet.

It may take a minute for your brain to "click" into this brainstorming mode. Keep on concentrating. Sometimes you are stating the obvious by identifying smaller roles you play at work. (For example, a primary role of Salesman might step into the secondary roles of Phone Caller, Email Sender, Blog Writer, Internet Researcher, or Social Media Maven.) At other times you are creatively recalling how you live your best life. (In my primary role of Explorer, for example, I could list secondary roles like Inquisitive Traveler, Virtual Worker, Magazine Reader, Journal Keeper, and Movie Watcher.) As you map your roles for the first time, you will probably start recognizing which ones require more of your conscious attention at this point in your life.

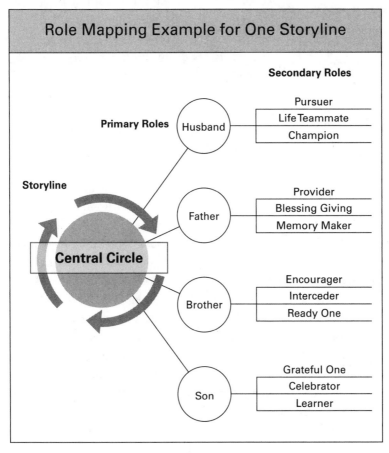

Figure 13.4

Role mapping is the single most helpful assessment to "point a flashlight" on an area of focus in your life. But let's continue to look at the other Rs as additional assessment lenses to refine and double-check what's happening in each of your storylines. As we do, be aware that these three Rs aren't looking for different areas of focus; they are just different lenses to help you best identify and name *one area of focus for each storyline*.

Resources

It's really easy for any person to miss how much God has provided them with. The sheer givenness of life itself and everything that makes up your Life Younique is loaded with all kinds of "capital" and, therefore, with all kinds of investment opportunity and growth potential. Once you decide what role you need to "step into" better, there will necessarily be a resource that you are increasing. Therefore, the resource "lens" will further clarify and strengthen your ability to focus in one area.

> These three Rs aren't looking for different areas of focus; they are just different lenses to help you best identify and name *one area of focus for each storyline*.

Let's start with this principle: everything you need to accomplish God's will in your life you already have, because you have him. Think about it: Why would your Father in heaven put you on this planet for unique purposes and not give you the resources to accomplish those purposes? The Bible is replete with promises that God is neither unwilling nor unable to supply us richly. "He did not even spare his own Son but offered him up for us all. How will he not also with him grant us everything?" (Rom. 8:32).

Now, it's generally easy to believe (though hard to remember) that if we are in Christ, our names appear with his on the ownership title to the new heavens and the new earth. It's harder to believe that we have everything we need and much, much more here and now. But it's true. So what makes it hard to recognize? In many cases, the vast wealth you have from God is currently in seed form. We're praying for trees, but God has given us seeds. Everything is there for an entire forest, but it has to be groomed, nurtured, and grown over time.

The question is, *how?* How do we learn to groom and nurture what God has given us in seed form? You learn to grow these gifts by using your time more effectively and learning to trade with everything God has given you. Both of these steps are illustrated by one of Jesus' most famous parables.

In the Parable of the Talents (Matt. 25:14–30), Jesus told of three servants whose master entrusted them with resources that he expected them to grow. While two servants aggressively used the money they were given to earn more, the third servant buried his in the ground to return it unchanged when the master returned. The servant's problem was laziness; his excuse was that his master was "a harsh man, reaping where you haven't sown and gathering where you haven't scattered seed" (v. 24).

Like the unprofitable servant, we misunderstand our resources for three reasons that were first articulated to me by Younique cofounder Dave Rhodes. First, we're afflicted by *insecurity*, because we undervalue what we've been given. The reason to assess resources as part of crafting LifeSteps is to expand your imagination to fully appreciate everything God has bestowed in your life today, even if it's in seed form. A complete view of your capital blows up your vision of what you've been given.

Second, we're afflicted by *fear*, because we overvalue what we could lose. One of the helpful insights from the Parable of the Talents is that the master is not worried about any of these servants taking risks. In fact, he expects it! Let's imagine that the servant with one talent actually "bet the farm" with a risk and lost it all. Do you think the master would have survived? Of course he would have! We can easily see that the master in the parable has a pretty diverse portfolio; after all, he just doubled his investments in two of his other "strategies." Most important, the master in the parable represents the universe's Creator, who has the resource base of a hundred billion galaxies—the same God who made you "to be fruitful and multiply" (see Genesis 1:28). The bottom line: God considers it a serious problem (wickedness and laziness) if you are paralyzed with your life's resources. He expects you to "make a move." He can handle losing what you might lose. And he can more than handle all of your needs in the process.

Third, we're afflicted by *deception*, because we misvalue who God is. The servant's perception of his master's character is all wrong. He plays the blame game rather than confessing his laziness. We must learn from his mistake and comprehend God accurately. He is not just good; he created us to seek increase for his glory. He will give us what we need to accomplish his will, and we won't need to be afraid of losing it or not having enough.

Years ago I was sharing a speaking platform with Os Guinness in a sermon series on personal calling. Os summarized the Parable of the Talents with a stunning phrase: he said that the parable reveals an "entrepreneurial assumption" that God has with human beings. The servants are given resources but are not told how to invest them—the master expects them to use creativity and initiative to bring a return. How is God's return on investment in your life these days?

The Five Capitals: To fully appreciate the wealth God has entrusted to us, it helps to clarify five different kinds of resources that he gives. In the Younique Life Plan we call them the Five Capitals:

- *Spiritual capital* consists of wisdom, power, and authority (reputation for holiness and integrity) you have as a follower of Jesus.
- *Relational capital* consists of the people you know. This includes your family, friends, and "followers" from your most intimate circle to your widest network.
- *Physical capital* consists of the physical capacity of your body, including your time, health, and energy level.
- *Intellectual capital* consists of your knowledge, intelligence, and creative capacity.
- *Financial capital* consists of your financial net worth, including your cash, assets, and investments. This certainly extends to your ability to borrow money if you need it.

We have each of these five resources in varying degrees, and if we need to increase one of them, we are going to need to invest in it, which requires either increasing the *effectiveness* of what we're doing with that resource or *trading* or *leveraging* the other ones.

The first way to think about increasing one of your capitals is to operate with them more *effectively*. You might hang out with a friend regularly, but are your conversational topics increasing the value of that relationship? You might spend a certain amount of relaxation time consuming entertainment, but is it replenishing you physically and mentally as well as another recreational activity would?

However, increasing effectiveness only takes you so far. Pretty soon you discover that if you're going to increase one resource, you're going to have pay for it from another one—you have to make a *trade*. For example, you need more intellectual capital, so you enroll in school to get a degree, which costs you financial capital (money). Or you need more relational capital, so you go out in the evenings with new friends, which cuts into sleep and exercise (physical capital).

The best deal is when you can *leverage* one capital you are rich in to make gains in another without losing anything in the process. For example, you have a friend who gave you a good reference for a high-paying job in his company, and you got the job. You used your relational capital to gain financial capital without losing relational capital or reallocating your time. Or perhaps your prayerful dialogue with God over Scripture stimulates a new way of thinking about some ideas at work. You used spiritual capital to increase your intellectual capital without becoming any less spiritually rich.

Let's put it all together with one example. Let's say that you want to increase your spiritual capital by seeing break-thru in your struggle with anger. First, you increase the *effectiveness* of what you're doing spiritually: in your prayers, you begin to pray more consistently about the fruit of the Spirit.

Next, you make a *trade*. You recognize that your inconsistent habits of eating, exercise, and rest make you more susceptible to anger. Furthermore, the end of the workday has been "stretching" later and later over the past eighteen months, making it harder to exercise and rest more. So you may take a hit in your financial capital by shortening your work hours in order to boost your physical capital. You also increase your intellectual capital by studying a book on anger. In this way, you're hoping to *leverage* that newfound physical and intellectual capital to increase your spiritual power and authority as a more kind, peaceful, and gentle human being.

Plot Your Present, Forecast Your Future: The Five Capitals is more than a theory; it's the practical basis for understanding what's missing in your life and what you already possess to fill it.

In the Younique Life Plan Journey, we give participants seventeen imaginary gold bars, and we direct them to distribute the bars among the Five Capitals to depict the state of their resources today. One person might assign two bars to financial capital and nine bars in intellectual capital, while another person might do the reverse.

Then we ask participants to pretend they'll have thirty-four gold bars three years from now. How do they hope those will be distributed among their Five Capitals? What do they want the resources of their life to look like then?

When people see their two lists, present and future, side by side, they instantly recognize where the biggest gaps are—which kinds of capital need the most investment. They also recognize the riches they already have and begin thinking creatively about how to use the one to grow the other.

The good news of the gospel is that you now have the Holy Spirit inside of you to help you wisely grow all the resources God has given you to accomplish his will in your life. With him you *can* grow them, and growing them will grow you.

Now that we have explored role mapping and resource increasing, let's take a look at the third lens for exploring the best area of focus for each storyline—replenishment. This additional perspective is especially helpful as you select one area of focus for each storyline so that you are being realistic with your total life energy in "life stepping" into a better future.

Replenishment

Replenishment is one more way that God has ordered all of creation to function. We see it on the first page of the Bible and it works its way through all of Scripture. Simply stated, there is a rhythm of rest and work that is to be the guiding metronome of your life.

The Heresy of Dividing Rest from Work: There is a time for rest. And there is a time for work. Unfortunately, most of us let either rest or work dominate our life.

Some of us work because we have to. Rest, relaxation, and "me-time" are considered the greatest good of life, and work is a miserable interruption to be concluded as swiftly as possible. But people with this mind-set misunderstand that rest exists to make work possible. Rest is what energizes us to do the multiplying, governing, nurturing, beautifying, and building that God made Adam and Eve—and you—to do.

It may be that your job is so awful that it feels like serving a sentence in a labor camp. If so, I hope this book challenges you that to remain in that relationship with work—*unless* God is intentionally shaping your character through that suffering—violates his purpose for your life. Apathy, complacency, cynicism, and hopelessness that inhibit your "value to show" and "risk to go" keep you from glorifying him. It's time to make rest do its job of replenishing you for work and to restoring work to its rightful honor in your life.

The rest of us, however—which I suspect includes most of the readers of this book—rest *when we have time,* rather than *making time to rest.* What if rest was the big rock in the river that every priority flowed around? This was one of the "Top 10" instructions God gave Israel—to keep the Sabbath (Exod. 20:8–11). In a mind-bending metaphor, God even said that *he* took the Sabbath to get replenishment after making the world: "in six days the LORD made the heavens and the earth, but on the seventh day he rested and was refreshed" (Exod. 31:17).

God's pattern in creation and redemption is simple: we receive rest that empowers us to work; we don't work to earn rest. It's not for nothing that in the account of creation in Genesis 1 it says for each day, "Evening came and then morning." Part of the grace of Eden is the pace of Eden. *Likewise, we lay our heavy burdens down when we come to Jesus, who promised us rest; only then are we able to "take his yoke" upon ourselves and do the active work of learning from him (Matt. 11:28–30).*

In the Bible, rest is best defined as re-Creation. There are certain things that give you life and fill you up, certain things that bring into being your personal Eden. Sleep is foundational for everyone, but there is a variety of possible replenishment activities that rejuvenate your Life Younique. It could be running to classic rock or walking to modern worship music. Your custom rest recipe may require a big dose of silence and solitude or it may revolve around a sound-filled siesta. When a time, place, person, or activity makes you leap like a second-grader at recess, your inner battery charger is blinking. Think about it—can't you list those special experiences that fuel your connection to God, to yourself, and to others?

Jesus built patterns of rest and re-Creation into his life (see Mark 6:31, for example). Yet many people are trying to run their lives on passion, intention, and striving. This all-too-familiar frenzy is not the way of Jesus. Pace is as important as passion.

God doesn't *need* you to accomplish his will, by the way. He can make the rocks do that. But he prefers to involve you. He wants you to run the race in a way that's sustainable. He wants you to posture yourself as a learner and live into the gracious reality that you really can't do the work of the kingdom apart from him.

Making replenishment a daily wellspring not only allows us to experience more and more of the kingdom with each passing day; it reminds us that God is the one holding the universe together. He's at the center of it, not me. He can accomplish his will in my life; my responsibility is simply to partner in what he's already doing. I don't know about you, but I need rest to rescue me from taking myself too seriously.

A Replenishment Audit: When it comes to replenishment, as with anything, you can't go where you need to go if you don't know where you are. You have to begin by taking a replenishment audit: comprehending what replenishment rhythms are and which ones are active in your life today.

For starters, understand that replenishment rhythms have two variables—replenishment and rhythm. (No surprise there, right?)

Think of replenishment as rest that recharges your energy supply. Like the battery in your phone, you're either discharging or recharging at all times. God has built into our natures the need both to fully discharge and to fully recharge. Unfortunately, people can get caught out of balance by doing too much of one or the other.

On the one hand, our world is go-go-go. People have never been busier, many of them frantically discharging all the time with only a sip of replenishment before draining themselves of energy again. On the other hand, our world is also an amusement factory. With a tap and a swipe you can install a game on your phone whose job is to alert you every few hours that you need to play it again. Some people spend so much time recharging with low-value leisure and entertainment that they don't feel the health that comes from getting downright tired from dedicated productivity.

Ironically, both the life of too much work and the life of too much rest make us feel exhausted. God made us to feel most energized when work and rest stay properly balanced and when we have seasons of thorough discharge and thorough recharge.

The way to tell the difference between work and rest isn't whether you get paid for it or not. The difference is, quite simply, whether the activity feels like work or rest. This not only varies activity by activity, but also from person to person, and even in one person's life at different times. For instance, for one person, going for a run is rest because she likes to run; it soothes and relaxes her. For someone else, going for a run is work because he doesn't like doing it; it's difficult and uncomfortable even though it keeps him healthy and increases his physical capital overall.

Another example: if you like engaging in conversation and you have a close and harmonious healthy relationship with your spouse, then a long, rambling talk with your mate is rest for you. But if conversation isn't really your thing or your marriage is distant or conflicted, then making time to talk is work. It doesn't come easily and it takes effort and focus even though it nourishes your relationship toward health and strength.

We find replenishment in restful activities that recharge us. But to get the most out of them, we need to build them into our lives in a rhythm. By "rhythm" I mean a recurring pattern at regular intervals—each day, each week, each quarter, or each year.

This is where the replenishment audit comes in. It consists of your thorough answers to this fourfold question: What rest activities are you doing to replenish your-self every day, every week, every three months, and every year? Answering this question gives you your current replenishment rhythms.

When you perform this audit, truths about your life immediately emerge. If you don't have many rhythms, is it because you aren't replenishing but just grinding it out? Or are you grazing on low-value replenishment continually but not getting bang for your buck out of richer, focused replenishment rhythms? Are there rhythmic intervals where replenishment is missing? What might belong there?

I recognize that there are people in circumstances that make it very hard to get the replenishment they need. I think of the single dad working the graveyard shift at night and watching his kids all day. I think of the mother of newborn twins for whom sleep seems like a distant memory. These exhausting demands enter our lives sometimes. But for every person I know who truly cannot find replenishment as a norm, I know many more who *think* they don't have time to rest because of choices, commitments, and obligations they think they can't say "no" to. For them, it takes courage to step into a new replenishment rhythm at the risk of disappointing others (or themselves). But God can be trusted. "In vain you get up early and stay up late . . . he gives sleep to the one he loves" (Ps. 127:2).

Find Your Focus

Everything we've looked at so far is about the fixed stuff of your life that changes rarely and gradually. It's a lot, I know! But it is the necessary base for the four areas of focus where you get leverage for the next ninety days. These are your LifeSteps.

To define your LifeSteps, start with one storyline. Consider its condition currently.

Now look at your Role Map. As you look over your secondary roles, is there one that jumps out at you that is clearly being neglected as it pertains to this storyline? If so, make a note of it.

Now look at your Five Capitals. Are you obviously lacking a resource that this storyline requires or is supposed to gain?

Finally, look at your replenishment rhythms. Is it evident that this storyline needs a boost through resting more deliberately or through working more deliberately? If so, note which of the two.

At this point you may have one item shouting for your attention—a role, a resource, or replenishment—or you may have two or three. If you have more than one, which stands above the rest? Which one is most central or foundational or critical to the prosperity of all three? That is your LifeStep for that storyline. Now use your imagination to consider how the other two fundamentals can support that LifeStep.

When you repeat this process for your other three storylines, you end up with a four-focus strategy. On the other side of the complexity of your life, you've arrived at a limited number of places to set your levers. Then, with the power God gives you, you can move your world.

 (To see an example of how I once put together four LifeSteps by analyzing my own roles, resources, and replenishment rhythms, go to WillMancini. com/LifePlanUpdate.)

PART FOUR

YOUR DIRECTION
How to Develop a Simple Plan for Tomorrow

HORIZON
STORYLINE

Ever been afraid of the dark? Don't feel bad—you were made to be.

Humans avoid darkness, especially in unfamiliar environments, because most of what we sense comes through what we see. About 80 percent of the sensory data from the external world that our brains have to work with comes from 20 percent of our senses, namely, from our sense of sight.

Fortunately, most people are able to see, at least with corrective lenses. But most people who see don't see *how* they see.

I began to "see how I see" when I watched my wife Romy paint a landscape. Artists are magnificent not only at seeing sights but at *seeing* and then using it to create. Romy showed me how she portrayed the depth of a three-dimensional landscape on a two-dimensional canvas by painting figures on three planes, at three levels of focus.

I learned that that's how our eyes function all the time. See for yourself (literally). Raise this book up to eye level. These words that you're focusing on now are called the foreground. Now look over top of the book to an object near you like a piece of furniture or a nearby wall. That's the midground. Now look beyond that—say, out a window in the wall or to the far end of a big room. That's the background (figure IV.1).

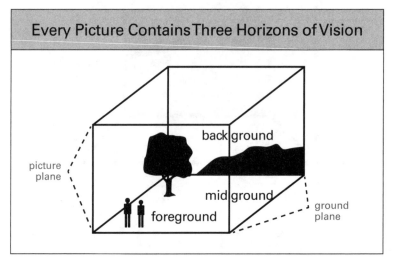

Figure IV.1

Do you see how quickly you can shift your focus from near to far and back again? That physiological phenomenon is called "accommodation," and you perform it in about a third of a second. It happens continuously without you noticing, but you can also direct it purposely if you choose.

That's exactly what I'm going to teach you in part 4: how to look into your future and rapidly shift your focus from close up to far away and back (figure IV.2).

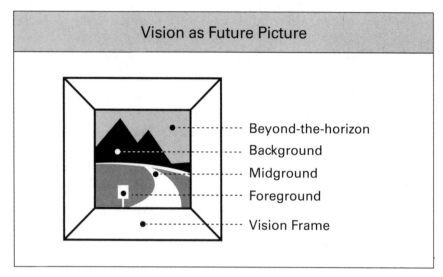

Figure IV.2

To do this, let me introduce you to another master tool: the Horizon Storyline (figure IV.3).

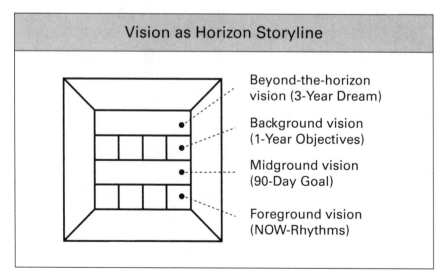

Figure IV.3

With the Horizon Storyline, you don't look ahead in space but in time. The foreground horizon is what you're doing now—today, this week, this month. The midground horizon is what's dead ahead ninety days from now. The background horizon is one year from now, the furthest ahead you can see; the details that far out are not clear.

To those three horizons we add a fourth, three years away, which I call "beyond the horizon." It's the next destination you're traveling toward, the place you'll settle down for the night. You can't see it yet, but you can *picture* it—it's where you want to be.

The midground and foreground horizons together tell the story of your short-range direction—one ninety-day goal and four "NOW-rhythms," the habits you install to get you there. The space beyond the horizon and the background horizon tell the story of your long-range direction—one three-year dream and four one-year objectives to get you there.

Note that your plan is never more complicated than ten elements—one dream supported by four objectives and one goal supported by four next steps. The nickname for the Horizon Storyline is the "1:4:1:4." Think of the Horizon Storyline as the right amount of vision content and the right amount of time in the future. It's the comprehensive yet concise way to know where you're going. Whether you're a cardiac surgeon or a college student, whether you're in human resources or homemaking, whether you're managing one thousand people or only one—yourself—ten elements provide the break-thru that you need to take the next step in your life (figure IV.4).

How the Horizon Storyline Works				
Horizon Storyline	Horizon Name	Life Plan	Long/Short Range	Max # of Ideas
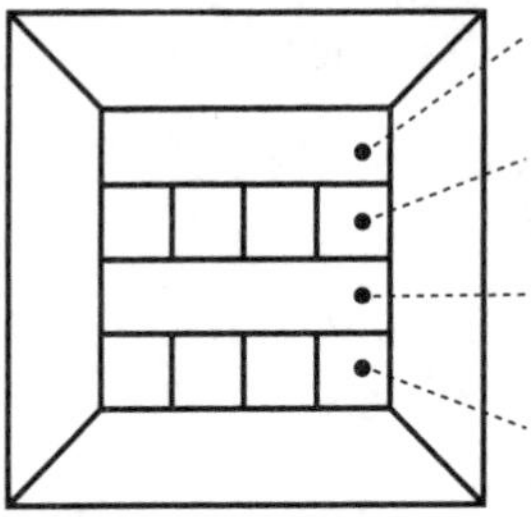	Beyond-the-Horizon Vision	3-Year Dream	Long-Range Visionary	1
	Background Vision	1-Year Objectives	Long-Range Strategic	4
	Midground Vision	90-Day Goal	Short-Range Visionary	1
	Foreground Vision	NOW-Rhythms	Short-Range Strategic	4

Figure IV.4

In the rest of part 4 we will walk through each time horizon of the 1:4:1:4 as the master tool for life direction. When we get to part 6 we will loop back to include some additional visionary perspective on a lifetime horizon. Those tools are more about *destiny* than *direction* and include topics like how to write a bucket list and how to discern your ultimate contribution.[1] But first, in the pages ahead, I'm going to teach you the tools to see where God is taking you with stunning clarity for today, ninety days, one year, and three years away.

You think I'm joking? You ain't seen nothing yet.

Chapter 14

DREAM

The Four Hidden Lessons of Today's Most Popular Bible Verse

"Questions of implementation are of no consequence until the vision can be imagined. The imagination must come before implementation. Our culture is competent to implement almost anything and to imagine almost nothing."
—Walter Brueggemann

If you are a human being, you are a visionary.

Is that claim too lofty? I don't think so. In my day job I often remind church leaders, "If you've ever looked forward to something and told others about it, you are a visionary." With rare exception, people always look forward to something. We look forward to vacations and date nights, to graduations and project completions. We look forward to relief from physical pain or a filled belly. It's important to see that vision has an almost infinite span: from grand proposals for how people will live on the moon one day to pondering what you'd like for lunch today. The ability to envision a better future, no matter the size and scope, is a significant part of what makes you human. It's a critical faculty that sets us apart from all the other living creatures God made.

As a result of our "visionary-ness," any person can live in multiple time zones. Every person can visit places their feet dare to tread. Imagination is our liberation from the tyranny of time and space. Have you ever sat in a seemingly endless, mind-numbing meeting and found yourself suddenly transported to a favorite beach? Have you ever talked with your spouse about a glorious summer vacation in the dark dead of winter? Every day births millions of daydreams.

Whether you consider yourself a "dreamer" or not, I bet you've spent some time in reasoned pondering or daydreaming. The bottom line: you are a visionary. You saw a picture in your mind's eye of something different and better than the present moment. And it wasn't just any picture: it was a future that called you to itself, a future that—if only you could—you would make real.

I'm convinced that our compulsion to envision, to imagine, to *dream*, is one aspect of what it means to be created in the image and likeness of God. You envision because God envisions. You dream because God dreams. You have to imagine something before you can make it, and that is exactly what God did when he made the world.

In Proverbs 8 Solomon crafts a monologue performed by Wisdom, who says, "The LORD acquired me . . . before ancient times, from the beginning, before the earth began. . . . I was a skilled craftsman beside him. I was his delight every day, always rejoicing before him" (vv. 22–23, 30). God used wisdom to imagine the world he wanted to make before he made it. Imagination isn't contrary to wisdom; rather, *imagination is essential to wisdom*.

Ready to have your mind blown? That wisdom, that imagination that God used to make the world—Paul says that it is actually a person. And not just any person: the "wisdom of God" is Christ Jesus, God's Son (1 Cor. 1:24, 30). "Everything was created by him . . . in [whom] are hidden all the treasures of wisdom and knowledge" (Col. 1:16; 2:3). So if God used his wisdom to imagine the world before he made it, and if Jesus is his wisdom, is it going too far to call Jesus the *Imagination of God*, the *Vision of God*, even the *Dream of God*? I don't think so.

Let's take it one step further still. Paul also says that "before the ages" God predestined his "hidden wisdom"—Jesus himself—*to be "our glory*. . . . What no eye has seen, no ear has heard, and no human heart has conceived—God has prepared these things for those who love him" (1 Cor. 2:7, 9). God imagines something we cannot imagine: that we human beings—created beautiful but broken by sin—would one day look like his Beloved Son. As a perfect prototype, the glorious person of Christ is God's dream of a glorious you!

God dreams a dream of you reflecting him like no one else—your Life Younique. And God dreams you to dream his dream of you.

God made you to be a visionary; you're going to envision your future somehow whether you try to or not. So do you want to envision your life distractedly, selfishly, haphazardly, despairingly, or uninterestingly? I doubt it. I'm here to help you to envision your future according to how God envisions it: to dream it thoughtfully, prayerfully, intentionally, hopefully, and magnificently.

That Verse about God's Plans That You Think You Know

Dreaming God's dream for you is quite different from the cliché, contemporary, commencement-speech advice to "follow your dreams." To illustrate the distinction and to take a step toward the practical, explore with me the profound meaning of one of the most quoted Bible verses of our time, Jeremiah 29:11: "'For I know the plans I have for you,' declares the LORD, 'plans to prosper you and not to harm you, plans to give you hope and a future'" (NIV).

I bet you didn't even read the quoted verse in the last paragraph once you read the reference, because that's how familiar it is. However, almost everything that most people think they know about that verse is wrong (or at least incomplete). And embedded in it are four disciplines for dreaming along with God.[1]

Discipline #1: Dream, Don't Fantasize

The story of Jeremiah 29 is a story of a true dream and a false dream locked in a duel for the imagination of God's people. Yet to fully appreciate the situation requires a little historical context.

In the years around 600 BC, a new Babylonian Empire under Nebuchadnezzar spread throughout the Middle East, compelling small nations like Judah (one of the two kingdoms of God's people) to swear allegiance and pay tribute or else be annihilated. Babylon was a massively intimidating superpower. And God's people were deeply divided: fight them or give in? Judah's policy wobbled between submission to Babylon and resistance, hoping for help from the nearer but weaker empire in Egypt.

A throng of patriotic false prophets rallied Judah to fight Babylon, imagining that Yahweh, the God enthroned in Jerusalem's temple, was with them. On the other side, standing alone, Jeremiah urged his countrymen to surrender to Babylon because God had decreed that empire's triumph. Yet Jeremiah also preached that Judah would never have been dominated by Babylon in the first place if its people hadn't committed "spiritual adultery." (That's the image the Bible uses to capture the heartbreak of God when the Israelites worshiped false gods rather than Yahweh, the God of Israel, alone.) Unfortunately, every time Judah's king ignored Jeremiah's prophecies and rebelled against Babylon, Nebuchadnezzar's army would invade, lay siege to its cities, and carry off plunder and hostages critical to Judah's war effort. Jeremiah was God's true prophet, and God's people suffered when they didn't heed his prophetic warnings.

Ten thousand of these Jewish hostages sat as refugees in the land of their enemy, perplexed over what to do next. Then false prophets who had been deported with them declared that God would deliver Judah and send them home soon. They urged the exiles to refuse to unpack their bags and settle down. These prophets claimed to have heard from God in a dream, but they lied; they simply told the people what they wanted to hear.

By all means, let's learn the lesson of these miserable Jewish exiles: *don't tell yourself what you want to hear.* It is crucial that any dream for your life emerge from God's dream for you and not from your independent wishes, hopes, and ideals. A dream that isn't from God is a fantasy, and following fantasy leads to bondage, not freedom.

Discipline #2: Dream Where God Is Taking You, Not Where You're Taking Yourself

While the unhappy captives clung to the false hope given by their false prophets, they received a shocking letter from Jeremiah in Jerusalem. It read:

> This is what the LORD says: "When seventy years for Babylon are complete, I will attend to you and will confirm My promise concerning you to restore you to this place. For I know the plans I have for you"—this is the LORD's declaration—"plans for your well-being, not for disaster, to give you a future and a hope . . . and I will restore your fortunes and gather you from all the nations and places where I banished you." (Jer. 29:10–11, 14)

Do you think this was good news or bad news to the exiles? On the one hand, God promised to take them home. On the other hand, nearly all those who heard it would be dead before it came true. One thing was certain: the destiny God dreamed for these exiles was beyond what they could achieve by themselves. To get there it was God or nothing.

Part 4 of the Younique process is about moving from the Vision Frame to the Vision-Inside-the-Frame, or what I call "vision proper." And when we make this shift, the subject changes in a big way. In chapter 11 I listed the Five Irreducible Questions of Clarity. The first four, which correspond to the four sides of the Vision Frame, are:

- What are *you* doing?
- Why do *you* do what you do?
- When are *you* successful?
- How do *you* get there?

But notice the fifth question, which corresponds to the Horizon Storyline: "Where is *God* taking you?" A true vision from God is what *God* has dreamed up for you to do, in the order and on the timetable that he has prepared. Your part is to design your life in accordance with his dream and align your activity to it.

To the astonishment of Judah's captives, a long exile wasn't the loss of their dream. It wasn't even the dream deferred: it was actually the dream defined. The worst day of your life over and over again—that's what exile felt like—can actually advance you toward the fulfillment of your dream, because it prepares you to receive it. God wanted to do miraculous ministry in and through them despite living in enemy territory.

Discipline #3: Dream Your Long-Range Future, Don't Plan It

God's "plans" for his people were not their hope; rather, his plans were to "*give* a future and a hope." The distinction is important, because God's plans for his people were short-term, while his dream for them was long-term. His plans were actionable; his dream was inspirational.

God's plans for the exiles were concrete: "Build houses and live in them. Plant gardens and eat their produce. Find wives for yourselves and have sons and daughters. Find wives for your sons and give your daughters to men in marriage so that they may bear sons and daughters" (Jer. 29:5–6). These were action steps for his people to get going on without hesitation, and it was in their power to do so. Waiting to enter God's dream is faith; waiting to act on God's plans is sin.

Conversely, the dream God has given you is not a goal to accomplish. This principle trips up many people who gain a vision of their favored future and set it as a mark to reach, come what may. It's the equal and opposite error of fantasy; while fantasy is escape from reality, planning that far ahead is demanding that reality fit into your mold. James gives a severe warning not to lay out plans too far into the future: "You do not know what tomorrow will bring—what your life will be! For you are like vapor that appears for a little while, then vanishes." He goes on to call such confident long-range planning "boasting," "arrogant," and "evil" (James 4:14, 16).

> Waiting to enter God's dream is faith; waiting to act on God's plans is sin.

The distinction between dreaming and planning is built into the division between the upper and lower portions of the Horizon Storyline master tool I described in the introduction to part 4. The upper half—three-year dream and one-year objectives—constitute the long-range vision; this is what you dream. The lower half—ninety-day goal and NOW-rhythms—compose the short-range vision; this is what you plan.

Long-range vision is about managing context of the future and attending to your imagination, not making a commitment. Describing your three-year dream isn't setting a goal but imagining a future state. Because it is over the horizon, it requires faith, because the very nature of godly faith involves apprehending something ahead that our physical eyes cannot (yet) see (Heb. 11:1). Your dream isn't what you're looking at while you're driving down the road; it's the reason you're driving.

You have a three-year dream to energize your day-to-day every time you picture it. If your identity—expressed in your LifeCall and your LifeCore—is the wind at your back, your three-year dream is the magnet on your heart.

Discipline #4: Dream for Others, Not Just for Yourself

Finally, God's short- and long-range vision for these Jewish exiles did not benefit them alone. A dream of God never does.

God ordered the captives to "pursue the well-being of the city I have deported you to. Pray to the LORD on its behalf" (Jer. 29:7). Unless you've been part of a conquered people (I haven't), you can hardly imagine the difficulty of keeping these commands. Consider that they were delivered to people who would soon sing:

Daughter Babylon, doomed to destruction,
happy is the one who pays you back
what you have done to us.
Happy is he who takes your little ones
and dashes them against the rocks. (Ps. 137:8–9)

But God was trying to give his people a vision of a virtuous cycle of mutual blessing: "when [Babylon] thrives, you will thrive." As the exiles blessed the city of their enemies, the city would bless them.

And it didn't stop there. Isaiah foretold that because of the return from exile, "Nations will come to your light, and kings to your shining brightness" (60:3). The Servant whom God would raise up to "[restore] the protected ones of Israel" would also be "a light for the nations, . . . my salvation to the ends of the earth" (49:6). Every non-Jew past, present, and future who belongs to God through Christ is a beneficiary of the dream God gave Jewish exiles over two and a half millennia ago.

This is always how it goes. True vision serves. Any vision that God gives you is for his glory and for the benefit of others. Though your vision blesses you, that blessing is bound together with the well-being of everyone around you and of the whole cosmos. If you can't see that in what you dream, return to God and dream with him some more.

Chapter 15

THREE YEARS FROM NOW

How to Prototype the Next Chapter of Life

*"If you want to build a ship, don't drum up people to collect
wood and don't assign them tasks and work, but rather teach
them to long for the endless immensity of the sea."*

—Antoine de Saint-Exupéry

In the introduction to part 4, I talked about how our sense of sight constitutes 80
percent of our perception. But it's even more important than that: it constitutes 80
percent of our inspiration.

I don't mean to knock the other senses, like the sense of hearing, for example.
Listening to a piece of music can be deeply moving. But sight is a unique motivator.
What you see can make you yearn to go or stop, to lean forward or to pull back, to act
or to wait. In fact, sound motivates mainly when our minds convert it into sight—
when we describe images as figures of speech, our metaphors turn hearing ears into
seeing eyes.

God built this into us, so he uses it repeatedly. Time and again in Scripture he
gives his people visions that change their direction and propel them forward.

Take Abram, for instance. In Genesis 15, after Abram had already obeyed God to
go to a land he had never seen before, God encouraged him that he was on the right
track. "Do not be afraid, Abram," God said. "I am your shield; your reward will be very
great" (v. 1). It's easy to say, "Don't be afraid," but it's hard to obey it. But surely Abram
could not help but picture a shield that covered him all around, turning this way and

that to deflect arrows and ward off swordstrokes. And he could not avoid imagining the pile of gold and silver that God said he was giving to the person who trusted him.

But that's not all. Abram lamented that he had no son to inherit his property, and God gave him something else to imagine. Directing him to go out of his tent into the night air, God said, "Look at the sky and count the stars, if you are able to count them. . . . Your offspring will be that numerous" (v. 5). God turned the ever-present starry sky into a non-stop personal vision IMAX. He could literally see—before his first son was even born—the "power points" of everyone who would come from him.

But God still wasn't done. He enveloped Abram in terrifying darkness and told him that his descendants would be oppressed as slaves for four hundred years. In the gloom Abram could not have mistaken the message. But then a torch in an oven flamed in the darkness and floated between portions of sacrificial animals that Abram had laid out. The light represented God himself walking between the pieces of meat, which was the ceremony for making a solemn covenant in Abram's world. God bound himself by an oath to Abram: "I give this land to your offspring" (v. 18). Forever after, every time Abram saw a cooking fire, he would remember God's promise burned into his memory.

A shield, a reward, stars, a flaming torch . . . these visionary images kept Abram trusting, hoping, believing, and obeying to his dying day.

God's people did not always have to see their own visions to be inspired to trust and obey. Often just hearing the vision from the one who saw it was enough; people's imaginations did the rest.

Take, for instance, Moses' full-color speech to Israel when the nation was on the threshold of the land God promised to their ancestor Abram (Abraham) centuries before:

> "The LORD your God is bringing you into a good land, a land with streams, springs, and deep water sources, flowing in both valleys and hills; a land of wheat, barley, vines, figs, and pomegranates; a land of olive oil and honey; a land where you will eat food without shortage, where you will lack nothing; a land whose rocks are iron and from whose hills you will mine copper. . . . When you eat and are full, and build beautiful houses to live in, and your herds and flocks grow large, and your silver and gold multiply, and everything else you have increases, be careful that your heart doesn't become proud and you forget the LORD your God who brought you out of the land of Egypt, out of the place of slavery." (Deut. 8:7–9, 12–14)

These few sentences were such a vivid description of the good place God was taking them that they could not forget it. It made them lean forward to take God's blessing by obeying him and giving him praise for it.

God has given his people visions for thousands of years, because he knows they compel us to press on to the good works he prepared in advance for us to do. This chapter is about how to gain the vision of the place you've not yet been that slingshots you into your future.

Seeing Your Beyond-the-Horizon Vision

Your Beyond-the-Horizon Vision (the top level of your Horizon Storyline) is a vivid picture of your life three years into the future (figure 15.1). It is a God-inspired sense of destination. If you could prototype your life after three revolutions around the sun, what would it look like? Keep in mind that a prototype is a preliminary model that can be evaluated, considered, adapted, and adjusted. Prototyping is a creative, fun, and even exciting process, allowing you to step outside of your life to create and re-create different scenarios or snapshots of a potential future.

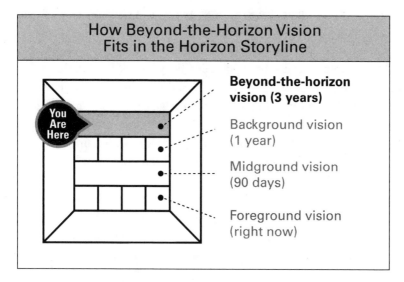

Figure 15.1

The final expression is one idea expressed by a short sentence and anchored by a picture or metaphor—that is, one image you can see in your mind's eye. Once you select a picture you can develop it like a Polaroid with vivid-description bullet points. Each vivid description statement should feel like God is leading you forward in some specific way. The end result is a moving snapshot of your life three years away. It's always designed for motivation and inspiration, not just for information.

Why three years? Three years is further into the future than most people proactively think about. It's further away than 99.9 percent of the events in your iCal or Outlook calendar. Yet it's accessible enough to consider key milestones, anticipate life events, and sense big ideas of God's leading in your life. It forces you to stretch your thinking and activate brain cells you don't typically use. Your three-year dream takes you one big step into the future from today toward an ultimate life legacy that could be decades away. It's a three-year fuel rod for daily activity and food for prayer every time you think of it. It infuses your life with deeper meaning. It stokes your hope. It stretches your stamina. It fires your faith. It inspires a deeper sacrifice for the things that matter most. And, as we'll see in the next chapter, it ramps you up to tackle the major obstacles sitting between where you are and where you want to be.

To sculpt your three-year dream, you'll have to flex your imagination muscles. Don't judge yourself if you think your effort isn't good enough. The very act of a deliberate dreaming exercise is a major accomplishment for most people. Know that it gets easier and easier to imagine again and again until you're living a vividly visionary life. I don't want you just to have a vision statement, I want you to have a visionary state of mind.

Take time to pray and submit yourself wholly to God—mind, heart, body, and emotions. Ask him to make his will clear. Release all of your requirements, self-expectations, and wishes to him so that his dream reigns supreme. Cultivate an internal confidence that God does not withhold anything good from those who walk uprightly (Ps. 84:11). Remember that God has already given you Jesus Christ, not sparing his life on your account. Therefore, he will certainly and graciously "give us all things" (Rom. 8:32).

Be sensitive to nudges in your feelings (especially the ones that are hard to explain) as you work on your three-year dream. Before starting, think back to your life three years in the past. What were you doing at that time? Try to feel the scope of a three-year slice of life. Then reflect on these questions to warm you up:

- What has God been making clear to you about the future as you've been reading this book?
- What promptings, ideas, or themes from God and his Word have you experienced repeatedly over the last year that have not been fully developed or fulfilled?
- When you picture the life you yearn for, what do you see that excites you the most?
- What will be the dominant theme in your life three years from now?

- What is the thing in your life that you most desire to be different three years from now?
- How do you hope your family will be different?
- How do you hope your work will be different?
- What are the obvious thresholds, turning points, or milestones coming over the next three years (for example, graduations, retirements, births, relocations, etc.)?
- Has God shown you anything about yourself as you've worked through this book? How will that revelation be included in your three-year prototype?
- What do you know beyond a shadow of a doubt that you need more of in your life? What do you need less of?
- What single greatest accomplishment in the next three years would make the biggest difference for the rest of your life?
- What might you regret for the rest of your life if it's left undone in the next three years?
- What has God been preparing you your entire life to do in the next three years?

Now consider, what picture in your mind best represents the life you hope for? What image could capture everything you just thought about with a dash of wonder? Is there a symbol that lights your countenance or grips your heart? Aristotle said that the soul never thinks without a picture.[1] Brainstorm ideas and try a few on for size. Find the one gives you that aha-moment jolt. Then write your soul-picture out as a single sentence.

While there are literally hundreds of jump-off points for future pictures, imagine the splendid variety with just the metaphor of water. In three years, is your life going to resemble:

- the rush and adventure of whitewater rapids?
- the serenity and beauty of a trickling brook?
- the expanse and unknown of open ocean?
- the power and immensity of unstoppable waves?
- the refreshment and renewal of desert rain?
- the peaceful pleasantness of a still pond?
- the joy and discovery of a walk on the beach?

With these sample images of water as a backdrop, consider the continued variety. If your life is a whitewater river, are you a kayaker navigating the currents or a salmon swimming upstream? If your life is playing in the waves, are you a competitive surfer or a child laughing and splashing with friends?

Next, it's critical that you amplify your vision-in-the-making with compelling specifics. Write out nine bullet points that together vividly describe the life you imagine three years in the future. Start the points with phrases like these (purely as examples):

- "My family is . . ."
- "I work for . . ."
- "I have . . ."
- "Every day I see . . ."

Finally, gather into one paragraph the sentence that succinctly paints the picture of your future together with your favorite vivid-description bullets. As you read the paragraph, does it evoke an inner yes? Does it tug on your heart? Reviewing this paragraph on a regular basis will imbue the nitty-gritty and highs and lows of your life with meaning that fires your soul.

How a Vision Changed My Life

Everything I have written over the last fifteen years is my attempt to express how much I believe in the power of vision. I simply cannot talk about it enough. But perhaps the best thing I can do to show you the power of a dream to change a life is to show you my dream. A few years ago I envisioned this:

Picture Idea: A Deep Well

Short Phrase: My life will be a deep well of blessing free to overflow to those around it.

Vivid Description Bullets

1. I see a giant pendulum swinging toward depth of identity from scope of activity.
2. My rally cry is, "Being more accomplishes more than doing more."
3. I will be closing out an extended "warrior" life stage (a focus on mastering my consulting work) and fully entering a "king" one (a focus on harvesting from my consulting work).
4. I see a freer man with more margin, spontaneity, and flexibility.
5. I see a day-after-day reality that I am never found in a rush, with more time between phone calls and more relaxation at meals.

6. I will focus on relational and spiritual capital by investing in four groups of people: my central circle (Romy, Poema, Jacob, Joel, and Abby), the Auxano team, the Younique team, and my neighbors.

7. When I arrive three years from now, I will be prepared for the next chapter of new initiatives with the strength of an established platform for Younique, including a Younique trade book, financial freedom, and replenished energy in my personal life domain.

8. I see more adventure travel for both personal and vocational time with at least four locations a year that create energy and anticipation every day.

9. I want to be known as much for my joy as I am for my tenacity.

Paragraph

*My life will be a **deep well** of blessing, **free to overflow**.* As I move toward depth of identity from scope of activity, my rally cry is, "Being more accomplishes more than doing more." I will be shifting my life stage from "mastering" to "harvesting" as I prepare for my 50s. I see a freer man with more margin, spontaneity, and flexibility to invest in my most important relationships. When I arrive, I will be prepared for the next chapter of new initiatives that center on building an ecosystem of organizations, master tools, and processes that multiply my life's contribution in the areas of clarity and vision for believers. I will engage in adventure travel quarterly and will greet each day from full, not partial, replenishment. I will be known as much for my joy as I am for my tenacity.

Rather than leave you guessing what difference this dream made in my life, I'll conclude this chapter by giving you examples. How about ten?

Top Ten Panel: 10 Ways Vision Transformed 1,000 Moments over 3 Years

1. My prayer life was guided countless times by the picture of a deep well.

2. In hundreds of little moments I chose "relationship" over "task," knowing that the momentum of my life needed to shift.

3. I smiled more than I ever have before. I learned how to experience more joy during more frustrating circumstances.

4. As three of my children entered early adulthood away from the home, I moved heaven and earth to be with them whenever I could be. I chose client work based on where my children lived.

5. I invested in extravagant moments and memories like never before: from Poema's first birthday to Jacob's graduation to Mom and Dad's 50th anniversary.

6. I learned how to enjoy walks with my wife, which used to go against the grain of my existence, as the activator and maximizer in me doesn't like strolls in the park.

7. I introduced more people to other people than ever using my influence to build the influence of individuals on the teams I serve.

8. I learned how to give more authority away to more people.

9. I made one of the biggest financial decisions of my life that looked like a step backwards to many people, but it fueled my vision like never before.

10. I set a total of twelve big goals for my life (four 90-day goals a year), each goal guided by the vision. During this time I aspired toward 156 moments of weekly reflection guided by the vision, which I accomplished a majority of the time.

As you ponder this list, I want to emphasize that it's not about getting vision perfect. It's about getting dreaming started. I still make mistakes, experience drifts, get overwhelmed, and run down an occasional rabbit trail. Storms still come and circumstances still happen. But the question I put to myself is: *Do I want all of this to happen in the absence of a vision-guided life or in the harness of one?*

Chapter 16

ONE YEAR FROM NOW

Four Things to Remember While You Revolve around the Sun

"If I could go back 20 or 25 years, I wish I would have known that there was no need to wait. . . . So if you're planning to do something with your life, if you have a 10-year plan of how to get there, you should ask: Why can't you do this in 6 months?"

—Peter Thiel

Have you ever driven from east to west across the Great Plains?

You drive for hours, across the even steppe and blunt cliffs of South Dakota, or the gently sloping rock-chalk hills of Kansas, or the mammoth pool table that is the Texas Panhandle. Then you see something dark on the horizon. *What is THAT?* you wonder. As the car hurtles closer, you realize that it's a range of *mountains*—or, as you later discover, mere foothills that still look gigantic to anyone who isn't from the Rockies. *Finally!* you think. *We're almost there.*

Only you're not. For hour after hour you continue to drive straight west, the declining sun nearly blinding your eyes. The imposing, jagged band of darkness on the horizon doesn't seem to be getting any closer. And then with startling suddenness, it's upon you: the road angles into a narrowing embrace like outflung arms of the range. Finally, your car is swallowed by a pass through the awesome, towering peaks.

Why open this chapter with a driving illustration? Even though the ultimate goal is to get to the other side of the mountains, all you can see for hours is the distant range getting closer and closer.

The Beyond-the-Horizon Vision that we talked about in the previous chapter is the destination you're driving to reach, but you can't see it except in your imagination. What you can barely see, however, as you squint through the haze of your future, are four mountains standing along the horizon, shielding your destination from view and guarding the way. These mountains form your Background Horizon rearing up one year ahead (figure 16.1).

One-year objectives complement your three-year dream to compose your long-range vision. As we shift our focus two years nearer in time, we move from the inspirational to the informational, from the pictorial to the practical. One-year objectives are problems to solve, steps you're eventually going to have to take. In other words, one-year objectives are the four strategic *hows* you have to have to reach your one visionary *what*.

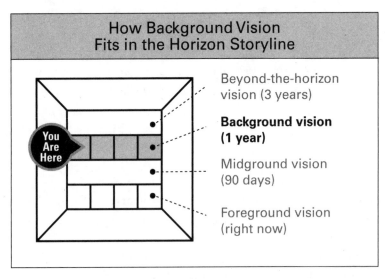

Figure 16.1

How One-Year Objectives Serve a Three-Year Dream

Here are four other ways to conceptualize Background Objectives.

1. One-year objectives are the four big obstacles to overcome on the way to the climactic scene of your three-year epic adventure. Think of your favorite fantastic, sweeping adventure movie or series—*Star Wars, The Lord of the Rings, Harry Potter,* or the Marvel universe movies, for example. Before the heroes reach the climactic showdown or test, they have to surmount multiple major challenges along the way. Similarly, your one-year objectives are roadblocks you know you're going to have to overcome in order to reach the destination three years away that you've been dreaming of.

2. One-year objectives are the four big rocks that go into the jar of your three-year dream. A small bucket of sand, one of gravel, a bunch of pebbles, a few big rocks, and a gallon-sized Mason jar combine to make a famous demonstration of the power of putting the important things first, popularized years ago by Stephen Covey. If you put the small things in the jar first—sand, then gravel, then pebbles—you can't fit all the big rocks in at the end. But if you reverse the order by putting in the big rocks first, then pebbles, then gravel, then sand, the smaller things flow around the bigger ones, and the jar holds it all.

Covey taught that if you continually devote your first and best minutes to the welter of small, urgent matters and hope you have time left over for what matters most, you'll never make progress on the "big rocks." But if you block out time to advance what is most important, the necessary to-dos of lesser importance will somehow still get done. Your one-year objectives are like your four big rocks: they may not be urgent, but they are the critically important issues to devote time to if you're going to make break-thru progress toward your three-year dream.

3. One-year objectives are the four legs that support the table of your three-year dream. I used the Horizon Storyline for years with church teams before I noticed that the diagram looks like a four-legged table sitting on top of another four-legged table. What a great analogy! Achieving your one-year objectives sets up and supports the Beyond-the-Horizon Vision you're headed toward. Once you've followed the process of ascertaining and articulating your one-year objectives, you'll immediately notice the resemblance between each one and an aspect of your three-year dream. It is the imaginative made concrete.

4. One-year objectives are the four horses that pull you toward your three-year dream. Though I've intentionally used the analogies of mountains and obstacles above, don't get the impression that one-year objectives are mainly about *stopping* you. In fact, they're mainly about *starting* you and *sustaining* you along the way. Deliberately and consistently marshaling your spiritual, relational, physical, intellectual, and financial capital toward your one-year objectives channels enormous power to do things you might have thought were impossible.

Simple Steps to Four Objectives

To crystallize your four one-year objectives, follow the steps of this simple but powerful exercise adapted from the work of Tom Paterson called "Four Helpful Lists."

Step 1: "Where am I now?" Brainstorm a list of observations about your life right now. Anything goes. Some observations will characterize the state of affairs while other, countable things (like money) will have numbers attached.

If you'd like a little more structure to this step, use Paterson's "Four Helpful Lists." For each of your four storylines, ask yourself four questions:

- What is working? *(celebrate it)*
- What is broken? *(fix it)*
- What is confused? *(clarify it)*
- What is missing? *(add it)*[1]

As you look at the intersections of these four questions with your four storylines, what do you see? Often patterns will emerge that bridge storylines and tie your life together. Make note of those.

Step 2: "Where am I headed?" Look at your three-year dream, especially noting the vivid description bullet points that you incorporated into your statement. Transfer these, perhaps with greater amplification or specification, onto a list that you can view side-by-side with your right-now observations.

Step 3: "How am I getting there?" Now compare each observation in Step 1 with any aspiration that seems to correspond to it in Step 2. For each, brainstorm one or more broad steps you might take over the next one year to advance from where you are toward where you're headed three years from now.

Step 4: Combine. Look over the items in your third list and group them into four clusters, each with a common theme. If you have trouble knowing how to group the items, try making a cluster for each of your four storylines to get started.

Step 5: Articulate. Write a short handle—a word or a short phrase—that captures each cluster. If it would help you, add a sentence or two or a hyper-concise bulleted list to each to flesh it out a bit more. The result is your four one-year objectives.

For example, the first year after I articulated my "Deep Well" dream I created the following four one-year objectives:

- *Objective #1:* REPLENISH: Fight for renewed physical and personal energy that has been eclipsed by over-activity on the road consulting. Start by resting adequately every night. Use any sense of renewal to fuel the time I spend with God before anything else.
- *Objective #2:* REALLOCATE: Adapt the Auxano budget year model in a way that shifts 20 percent of my time to working "on" Auxano, coaching the team, rather than working "in" Auxano, as an onsite consultant.
- *Objective #3:* RESOURCE: Develop a holistic financial strategy for my family and for future initiatives. I must secure a financial advisor and part-time administrative support for my rental properties.

- *Objective #4:* REMARK: Achieve enough progress with time margin in one year that my wife, my children, and my assistant all remark, without any prompting from me, that something in my life has changed.

Critical Benefits of One-Year Objectives

Naming your one-year objectives yields great benefits. They bridge the gap between your favored future and your particular present. They provide the context that makes your day-to-day activities meaningful. They outline the priorities for aligning your short-range areas of focus, which we'll look at in the next two chapters.

One-year objectives are especially valuable for uncovering blind spots or life issues that don't naturally motivate you. Your three-year dream depicts what you *want* to happen, but your one-year objectives detail what *must* happen for the dream to become reality. When we gear up to set a short-term goal, we sometimes rush toward what we *want* to do, but our one-year objectives remind us of what we *must* do to get where we want to go, whether we enjoy it or not.

Chapter 17

NINETY DAYS FROM NOW

How Anyone Can Accomplish Dramatically More without Working Harder

"Whenever anything is being accomplished, it is being done, I have learned, by a monomaniac with a mission."

—Peter Drucker

People think I work hard. But I have a secret: I don't actually work *hard*; I work *focused*. And there is a big difference.

This chapter is all about that difference, and it reveals one of the most important practices in the book.

You know by now that I'm passionate about simplicity. So despite the inescapable complexity involved in knowing and naming a life's identity and direction, I am obsessed with summing it all up in a simple, supple, actionable way.

I believe that all elements of the master tools of the Vision Frame and the Horizon Storyline achieve this, but I especially love the radical simplicity of the LifeCall and the ninety-day goal, which sits in your Midground Horizon (figure 17.1). Both are incredibly concise. And both are irresistibly motivating.

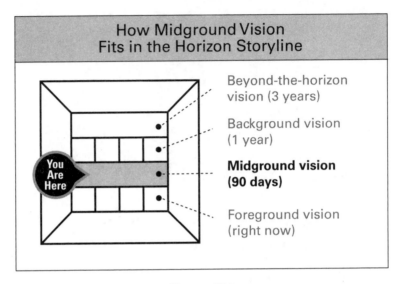

Figure 17.1

Your LifeCall tells you what's important always. Your ninety-day goal tells you what's important now. Both stand with succinct singularity.

If the only things you did to put this book into practice were to (1) align your emotions, habits, and commitments repeatedly to your mission in life and (2) devote yourself to one new goal every ninety days, your life in ten years would be indescribably richer than it is right now.

Why do a strong LifeCall and a gripping ninety-day goal each have such a powerful influence on a person's life? The Power of Focus.

The Power of Focus

In fourth grade I learned a lesson in optics that was indelibly etched on my memory. I certainly wasn't the only kid in history to learn it, but I've never forgotten it.

I learned it the first summer day I took a magnifying glass outdoors. Positioning the lens between the sun and the earth, I slowly raised and lowered it and watched the circle of sunlight beaming through the glass expand and contract on the ground. The smaller the circle got, the brighter it got. Condensing the light to a brilliant pinpoint, I watched the dry leaf under it start to smoke and catch flame.

It amazed me how much energy was silently pouring through that magnifying glass the whole time, whether the light was concentrated or diffused. And it amazed me how merely focusing the energy would start a fire.

I'm still amazed by it. I don't believe any of us know how much energy is coursing through our lives, even if we're experiencing a prolonged period of weariness and fatigue. We don't recognize how much power we have to harness it, because it usually stays unfocused. But when all that energy gets directed toward one target, a fire starts that changes us and the world around us.

Through Auxano we have seen this practice repeatedly reap bountiful fruit with teams. Attack one big goal at a time together—not five—and teams surprise themselves with their mountain-moving mojo. Other organizational consultants practice the same thing. Patrick Lencioni counsels leaders to set what he calls a "thematic goal" or a "rally cry" as a singular point of focus. The team at Franklin Covey calls it a "wildly important goal"—"WIG" for short. Nailing that singularity-with-specificity to the door is the open secret of the productive life. As Tim Ferriss put it, "Life favors the specific ask and punishes the vague wish."[1]

> Your LifeCall tells you succinctly what you're supposed to be doing always. Your ninety-day goal tells you succinctly what you're supposed to be doing now.

Focus enables us to do more. It also enables us to travel further. In short, focus expands. I learned that from my other big optics lesson.

If we were standing in a room together with daylight streaming through the windows, and if I shined a flashlight at a wall twenty feet away, you might faintly see the circular beam it would cast on the wall. But if I pointed a laser with the same energy as the flashlight up at the moon, an observer with a powerful enough telescope could mark its red dot on the lunar surface *238,900 miles away*. Hard to imagine that distance? Well, it's like traveling across the contiguous United States at its widest point in a straight line eighty-nine times—does that help?

Focus especially enables us to go further faster when it is linked to another superpower of Midground Vision: the Power of Ninety Days.

The Power of Ninety Days

There is something about a ninety-day period—approximately one quarter of a year—that is entwined deeply with the operating system of human beings. Ninety days is roughly the length of a season in temperate climes. It is about the length of a school semester and the span of the business quarter.

Ninety days also has the intriguing characteristic of being just out of reach. It is far enough away from the here-and-now to imply a substantial journey but close enough that we can cross it with a solid burst. It is enough time for an individual to accomplish something truly significant. You would not believe what people can achieve in three months. (A list of my favorites is in the Top Ten Panel below.)

Top Ten Panel: Big Accomplishments in Ninety Days

1. A Moscow architectural firm will build you an environmentally friendly, 1,300-square-foot home within ninety days of order.

2. Boot camp turns a couch potato recruit into a ready Marine in just under ninety days.

3. Thru-hikers walk the Pacific Northwest Trail from the Continental Divide to the Pacific Ocean within ninety days.

4. A human baby *in utero* is fully formed and can open and close its hands and mouth by ninety days after its conception.

5. Blogger Maneesh Sethi developed and lived out a plan to become fluent in a new language (in his case, Italian) in ninety days.[2]

6. In FDR's first ninety days in office in 1933, he saw passage of the Emergency Banking Act and the Federal Emergency Relief Act; created the Civilian Conservation Corps, the Tennessee Valley Authority, and the Securities and Exchange Commission; and nominated the first female Cabinet member, Frances Perkins.

7. John Steinbeck wrote the first draft of *The Grapes of Wrath* in ninety days in 1938.

8. In 2004–05, Frenchman Vincent Riou became the first person to sail around the world in a monohull vessel, solo, in under ninety days.

9. On July 8, 1914, the Boston Braves baseball club had a record of 29–40, dead last in the National League. Over the next ninety days they won a whopping 74 percent of their games to win the league pennant and eventually a World Series championship.

10. Mozart composed two piano trios; a violin sonata; two piano sonatas, including his most famous; his last three symphonies, arguably his greatest; and three other pieces of music in ninety days in 1788.

This crucial principle is missing in so many life-planning approaches, but businesses are beginning to figure it out. The fourth quarter of the year is almost always a company's most productive, sometimes more than the previous three put together. That's because year-end deadlines ratchet up the urgency. Brian P. Moran teaches organizations to redefine their "year" to be twelve weeks long and to repeat the cycle every three months to capture this kind of momentum and lock down execution over and over.³ Setting a ninety-day goal makes the "Important" into the "Urgent."

The Power of Ninety Days is harnessed by setting one—*exactly* one—just-out-of-reach goal and driving toward it with laser-beam focus. It is simply incredible how much you can do when you use this method—especially when you use it repeatedly. Ride a rifle bullet into the future, not a scatter shot.

The Power of Stacking Goals

My favorite illustration of this principle is the ingenious technique devised by General Erwin Rommel to move his German armored division across North Africa during World War II. Rommel—a brilliant tactician employed by an evil regime—was nicknamed "the Desert Fox," and his tank division was called "the Ghost Division." How did Rommel and his force earn such awe-inspiring nicknames?

Imagine you're a tank driver, enclosed in a cramped, dark, metal box with three men, broiling all day under the fierce North African sun. Your lips and face are chapped; your mouth tastes like grit. All you hear is the loud, dull roar of the diesel engine and the squeak of the churning tracks under you. All you smell is fuel, oil, and sweat. All you see out of the slit before you is featureless sand—no rivers, no vegetation, no animals—reflecting blazing sunlight so bright that it burns your eyes.

Then, after one hour of creeping across the desert, everything looks exactly as it did sixty minutes before. And this continues for hundreds of miles. It's more than enough to sap the fighting spirit out of anyone and to slow progress to a crawl.

Rommel's brilliant innovation was to send a fleet of Kübelwagen—the German Jeep—ahead of the column to place a line of fifty-gallon drums, each with a huge flag sticking out the top, at intervals so that a tank driver could just see the one ahead. With the remarkable shift of focus those flags provided, the driver was no longer driving to some distant place he had never seen, miles and miles away. Instead, he was just driving to the next flag . . . and the next . . . and the next. Each flag passed was an accomplishment—it meant progress.

The psychological boost this gave Rommel's men was enormous. It compelled them to drive their tanks straight and swiftly. It enabled the entire force to come upon its enemies by surprise, traversing vast distances to appear seemingly out of nowhere.

In the same way, you can do amazing things when you focus on one single goal after another. Do a quick calculation. Let's pretend, following Moses' remark in Psalm 90:10, that you have eighty years to live, total. With four ninety-day periods every year, how many do you have left to work with? I have 127. Imagine what I could do if I accomplished 127 substantial goals over the course of the rest of my life. Imagine what *you* could do!

See, just as with Rommel's oil drums, those goals aren't a scattered, random assembly. Focused by your LifeCall, they trace a line that takes you somewhere. I repeat, *focus expands*. It's paradoxical and not what you'd expect, but the tighter you narrow what you're trying to accomplish, the wider the vistas that open up before you down the road.

Goals also "stack" when you take them one at a time. They create a flywheel effect when you accomplish one goal after another. Have you ever set up dominos in a long, serpentine line for the joy of seeing them fall in a swift, steady wave, one after the next, after you toppled the first? Well, did you know that the momentum of a falling domino can knock over a domino about 50 percent larger than itself? If you line up a series of dominos each one-and-a-half times larger than the one before, the first domino—even if it is the size of a Tic Tac—can set off a chain reaction that eventually topples the 29th domino, with the height of the Empire State Building![4]

In the same way, a sequence of ninety-day goals, even very modest ones, compound over time. They multiply your Five Capitals in ways you couldn't imagine and make your dreams come true.

If your one-year objectives are the mountains in the distance, and the "NOW-rhythms" of your Foreground Horizon (which I'll talk about in the next chapter) are your dashboard, then your ninety-day goal is what you see a quarter-mile ahead as you're driving down the highway. It's worthwhile to enjoy the view of the mountains, and you need to check the dashboard frequently. But if your eyes don't spend most of their time watching where you're going, you'll wreck. If you *do* stay focused on the road ahead, however, you will eventually reach the destination beyond the horizon that you've been dreaming of.

Top Ten Panel: Benefits of Focusing on One Goal Every Ninety Days

1. One ninety-day goal makes it easy to focus attention daily without having to adopt a new system or tool or app.

2. One ninety-day goal powers your prayer life in new ways.

3. One ninety-day goal stretches your faith in a meaningful direction rather than leaving it complacent in seven.

4. One ninety-day goal eliminates the false optimism of assuming you're getting somewhere and the discouragement of feeling you're going nowhere.

5. One ninety-day goal regathers personal energy that has been dispersed and fragmented.

6. One ninety-day goal creates an "eye of the storm," as a center of calm singularity amid the swirl of needs and responsibilities competing for your time.

7. One ninety-day goal, repeatedly set, gives you plenty of time to create a splendid variety of goals in many aspects of your life.

8. One ninety-day goal—after another, after another—grows you to attempt things ten, twenty, and thirty years down the road that you would never imagine you could accomplish today.

9. One ninety-day goal set and reset over time builds a track record to chronicle your journey with God like none you've ever seen.

10. One ninety-day goal at a time is easy to track and celebrate with yourself and others.

How to Set a Ninety-Day Goal

Your ninety-day goal is teed-up inside your Vision Frame (identity) and fed by your longer-range dreaming. Now it's time to plan and act. You have all the context you need to commit. Meditating on the three sets of questions below—while bathing them in prayer, as always—helps you brainstorm a range of emphases for your next ninety days.

Life questions to jump-start your brainstorming:

- What is the next best step for my life right now?
- What has God been up to lately and how is that providing direction?
- What is my life asking me to do differently?
- What am I now ready to achieve?
- How have I been getting in my own way?
- Who needs dramatically more attention from me?
- What needs dramatically more time from me?
- If I woke up tomorrow and all of the sudden my life was wonderful, what would have changed?

Vision Frame and Horizon Storyline questions for "quality control" and integrative planning:

- What LifeCore (value) do I need to realign or strengthen?
- Which LifeScore storyline is thriving that I want to accelerate?
- Which LifeScore storyline is just surviving that I want to see revived?
- When I look at my one-year objectives, which one is most urgent?
- Which one is most important?
- Which one am I most motivated to accomplish?
- What am I tolerating that is delaying a one-year objective?
- What single goal would have the greatest impact on *all* my one-year objectives?
- What aspect of my three-year dream am I energized to advance right now?
- What is holding back my three-year dream from being fulfilled?
- What goal would produce the most progress toward my three-year dream?

Questions to reduce your list and validate your top ninety-day goal selection:

- What goal would still motivate me six weeks from now?
- What goal would bring a smile to God and my loved ones the most?
- What goal, if accomplished, would set me up best for my next goal?
- What goal makes the most sense given the unique timing of the next three months?
- What goal would most super-charge my LifeCall (mission)?

When you have a healthy list, select one emphasis to move ahead with. Your ninety-day goal can be directed toward a difficult target or it can be dedicated to an area where you already have a lot of momentum—it doesn't matter. While selecting wisely is as important for a ninety-day goal as it is for anything else, don't lapse into paralysis by analysis. Peter Drucker was exactly right when he wrote, "It is better to pick the wrong priority than none at all."[5]

Once you've settled on your emphasis, convert it into a goal that's "S.M.A.R.T.": *Specific, Measurable, Attainable, Relevant* (to the long range), and *Time-Based.* One issue to pay attention to is how ambitious the goal is. Do you tend to play it safe or bite off more than you can chew? Do you need more faith, or do you need less folly?

Another thing to pay attention to is whether the goal grabs your gut and doesn't let go. Is it the sort of thing you're going to want to pray for every day? Are you eager to share it with family and friends?

Once you decide on your ninety-day goal, own it even more. Write it on a card for the car dashboard or scribe it on your bathroom mirror with a dry erase marker. Add it to an inspiring photo and make it the lock screen on your phone. Eat, sleep, and breathe it for the next ninety days.

Having a ninety-day goal, however, is only half the battle to achieving it. You also need practical steps to reach it. Forging them is what the next chapter is all about.

Chapter 18

NOW

The Best Approach to Tackle Today Every Day

*"The future is not the result of choices among alternative
paths offered in the present. It is a place created—created
first in the mind and will; created next in activity."*
—Walt Disney

Budd was a collegiate cross-country runner. Unlike his teammates, he had a weakness—a left hip flexor that caused frequent pain and forced him to miss practice. As a result he spent weeks at a time on a stationary bike while the rest of his team was out running. Decades before "spinning" was a thing, Budd toiled away, going nowhere in the campus physiology building, to keep himself conditioned.

After Budd worked out, he would read articles in scientific journals, hunting for a solution to his recurring injuries. That's when he discovered an intriguing truth about what happens when humans breathe.

As all of us do, Budd inhaled when his diaphragm—the arched, sheet-like muscle positioned under his lungs—compressed downward, opening up space in his lungs that sucked air in. He exhaled when his diaphragm relaxed back into its upward arch shape, compressing his lungs and pushing the air out. With every breath in, Budd's core muscles flexed tight, and with every breath out they went slack.

Budd had never given much thought to how he breathed when he ran. Like most runners, he breathed along with his footfalls—at race pace he inhaled for two steps and exhaled over the next two. But now he realized that at the moment he began exhaling, his left foot was hitting the ground. In fact, every exhalation—and, therefore, every *relaxation*—came when his left leg absorbed its greatest shock. Over and over, the same leg absorbed the impact of the ground without firm support from the strong muscles of his core. No wonder his hip hurt!

So Budd experimented with new rhythms designed to spread the impact evenly between his left leg and his right. He inhaled for three steps and exhaled for two. Then when he needed to pick up his pace or power up a hill, he inhaled for two steps and exhaled for one. As a result, his left and right legs took turns taking the beating from the ground when his core muscles went slack.

With a new rhythm in place, Budd recovered from his hip injury and went beyond his team's activities to run a marathon. In the years that followed, he continued to refine his rhythmic technique and began training others. He now has been coaching distance running for thirty years and has run sub-three-hour marathons in five different decades. His personal best is 2 hours, 13 minutes, and 2 seconds.[1]

Budd discovered a truth that applies not just to running but to everything: *you go furthest fastest when you repeat the right action in the right rhythm.*

As with Budd's running career, so also with life planning: the most problems— and the least instruction—come at the point where the rubber meets the road.

Remember Mia from chapter 6? In frustration, she abandoned her life plan because she couldn't get traction on the thirty-two goals she had set for herself during her weekend retreat in the mountains. In that chapter I diagnosed her problem as a lack of known-and-named *identity* as the bridge between her *inventory* and her *implementation.* Now I'll identify the other reef she foundered on: she had thirty-two goals.

Thirty-two goals. Can *anyone* make progress on thirty-two goals? When Mia was writing them down, she felt a boost of energy because she felt like she was getting somewhere. But when she actually tried to accomplish them, she lapsed into despair.

> You don't change until you change something you do daily.

With the Younique Life Plan, you set and strive for one goal every ninety days, as I explained in the last chapter. That's enough. But the impulse that gave rise to Mia's impossible catalog of thirty-two goals is legitimate. The ninety-day goal of the Midground Horizon is not near enough or small enough to act on immediately; humans can't take a mental breath, dive underwater, and wait thirteen weeks to come up for air. You *aim* at a longer interval than you *act.*

For a more immediate action step in your Life Plan, we employ a rhythm with the potential to work every twenty-four hours. It has been said that you don't change until you change something you do daily. The Foreground Horizon is designed to put into practice right now four *NOW-rhythms.*

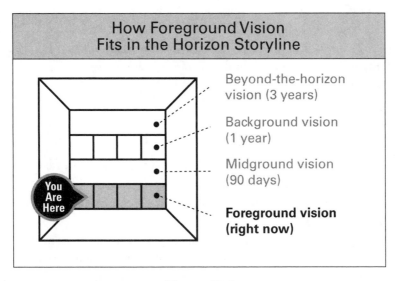

Figure 18.1

Introducing the NOW-Rhythms

Your Foreground Horizon does not comprise an exhaustive list of everything you have to do in your life. It's not a proper to-do list at all. Instead, it consists of four "NOW-rhythms"—one for each storyline. Each NOW-rhythm is a habit to add to your life for the next ninety days to advance you toward your destination. Whether you continue the intentional routine after those three months is up to you—the purpose of the habit or rhythm is simply to give you traction where you need it right now. Think of "NOW" as an acronym: your Next Opportunity to Win.

NOW-rhythms accord with the rhythms God built into creation. While one-year objectives line up with the astronomically determined year and the ninety-day goal lines up with the tilt-of-the-earth season, each NOW-rhythm lines up with the month, the week, or the day, whichever best suits the habit you adopt. (Occasionally you may also have a single big NOW-rhythm that you plan to act on one time during the quarter.) Not all your NOW-rhythms have to conform to the same interval—for example, you could be applying one daily NOW-rhythm, two weekly NOW-rhythms, and one monthly NOW-rhythm over the same period of time.

The nature of the NOW-rhythms requires more explanation and illustration, but before moving forward let's revisit our handy 1:4:1:4 napkin sketch. You now have all four horizons symbolized by the four rows inside your personal Vision Frame.

"Underneath" your three-year dream, you have four 1-year objectives and one 90-day goal. Your four NOW-rhythms at the very "bottom" are the immediate rhythmic actions you embed into your life. To make your Life Plan simple, you choose one NOW-rhythm for each storyline at the top of your Vision Frame (figure 18.1).

You gain momentum like magic when the habit you invent serves other elements of your Life Plan in one of the following four ways.

1. Tie a NOW-Rhythm to the Ninety-Day Goal

Remember, you have a single target you are focusing on for ninety days. By aiming your NOW-rhythms toward that goal—especially if you aim all four of them—you harness an enormous amount of energy toward reaching it as you work those habits daily, weekly, and monthly.

When my ninety-day goal was to prepare to put my house on the market in stunning condition in three months, I found ways to align all four of my storylines toward that goal. As a Beloved Son (personal health storyline), I practiced "HGTV with Jesus" by *praying for the house three times a week while watching HGTV and reading my Bible.* With my Central Circle (family and friends storyline) I *set aside every Friday night to review progress* with my wife, Romy, and my daughter Abby. Pertaining to my Olympic Contribution (work storyline), I planned to *take two weeks of vacation that quarter* to work on the house. And for my Epic Adventure (recreation storyline), I *made one phone call each day* acting as my own general contractor for the project.

That last habit might not seem particularly "recreational" to you (you're right—it wasn't), but the decision to move was itself born of a desire to free up more physical and financial capital for recreation in my life. Also note that I didn't start the month with a huge to-do list of everyone I needed to call to make arrangements for readying the house. Instead, I knew at the outset that if I simply made one call per day, the whole project would get done in time, and it did.

Finally, notice that each of these NOW-rhythms addressed my goal of putting my house on the market from a very different angle. That's the genius of this approach: by pointing all your storylines toward one goal, the whole breadth of your life is brought to bear on it with amazing alignment and harmony.

2. Tie a NOW-Rhythm to a LifeStep

Your LifeSteps are the four ingredients in your recipe to feed the biggest needs in your life over at least the next ninety days. That makes them a terrific source of inspiration for this quarter's NOW-rhythms.

Let's take the example of Cory whose storylines I outlined in chapter 15. One quarter of his ninety-day goal belonged entirely to his Magnum Opus (work) storyline. His other storylines didn't have any obvious way to contribute to it, so he set each of them to work on their respective LifeSteps.

His Whole Soul (personal storyline) LifeStep was to improve his Rest Replenishment Rhythms, so he adopted the NOW-rhythm of *taking solitary rest for one hour each day*. Since his Building a House (home and family storyline) LifeStep was his role as "Smile-Maker" to his children, he prioritized *spending at least one hour doing nothing but having fun with them at least three times each week*. And as his Disciplefriending (relationships storyline) LifeStep was to grow in his role as a "Discipler," he planned *to get together twice a week with* friends who aren't involved in disciple-making yet, a group that included Christians and non-Christians alike.

If in a given week he spent less time with his friends, he'd spend more with his kids, and vice versa. But the combination of all these NOW-rhythms kept his life running steady at a time when his work-related ninety-day goal could have driven him to run out of gas or caused him to overheat.

3. Tie a NOW-Rhythm to a One-Year Objective

Your one-year objectives are challenges to overcome within the next year. A succession of ninety-day goals may conquer them, but may not. Some of your objectives may by nature require steady, patient work over a longer haul. Or you may need to do some prep work this quarter to set up a ninety-day goal in the future. If any of those cases apply, then while some of your NOW-rhythms are aimed at the next ninety days, you might aim others at a challenge on the further horizon.

4. Tie Multiple Elements Together with One NOW-Rhythm

This option comes last on the list for the sake of clarity, but it comes first in priority. The steak really sizzles when you create a NOW-rhythm that is built on a LifeStep *and* that drives you toward your ninety-day goal. Or you could take the activity inherent in reaching a ninety-day goal and double it to serve a LifeStep. Stir in a one-year objective that you're making progress on at the same time, and you're really cooking.

There are all sorts of creative ways to use NOW-rhythms to tie your Life Plan together. Once I had a ninety-day goal to finish writing this book. The LifeStep for my Central Circle (relationships) storyline at that time was to step into the role of Encourager. I connected the dots between the Midground Goal and the LifeStep with the NOW-rhythm of *writing one letter of encouragement to a member of my family each week*. While that habit didn't advance me toward my goal directly, I took advantage of the writing groove the book-writing goal put me in to do something important for my family.

It's funny how things work out; I actually didn't meet my goal that quarter. (Missing goals is an important topic I'll address in a later chapter.) But that period coincided with my daughter Abby starting college. Abby went off to school carrying five letters from me for her to open her first five days away from home. Those letters became a precious way to show her I love her at a pivotal time, and they wouldn't have been written if I hadn't associated the LifeStep pertaining to my family with my goal to finish writing *Younique*.

The Future Is Now

The four habits you invent for your next ninety days are more than to-dos. Though you perform them now, they are for more than now. The NOW-rhythms of your Foreground Horizon make your vision of what lies beyond the horizon real today, for ten minutes here and an hour there.

Thoughtfully chosen NOW-rhythms are the behaviors that accord with your future life thrown back into the present, and they get you to that future life as you practice them. As you work your ninety-day habits, you live in the "future-perfect tense"—you are doing what you *will have done* when you've arrived at the destination you're journeying toward. You walk by Hebrews 11 faith, taking actions in the present according to "the reality of what is hoped for, the proof of what is not seen" (v. 1).

It's been said that when you break the pattern, a new world can emerge. Our lives are filled with patterns that become ruts. The way we always do things—habits, some good, some bad, some neutral—make up the flow of our lives. Walking the Clarity Spiral breaks the pattern of your life and enables you to see beyond the old world. But you must rebuild the patterns, and when you do, you want to use the rhythms that God built into the universe. NOW-rhythms are the way you reset those patterns anew.

Chapter 19

SNAPSHOT

The Most Important Single Sheet of Paper in Your Life

"God sees everything at once and knows what you are called to do. Our part is not to play God, but to trust God—to believe that our single, solitary life can make a difference."

—Zig Ziglar

One of my favorite scenes in the movie *The Matrix* (spoiler alert) is when a technician named Cypher sits watching a computer monitor. The display depicts an inconceivably complex virtual reality running on a vast computer network, but it doesn't use pictures to do it. Instead, it projects a mesmerizing sequence of exotic pictographs and characters that drip vertically from the top of the screen to the bottom like rivulets of green rain.

The main character, Neo, asks Cypher why he looks at the weird green characters instead of the jerky, fuzzy display of the action on another monitor. "There's way too much information to decode the Matrix," Cypher replies. "You get used to it, though. Your brain does the translating. I don't even see the code. All I see is blonde, brunette, redhead."

This scene reminds me of how extraordinarily complex each life is. There's so much that makes us who we are and there's so much to describe about where we're going that we can't get our minds around it. But once you get break-thru clarity, your life's dimensions can be circumscribed with a one-page diagram. I call it your Life Plan Snapshot. It's your personal plan-on-a-page.

The Life Plan Snapshot trains your mind to translate the complexity of your life into simplicity that isn't simplistic. One diagram, combining your Vision Frame and

201

your Horizon Storyline, encompasses who you are and where you're going. With one look at your Snapshot, you see the whole thing at once. You can understand it. You can share it. Most of all, you can *act on it.*

I hope the Snapshot examples in this chapter get you pumped to take The Journey to create your own. If you need more inspiration, check out the Top Ten advantages to capturing your life in one Snapshot.

Top Ten Panel: 10 Greatest Advantages of Capturing Your Life in One Snapshot

1. *Your Snapshot is simple.* The most important things about your life right now fit on one page and can be captured in one glance.

2. *Your Snapshot is inspirational.* When you look at your Snapshot, you want to take the next step. When others see it, they glimpse that they have a Life Plan inside themselves waiting to come out.

3. *Your Snapshot is accessible.* It communicates your core identity and direction with three single ideas: One LifeCall idea, one three-year dream and one ninety-day goal.

4. *Your Snapshot is whole.* It encompasses all aspects of your life, including those that aren't front-and-center to your attention right now.

5. *Your Snapshot is gradual.* It projects your direction in life across four easy-to-understand horizons.

6. *Your Snapshot is equitable.* The visionary plan for your life has exactly ten elements whether you're a homemaker, a Fortune 500 CEO, or anything else.

7. *Your Snapshot is pictorial.* It uses words to paint the attractive landscape of where God is taking you, as a preferred future.

8. *Your Snapshot is memorable.* The geometric layout of a frame and the numeric balance of 1's and 4's makes your Life Plan super-sticky.

9. *Your Snapshot is beautiful.* Instead of creating a long list of "to-dos," your Life Plan brings simplicity and power together in an aesthetic way; your plan is actually pretty to look at.

10. *Your Snapshot is sharable.* Have you ever been able to draw your entire life on a napkin for a friend using a simple, sketchable tool? Now you can.

If you want some help building your own Life Plan Snapshot, the Younique team will walk you through it step by step in an online course entitled *Life Planning 101*. Check it out at LifeYounique.com/courses.

Life Plan Snapshot Example 1

◎ LifeScore

	Storyline 1	Storyline 2	Storyline 3	Storyline 4
	Beloved Son	Central Circle	Olympic Contrib.	Epic Adventure

🔥 LifeCore

INTIMACY
"The Ultimacy of Intimacy"
...because friendship is the center of reality

FOCUS
"The Secret of Elimination"
...because I live more by choosing less

LEARNING
"The Opportunity of Growth"
...because I feel most alive when I am gaining new perspective

COURAGE
"The Life of No Regret"
...because maximizing my one and only life requires risk

BEYOND THE HORIZON: 3-YEAR DREAM
By March 2018, my life will be a DEEP WELL of blessing, FREE to OVERFLOW with more margin, flexibility and spontaneity to invest into my most important relationships.

BACKGROUND HORIZON: 1-YEAR OBJECTIVES

REPLENISH	REALLOCATE	RESOURCE	REMARKS
Re-establish patterns of rest especially in my beloved son storyline.	Shift the Auxano budget for me to work "on" the business with 20% more time.	Develop a holistic financial strategy with an advisor and admin support for real estate.	Achieve central circle rhythm success in a way that people remark about it.

MIDGROUND HORIZON: 90-DAY GOAL
Prepare my home on Heather Springs to be put on the market in excellent condition by July 11, 2016

FOREGROUND HORIZON: NOW-Rhythms

HGTV with Jesus (3X weekly spend time with God & pray for house)	Friday "family night" to review progress with my "green" girls (1X weekly)	Take 2 weeks of vacation to work on the house (1X quarterly)	Make one phone call per day as a "general contractor" to advance house preparation (daily)

◇ LifeCall

Making a life of more meaningful progress more accessible to every believer

◀ LifeSteps

LifeStep 1	LifeStep 2	LifeStep 3	LifeStep 4
trust builder	provider	team leader	financial

Figure 19.1

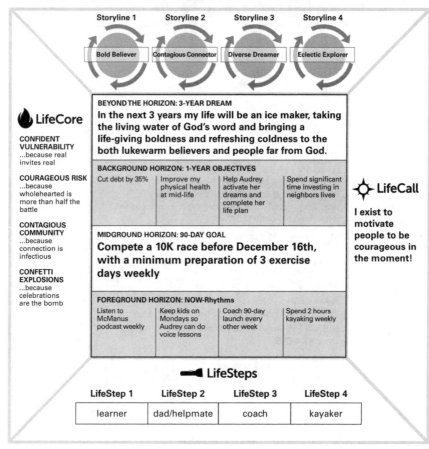

Figure 19.2

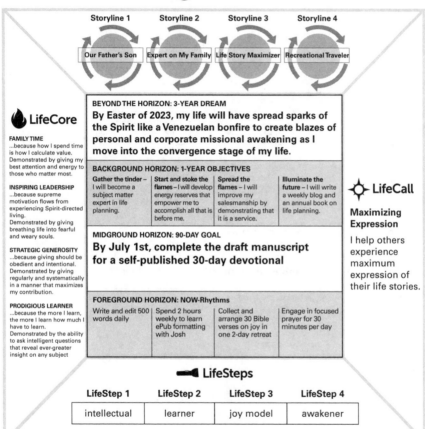

Life Plan Snapshot Example 3

LifeScore

Storyline 1	Storyline 2	Storyline 3	Storyline 4
Our Father's Son	Expert on My Family	Life Story Maximizer	Recreational Traveler

LifeCore

FAMILY TIME
...because how I spend time is how I calculate value. Demonstrated by giving my best attention and energy to those who matter most.

INSPIRING LEADERSHIP
...because supreme motivation flows from experiencing Spirit-directed living. Demonstrated by giving breathing life into fearful and weary souls.

STRATEGIC GENEROSITY
...because giving should be obedient and intentional. Demonstrated by giving regularly and systematically in a manner that maximizes my contribution.

PRODIGIOUS LEARNER
...because the more I learn, the more I learn how much I have to learn. Demonstrated by the ability to ask intelligent questions that reveal ever-greater insight on any subject

BEYOND THE HORIZON: 3-YEAR DREAM

By Easter of 2023, my life will have spread sparks of the Spirit like a Venezuelan bonfire to create blazes of personal and corporate missional awakening as I move into the convergence stage of my life.

BACKGROUND HORIZON: 1-YEAR OBJECTIVES

Gather the tinder – I will become a subject matter expert in life planning.	Start and stoke the flames – I will develop energy reserves that empower me to accomplish all that is before me.	Spread the flames – I will improve my salesmanship by demonstrating that it is a service.	Illuminate the future – I will write a weekly blog and an annual book on life planning.

MIDGROUND HORIZON: 90-DAY GOAL

By July 1st, complete the draft manuscript for a self-published 30-day devotional

FOREGROUND HORIZON: NOW-Rhythms

Write and edit 500 words daily	Spend 2 hours weekly to learn ePub formatting with Josh	Collect and arrange 30 Bible verses on joy in one 2-day retreat	Engage in focused prayer for 30 minutes per day

LifeCall

Maximizing Expression

I help others experience maximum expression of their life stories.

LifeSteps

LifeStep 1	LifeStep 2	LifeStep 3	LifeStep 4
intellectual	learner	joy model	awakener

Figure 19.3

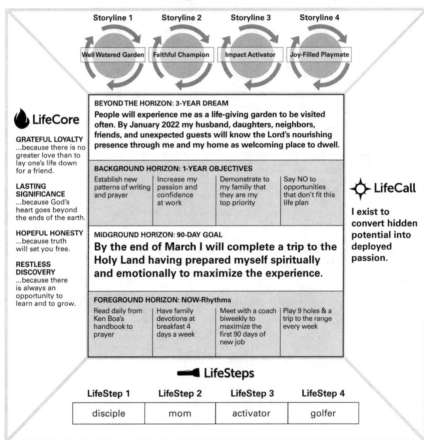

Figure 19.4

PART FIVE

YOUR RENEWAL
How to Live with Clarity Every Day

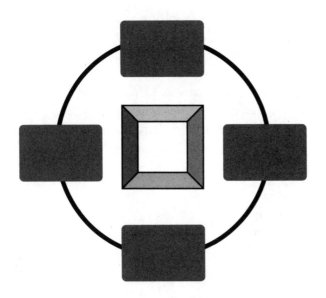

LIFE-MAKING
CYCLE

When Younique cofounder, Dave Rhodes, and I were developing the Younique Life Plan, a question kept nagging at me and wouldn't let me go. I knew we had to solve it; it would make the difference for people between break-thru and letdown.

The question was: *What makes the difference between a plan that lives in a drawer and a plan that lives in a life?*

This was not a small issue. I know many people who have attended seminars, workshops, and retreats, who have read books and followed all their instructions, who have binders and folders of great plans for their life, but they haven't done a thing with them. All their study and strategic planning made no impact on their lives.

We knew that people (including ourselves!) needed something more. We need more than the tools to make a simple Life Plan Snapshot. We need the tools to live it out, adjust it as needed, and live it out some more. We need a way to make our special calling so completely wrapped around our lives that we can't conceive of living without it.

That's the extraordinary value of the last master tool I want to introduce you to, the Life-Making Cycle.

The goal of the Life-Making Cycle is to make you *unconsciously competent* at living out your known-and-named Life Younique. Unconscious competence means being so deeply shaped by your Vision Frame and Horizon Storyline that you continually, subconsciously refer to it every day in your relationships and decision-making. It is not something forced or appended to your life, but it is seamlessly integrated into how you think and act. The Life-Making Cycle that develops that kind of competence is built on four rhythms:

1. allocating daily
2. reflecting weekly
3. planning quarterly
4. retreating annually

Following this pattern, in the pages to come I'll give you ultra-practical direction for weaving your Life Younique into every day, week, season, and year of your life.

Chapter 20

CALENDAR

An Easy, No-Cost Step to Foster a Rich Life

*"People spend too much time doing and not enough
time thinking about what they should be doing."*
—Naval Ravikant

Let me introduce you to the 4% Life.[1]

Let's say that before you finish reading this paragraph, you get a text message. It's an old friend you haven't talked to in ages who (you're delighted to hear) is coming through town this evening and wants to go out for dinner. How much time will you take to figure out where to meet, when to meet, and what arrangements to make with your family to bring them along or leave them behind? Five minutes seems reasonable. That's about 4 percent of the length of a two-hour dinner.

New situation: you're planning to take a week's vacation. How much time do you take to figure out where to go, what to do, where to stay, how to get there, and how much to spend, and to make all the reservations and arrangements needed for it to happen? Seven hours seems reasonable. That's about 4 percent of the length of a seven-day vacation.

Interesting—maybe we're onto something here.

One more situation: you're graduating from high school or college or graduate school, looking for your first "real job." How much time do you take to figure out what your career is going to look like and what you have to do to navigate it?

A full-length career consumes about eighty thousand hours, so let's apply the 4 Percent Rule. That comes out to thirty-two hundred hours. Reasonable? That would translate to four hundred days of planning spent a bit at a time for more than forty years of vocational contribution. It might sound a little crazy, but it's actually a crazy-good recipe for living your utmost.

If you're wondering, you could spread out that investment of time into tens days a year, or less than three days per quarter. The time would include dreaming, planning, assessing, reflecting, task-listing, calendaring, and training for your vocational future. When you break it down, it's really not *that much* time. Yet most people spend vastly more time and care, proportionally speaking, planning a nice meal or a nice vacation than they do planning a career in which they will spend a huge portion of their time on earth.

We must use time in order to invest time.

The ancient Roman philosopher Seneca wrote that most people are like a man who boards a ship and goes below deck. For weeks he feels the pitch and roll of the waves, sometimes violently, as the ship is tossed about by storms. At the end of his journey he disembarks and tells his friends about his eventful and harrowing voyage, but unbeknownst to him, his ship never left the harbor. This, Seneca says, is the picture of a busy life that isn't meaningful because preoccupation crowds out reflection. There's a lot going on, but nobody goes anywhere.

Seneca wrote this story in a brief work entitled *On the Shortness of Life*. The title is ingenious "clickbait": the ancient reader picked it up expecting the author to com-miserate with him on how short life is, but in it Seneca asserts that life is plentiful if you use your time to make the most of it.

So, what is the minimum reflection time required over the rest of your lifetime to make it meaningful?

The Secret Ingredient

I want to share with you the top secret truth of how to live meaningfully and purposefully. It is so important that without it, everything else that I've written in this book so far—which I deeply believe in—is worthless. It is a tool of critical importance. Are you ready for it? Pay close attention.

The secret ingredient of a rich life is . . . calendar blocking.

(This is the part where I wait for you to get it, then I notice the blank look on your face.)

I'm serious! Calendar blocking is the tool you can't live—*really* live—without.

(I'm waiting again. . . .)

Okay, maybe you don't know what I mean by the term. Calendar blocking is when you make appointments with yourself in advance to think about your Life Younique, and you bolt those onto your calendar. Specifically, you schedule twenty minutes every week, a half-day every three months, and a full day every year. That's the bulk of what we call the Life-Making Cycle.

Scheduling the Life-Making Cycle in advance is *the* difference between those who have a wonderful time on the Younique Life Plan Journey and then go about their lives unchanged and those whose lives change permanently, irrevocably, and continuously from then on.

Pre-blocking time is how all major changes for the better happen in a person's behavior—changes that last, that is.

For example, if you ask me what I'm going to be doing Sunday morning, June 26, 2050, I can tell you. I'm going to be worshipping in church.

Now how could I possibly know what I'm going to be doing that far in the future? Well, I don't know *for sure*. There could be some highly unusual occasion or opportunity that has me doing something else. I may be too sick or disabled to make it. Heck, I could be dead.

But I can predict with confidence that I'll be worshiping many years in advance because I've pre-blocked the time. I am a Christian; therefore, I worship with the saints on Sunday morning. Period. Except in rare circumstances, I don't schedule anything else for that time—not this week and not years from now.

Importantly, *that blocked-out time changes me*. I am a different man than I would be if I did not pre-block the time to worship the Lord and listen to his preached Word with the family of God every week. I can hardly imagine how much that difference has compounded upon itself as I look back over hundreds of weeks of my Christian life.

I maintain that blocking the time to reflect weekly, plan quarterly, and retreat yearly makes the same magnitude of difference for the better in your life.

> Calendar blocking is built on the natural rhythms of Sabbath, season, and solar revolution that God built for us.

Calendar blocking isn't the arrogant sort of long-range planning that James criticizes when he says, "You do not know what tomorrow will bring" (James 4:14). Calendar blocking isn't planning to *do*. It's planning to *think about what you do*. It's pre-building in discovery, reflection, prioritization, and commitment as a rhythm of life. I use the term "rhythm" intentionally, because it is built on the natural rhythms of Sabbath, season, and solar revolution that God built for us.

With a smartphone you can block repeating appointments for the next three years in about thirty seconds. That will take you from now to your Beyond-the-Horizon. There's nothing stopping you but you.

Do Less to Do More

There's a fable about two lumberjacks engaged in a day-long competition to see who could chop the most wood. The first lumberjack prided himself on his stamina, and, amazingly, he worked solidly without a break the whole day long.

The second lumberjack took a ten-minute break after a mere fifty minutes of work, calmly sitting down and taking out a whetstone. The first lumberjack scoffed at him, confident that his superior work ethic would win the day.

But the second lumberjack used his break not only to rest his muscles but also to sharpen his axe.

At the end of the day, the first lumberjack was astonished to find that he had lost the competition badly. The second lumberjack had cut far more wood than the first because his blade was sharper and bit into the wood more deeply with each swing. His blade was sharper because he planned in advance when to stop what he was doing and prepare for the next leg of the long race. By planning to do less, he ultimately did more.

In the end, the entire Younique Life Plan Journey, with all its tools and questions, is my attempt to help you sharpen your axe—not just for a mountaintop moment but for every mile marker for the rest of your life. But all I can do is give you the whetstone. You have to block out the time to use it.

Chapter 21

ENERGY

Ten Tips to Manage Attention Instead of Time

"Time management is an oxymoron. Time is beyond our control, and the clock keeps ticking regardless of how we lead our lives. Priority management is the answer to maximizing the time we have."
—John C. Maxwell

Cory is a solo entrepreneur and writer. On an ordinary day—which sometimes happens—he gets up at 6:00 a.m. to read the Bible over breakfast, and he prays as he walks to his office. He devotes himself to billable hours before noon, manages communications and social media and sometimes reads in the middle of the day, puts time into sales, then goes back to paying work to round out his typical workday. When he gets home, anything goes, often hinging on which of his four children needs to go where. He grabs a few items from an à la carte menu of exercise, meal preparation, laundry, spending time with his kids, hanging out with a friend, going to a small group, catching up with the news, and plowing through personal emails and bills with the baseball game sounding from the radio. He rounds out the day with some solitary leisure time in a book or on the piano and an hour or so of quality time with his wife Kelly before hitting the sack at around 11:00 p.m.

Before Cory leaves for work the next morning, he kisses Kelly on the cheek while she sleeps. Kelly teaches voice and piano out of their home and serves as music director for school and community musical theater productions. When the rehearsal schedule gets intense as a show's performance draws near, she rises between 9:00 and 10:00 a.m. and spends some time doing Bible study alone or with a friend. Then she does a combination of volunteering at the kids' schools, talking with friends and family, shopping for groceries, doing home projects, and handling emails of all kinds until mid-afternoon when her students begin to arrive. She uses cancellations and cracks between lessons to get supper started and catch up with the kids after they get home from school. When her last lesson ends at around 6:00, she grabs a bite (maybe) for her drive to rehearsal. Upon returning home hours later, she spends a few minutes with Cory before he crashes, then enjoys the quiet of the house to watch TV, browse social media, and read a devotional book until 1:00 a.m. or so.

What daily planning regimen works for both Cory *and* Kelly? And for a manager of a manufacturing plant, a dairy farmer, a mother of preschoolers, a retired hospice volunteer, and a college student?

News flash: there isn't one.

The Younique Life Plan doesn't prescribe a daily tool but gives you space to fill in your own. This isn't because I couldn't make a tool to put here—in fact, I've manufactured and modified numerous daily tools for myself over the years. Rather, I leave it open because your uniqueness has to define how you allocate your energy, imagination, intelligence, and love each day. (Be sure to check out Younique's 90-day Planner at lifeyounique.com/planner.)

I also don't leave the daily planning space unfilled because it's unimportant. Nothing could be further from the truth. Despite the enormous power of dreaming long-range vision and planning short-range vision, and despite the critical necessity of calendar blocking your future times of reflection, the only day that you know for sure that you have is this one. (And since the Lord will return as unexpectedly as a thief, we don't even really know we have *that*.) Since the only day you will ever have is called "today" (Heb. 3:13), if your Life Younique does not impact today, it makes no impact at all.

> If your Life Younique does not impact Today, it makes no impact at all.

Most of your best planning for today happens when you plan your whole week, which we'll talk about in the next chapter. That's when you sort out what precious molten alloy you're going to pour into the next seven days. But that liquid metal needs a mold to capture and shape it each day. The mold is the routine, the philosophy, the operating principles you live by consistently to make the most of the wondrous gift of a new day, every day.

Only you can shape the mold that's right for you, but I want to share with you my ten best tips to get you started. I don't assert that all of them apply to every person, so select the one that will give you the most break-thru and put it into practice this month. Then come back to the list and weave another into your every day.

Top Ten List: 10 Tips to Make the Most of Today

1. *Take inventory.* What is not known cannot be improved. Use or adapt a time-tracking app such as Harvest to record what you do with your work time, your productive off-work time, or all your time for two weeks, then review. Are you allocating your time the way you want to?

2. *Create day templates.* Executive coach Dan Sullivan advises people to design three kinds of days. On a "focus day" you concentrate on your most important and productive work. On a "buffer day" you plan, learn, and handle the administrative details that pile up. On a "free day" you relax, recharge, and renew yourself.[1] How many of each fit in your week, and what days are they scheduled for? I have used these templates for the last fifteen years of consulting as I've built my vocation around the eight to ten focus days monthly that I serve church clients onsite.

3. *Keep your Vision Frame visible.* Remember why you're living each day. Reread your Life Plan Snapshot. Laminate a copy for your desk. Write your LifeCall on your bathroom mirror.

4. *Find your task list mojo.* Take some time every day to think about what you're doing that day, set priorities, and make adjustments. Not every person is wired to appreciate and utilize task lists the same way. Yet anyone will benefit greatly from "thinking on paper" daily. My wife, Romy, likes to use sticky notes and I like to record notes in iCal. Brian Tracy asserts that for every minute of planning in your day, you will save ten minutes of execution. That principle translates to saving two hours during a day with only twelve minutes of making a mini action-plan.

5. *"Eat frogs first."* This little quip comes from Mark Twain, who once shared that if you were forced to eat a live frog at the beginning of the day, all other tasks would be easier that same day, because the worst would be behind you.[2] A frog is either the most important or the most difficult thing to get done for the day. The intimidation naturally leads to procrastination. But when you eat frogs first, you turn anticipation into acceleration—knocking out your important yet challenging tasks first hits the gas pedal of your day. In fact, my greatest seasons of accomplishment were guided by this practice. I would determine the two most important things for the day and aim to accomplish them by 11:00 a.m. before reading email.

6. *Know your golden hour.*[3] Photographers call the first thirty minutes after the sun rises and the last thirty minutes before it sets "the golden

hour" because of the almost magical quality of the light. The right light makes all of the difference for capturing the subject. In what hour of the day do you do your best work? Lodge your most important activities there. For example, Jeff Bezos—the founder of Amazon and currently the wealthiest man in the world—places his most demanding meetings at 10:00 a.m. every day. If the need for an important decision arises later in the afternoon it is usually scheduled for a 10:00 a.m. interchange for the next day. He knows he will not be making his best decision outside of his personal "golden hour."[4]

7. **Make a task sandwich.** Are you the sort of person with abundant "red" energy to get things done (see figure 6.2 on page 65), but you know you ought to carve out time to listen appreciatively to a team member going through a rough patch (a "green" job)? Pump yourself up by briskly accomplishing a few tasks, then talk to your team member, then hack through some more of your to-do list to boost you again. (This tactic works for *all* personality types with their differing favored and unfavored tasks.)

8. **Reward your accomplishments.** Rather than work yourself to exhaustion and then binge on some time-wasting distraction, get yourself a small "attention snack" to do or view something fun when you complete a task but still have some energy left. It will propel you through one task and give you refreshment for the next. For example, when I am writing in Santa Fe, where I go to get undisturbed creative time, I take thirty- to sixty-minute breaks for every three hours of writing to snack, shop, gaze through art galleries, or ride my mountain bike.

9. **Say "no" to notifications.** The boxes that pop up on your screen ("banners") and the red or blue dots that sit in the corner of your app icons ("badges") are cruel taskmasters for many people. Go into Settings on your device and turn them off for high-traffic apps. (Did you know you can do that?) Switch on Do Not Disturb when you need a period of no interruption at all. And mute busy group texts. You can survive without knowing what's going on every moment, and the world on the other end can survive without you for longer than you think. Open your apps when you're good and ready to.

10. **Concentrate communication.** Set aside one to three short blocks of time each day to handle texts, emails, phone calls, and social media, and *only* do so then. Schedule these periods as late in the day as allowable. Will your social media empire collapse if you don't live-tweet your entire day? Probably not.

Chapter 22

SABBATH

Master This One Keystone Habit to Master Everything in the Book

"Knowing is not enough; we must apply.
Willing is not enough; we must do."
—Johann Wolfgang von Goethe

The story of Sisyphus in Greek mythology presents an unsettling picture for any human being. As the supposed founder and king of Ephyra (an alleged early name for Corinth), he was a legendary bad guy. His life was marked by insatiable greed and callous murder. Sisyphus even believed himself to be even more crafty than Zeus, the king of the gods.

Ancient Greeks didn't look down on crafty deceit—they actually thought it was pretty cool—but they did warn people against classing themselves with the gods. So when Sisyphus died, as the story goes, Zeus got his revenge by compelling Sisyphus to roll a boulder to the top of a hill in the underworld. But just before Sisyphus reached the summit, Zeus made him lose control of the boulder so that it rolled all the way back to the bottom . . . over and over again. Sisyphus was doomed to this futile task for eternity.

A myth like this one makes me grateful for the gospel that tells me I've escaped the futility of death through Christ. Yet it is still disturbingly easy for God's servants to fall into a groove of futile, repetitive action that goes nowhere.

217

The Most-Overlooked Reason That People Aren't Transformed

Any inspirational message—a sermon, a blog post, a talk with a friend—succeeds at the most basic level if it makes people aware that things might be different in their lives. It's communication that paints a contrast between "what is" and "what could be." And it's relatively easy to create and activate a vision for change in a simple communication event.

But what does progress really look like between desiring change and actually changing? Let's imagine a possible progression of steps after you hear a motivational message like you might on Sunday morning at a local church.

Some motivated people—especially those who have heard the message repeatedly—become interested enough to want to know more. They try to understand what they're hearing. Some come to love the idea that life could be different. They feel good about it just by knowing about it. They might feel so good about it that they tell their friends about it. They receive especially good vibes when they talk it up with others because of the social reinforcement they get. The vision for a new way of living even creates a sense of belonging among the group that is attracted to the new idea.

What happens next? Some people in the group value the new learning enough to act on it. They will take a step or two to try to apply the teaching or principle or vision to their lives. They want something to change for the better. At this point, they think—and the preacher or author or friend hopes—that the message has changed their life.

Except that it hasn't.

The communicator has actually only empowered a Sisyphus-like scenario. Their motivational message inspires people to push a boulder up the hill of life-transformation. People may even want to learn more about moving boulders. They read a book about the best place to put your hands on the boulder. They take a 201 class on the best stance and pace for pushing a boulder up the hill. Then they take action. On the next day they actually get out of bed and start rolling the boulder up the hill.

But before it reaches the top, they get distracted. They start working on another project and the big rock rolls back to the bottom. They're wild about the idea—they might even think they're succeeding—but nothing has really changed. Next week the boulder will have to be pushed up the hill again . . . and again . . . and again . . . going nowhere.

If you're a communicator and this thought discourages you, take heart: Jesus knows exactly how you feel. He received heaps of acclaim for the messages he delivered, which were largely intended to inspire people to submit to life-transformation (that is, to repent). Huge crowds came to hear him and "listen[ed] to him with delight" (Mark

12:37). They thought his teaching was so powerful that they would hang around for days and walk miles to hear him.

But were most of them transformed? Not at all. In fact, it is safe to estimate that those who fully embraced Jesus as their Teacher—those who were counted among his disciples after his execution—numbered fewer than 1 percent of the total who enjoyed his talks, possibly much fewer. Jesus revealed it bluntly when he asked his audience, "Why do you call Me 'Lord, Lord,' and don't do the things I say?" (Luke 6:46).

If you try to communicate for life-transformation, but it doesn't take, what's missing? Commitment? Yes. Surrender? Sure. But it's not just the proper disposition of heart that's missing. Even if the heart lands in the right place and wants to commit and surrender, a person needs something concrete to commit and surrender *to*.

> A keystone habit bridges the gap from liking a truth to living it.

For Jesus' followers, that concrete thing was literal following. The physical acts of walking around with Jesus, sleeping under the stars with him, doing what he told them to do, and going where he told them to go—these daily actions catalyzed their commitment and triggered their transformation. Jesus told his hearers to believe, but he never told them, "*Only* believe."[1] He said, "Follow me" (Matt. 4:19).

The Keystone Habit of Life Younique

The disciples' act of following Jesus is what we call a "keystone habit." A habit is any practice that becomes a regular, recurring feature of your life. A *keystone habit* is one that takes a new truth that you want to live by and makes it real and practical to the point that you embody it.

A keystone habit is so called because it fits in the process of life-transformation like the stone at the top of an arch that keeps the whole structure supported. It bridges the gap from liking a truth to living it (figure 22.1).

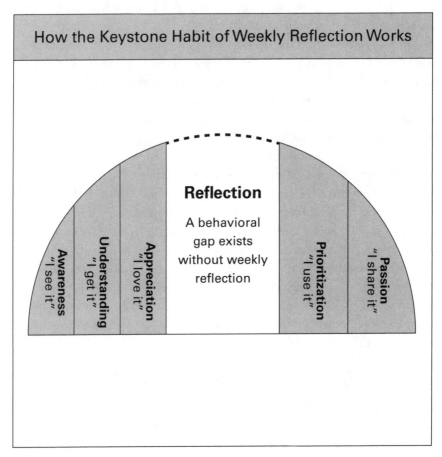

Figure 22.1

When people embrace and practice a keystone habit that fleshes out their new understanding, they deliberately expend time and effort to use it consistently. Eventually, it becomes such an intimate part of their life that they're able not only to tell their friends about it but also to guide them in living it out themselves, drawing on their own personal example.

The chief keystone habit in the Younique Life Plan is the *weekly reflection*—a focused, fifteen-minute, stand-up meeting with yourself. This is the practice that makes the difference between living your call and leaving your call on the shelf.

I didn't invent weekly reflection, of course. God did when he created the universe and stopped what he was doing at sundown on the sixth day (Gen. 1:31—2:3). He wanted to stand back and take a good look at it. He made it Ten Commandments-level clear to Moses that weekly reflection is a good habit for humans too. Jesus' teaching and life example continually emphasized the Sabbath, which became flexibly dependent on his lordship (which the early Christians took advantage of by making Sunday "the Lord's day," Rev. 1:10; see also Rom. 14:5–6). Jesus even insisted that the Sabbath is "made for man" (Mark 2:27–28). It's not some arbitrary rule we have to follow at pain of penalty; it's a privilege meant to provide for our flourishing. If we abandon the privilege of weekly reflection, we reject a gift that God made specially for us.

The purpose of weekly reflection is to put the "Important" in its rightful place in its eternal struggle with the "Urgent."[2] Everyone knows instinctively that problems that are both important and urgent must be addressed first. Everyone knows that problems that are neither important nor urgent are to be addressed last or (probably) not at all. The battle for break-thru in your life is waged over what to do *second*: Do you do what is important but not urgent, or do you surrender to what is urgent but not important?

Your Life Plan Snapshot reminds you of what is important *to* your life. Weekly reflection ensures that what is important gets *in* your life.

Mirrors for Reflection

At its simplest, weekly reflection consists of four elements:

- *Storyline review*—reflect on each of your four storylines as to whether you are *thriving, surviving,* or *reviving* in that area of your life
- *Ninety-day goal review*—assess whether progress toward your goal is on target, ahead of schedule, or behind schedule, and by how much
- *Review of obstacles*—consider the frustrations you faced during the week that's ending and *develop new ideas* for the week ahead
- *Prayer*—close by thanking God for sustaining and growing you in the previous week and asking for his guidance in the week to come

The fifteen minutes you take for these four elements can transform your week, but some veterans of The Journey don't stop there. If you block out more time, you can add other pieces to this liturgy of reflection to gain ground on what's important in your life.

Here are seven ideas. Sample what works for you without bloating your reflection and deterring yourself from doing it. (Remember, doing it is more important than doing it perfectly.)

- *1. Add identity and direction review.* This is almost a no-brainer. Ensure that at least once a week you remind yourself of your LifeCall, LifeCore, LifeSteps, and LifeScore, then review your LifeMap (1:4:1:4). That's what your Snapshot is for! And it provides a basis for the evaluations of your weekly reflection.

- **2. Add a spiritual discipline.** Add an extended time of private worship or intercessory prayer to your weekly reflection, or do your reflection on a day you set aside to fast.

- **3. Add a health habit.** I know someone who has struggled with depression and anxiety. He takes a diagnostic questionnaire as part of his weekly reflection to keep his finger on the pulse of his emotional health.

- **4. Add a relationship review.** Think about the people in your closer friendship circles and old friends who maybe live far away or have fallen out of touch; who do you need to schedule time to catch up with? Think about casual friends and new acquaintances; who do you need to schedule time with to get to know more deeply?

- **5. Add project management.** Most of us have multiple projects in our personal and work lives at any one time that take more than a week to complete. You can use your weekly reflection to do a status check on these projects and identify a discrete step or two you're going to take to make progress in the coming week.

- **6. Add to-dos.** Draft one list of what's important *and* urgent in the coming week and one list of what's important but *not* urgent as your basis for the coming week's activities. Also draft a list of to-dos to put off until the following week—you'll feel relieved when they're out of your head and into print, knowing that you can forget about them for the next seven days.

- **7. Add scheduling.** Is there a habit you're trying to establish? Schedule it on your calendar for the coming week to ensure it gets done. If you want, go further and block out all kinds of activities for the week, making adjustments as needed when you allocate your energy at the beginning of each day.

The Big Payoff of Intentionality

Intuitive leaders have a tendency to enjoy the Younique Life Plan because they instinctively resonate with the break-thru it provides. They move swiftly and smoothly through the tools of the process and produce eloquent language with notable clarity. The journey is a powerful "mountaintop" experience that sends them soaring.

But ironically, the most talented intuitive leaders are most tempted to fall short of the totality of the break-thru life-transformation available to them. You don't wring all the break-thru you need out of the Younique Life Plan until you move beyond *intuitive* application to *intentional* application. That includes concretely instilling your Vision

Frame and Horizon Storyline into your life every week. My life is a great example. I can get away with a lot of life design in my head; I can easily rely on hunch and instinct when making decisions, a great strength for sure. But my strength becomes a limiter if I don't practice intentionally what I can do intuitively.

Highly talented leaders often surpass the people working beside them on sheer intuition. But that advantage doesn't last forever. Success invites promotion, but at every level you move up, you find yourself rubbing shoulders with leaders as talented as you. Eventually, intuition is not enough to keep rising, and if you haven't established the habits of intentionality already, it becomes harder to start.

Remember—I want you to go pro in living your life. The athletes, actors, and artists whose graceful performance makes them look like "a natural" are actually incredibly disciplined. Music professor Percy C. Buck divulged the secret when he wrote, "An amateur practices until he can do a thing right, a professional until he can't do it wrong."[3]

You can compare the Younique Life Plan Journey to a spiritual retreat. A dynamic weekend retreat can yield huge spiritual break-thru. But the weekly discipline of corporate worship—which might seem awfully ho-hum the first time after the retreat—has a far greater impact on your life in the end.

Similarly, the payoff you get when you discover your Life Younique is huge. By contrast, the payoff you get the first time you do a weekly reflection might seem small. But over the course of your life you have many more weekly reflections than you have mountaintop clarity experiences. Over time, weekly reflections pay even bigger, compounded dividends. Install the keystone habit of weekly reflection and turn your Life Plan Snapshot into an every-day slingshot toward a better future.

Chapter 23

PRIORITY

How to Build Pit Stops for High-Performance Living

"Plans are worthless, but planning is everything."
                                        —Dwight D. Eisenhower

"Do it again!" Aren't those some of the best words to hear from a child?

I joined the old dads' club when my little Poema was born over two years ago. (Her older brothers and sister are out of the house already.) Being a father again after raising one generation is full of special treats and surprises. When do those "do it again" chants start sounding these days? When she escapes from the scissor trap (legs) with her special maneuvers. When we go down the slide, side by side. When she runs with unstoppable giggling around the kitchen island after a round of hide-n-seek. I may get worn out faster in my late forties but I still love hearing those words once more: "Do it again! Dadda, do it again!"

In chapter 20 I claimed that the supreme discipline for life progress is setting and chasing a single, focused goal every ninety days. So let's say you take my advice. What do you do when those ninety days are up?

Isn't it obvious? *Do it again!*

I'm not going to review here all the compelling reasons to set a ninety-day goal that I shared with you in that earlier chapter. Instead, I want to give you a practical process to "do it again." It's called *quarterly planning*.

Look Back, Look Forward

The basics of quarterly planning are simple. Its purpose is to review your last ninety days and to determine your next goal and the four NOW-rhythms you're going to practice on your way there.

Schedule a date every three months to get away by yourself. I recommend that you block out a solid half-day for it. The quarterly planning session will replace your weekly reflection for that week, but it doesn't have to fall on your normal reflection day if a different day of the week is more suitable.

Also, make it enjoyable; make it something you look forward to. Do your planning in a place you love to go, or treat yourself to something fun when you wrap up.

Your quarterly planning session has five movements.

Movement #1: Review your last goal

The first step is to look at your last ninety-day goal, evaluate whether you achieved it, and reflect on the path you took over the previous three months.

You get benefit out of this review when you do more than just check a box that says "Mission Accomplished" (or not). You benefit when you consider what God wanted to teach you and what he revealed to you about himself and about yourself over the last leg of the journey. Ask him about it.

Believe it or not, your contemplation can actually be even richer if you *didn't* achieve your ninety-day goal. This is an important topic, because the truth is, this is going to happen sometimes, and the last thing you need is to get demoralized by it.

I'll be honest: I probably only achieve my ninety-day goals about half the time—I tend to be pretty ambitious. But I've never regretted a single goal I've set or the fact that I set it. Remember, setting a ninety-day goal is something you *get* to do, not something you *have* to do. I want you to become your best cheerleader, not your worst slave driver.

When you don't achieve your ninety-day goal, first of all, celebrate the fact that you set a goal in the first place. Feel good about the fact that you have any basis for measuring progress at all—most people don't. Then think about why you didn't reach it. One possibility is that you sustained focus toward your goal, but your goal was too big to accomplish in ninety days. There's no shame in that. Celebrate the focus you sustained, and learn to set a better-sized goal. You may have a tendency to bite off more than you can chew. In any case, you're learning lessons about yourself that you can apply next time around.

On the other hand, maybe your goal was the right size, but you didn't sustain focus toward it. Sometimes this happens because life happens. Big surprises come along—crises like a cancer diagnosis or a layoff, or a sudden, surprising revelation of where God wants you to serve and what he wants you to do. If God allows or brings something into your life that diverts your attention from your ninety-day goal, that's not your failure; it's His sovereignty.

But by "life happens," I *don't* mean we should excuse ourselves on the basis of the myriad distractions that arise in all of our lives. Don't excuse yourself from the daily battle of deliberate decision-making. And remember the sage advice of the essentialist mind-set: You cannot overestimate the unimportance of practically everything.

Movement #2: Review raw materials for your new goal

After you close the book on your last goal, it's time to prepare to set a new one. Prayerful meditation and communion with God are a must here also.

While you're still looking backward, check the vital signs on your four storylines— are they thriving, surviving, or reviving? Then plot the progression of each one over the last quarter. What do you see? How has your relationship with God shifted over the highs and lows of the last three months?

Then look ahead at your long-range vision—your three-year dream and your one-year objectives. Now is not the time to overhaul these, but it may be appropriate to make small adjustments to details or wording.

Finally, take a fresh look at your LifeSteps. You don't have to plot your Role Map, set a target for your Five Capitals, and structure your Replenishment Rhythms all over again. Simply look at each storyline to ascertain which role, resource, or rhythm is the most important area of focus for this moment. It might be the same as the last ninety days, but very likely it will be something different.

Movement #3: Determine your new ninety-day goal

With prayer and reflection on your recent spiritual journey and long-range vision at the front of your mind, use the same process for setting a ninety-day goal that you used the first time you set one.

Movement #4: Determine your new NOW-rhythms

To begin to put practical actions toward your ninety-day goal in place, define a new set of NOW-rhythms that feed your ninety-day goal, your LifeSteps, your one-year objectives, or (ideally) that tie all of them together.

Movement #5: Set priorities for your week

Wrap up your quarterly planning session as you do your weekly reflection: by brainstorming new ideas for how you're going to approach this week and doing whatever other planning and review you've integrated into your weekly routine.

Remember Rommel's flags? Your quarterly planning session is your time to celebrate the achievement of reaching a flag—whatever condition you're in—and press ahead at full speed to the next one. Your destination beyond the horizon awaits.

Chapter 24

PERSPECTIVE

My Recipe for a Favorite Weekend of the Year

> *"Language . . . has created the word 'loneliness' to express
> the pain of being alone. And it has created the word
> 'solitude' to express the glory of being alone."*
>
> —Paul Tillich

Ruth was a wife, a mom, a church volunteer, a writer, and a seminary student. She was busy, busy, busy. Poured into the crucible of her responsibilities was the molten alloy of hot, bubbling questions shooting out of her like angry sparks. Her questions were charged by the frustrating gap between the faith she was studying academically and the spiritual impotence she found within herself.

It seemed as if she failed over and over to perform the most basic instruction—to love—toward the most immediate people—her husband and children. This was especially true if loving caused her any discomfort or inconvenience. She also felt like an unquestioning slave to every person who asked her to do something no matter how much she might want to say "no."

Under her disappointment in her own behavior swirled frightening emotions—anger, confusion, loneliness, desire. Ruth clamped down and turned away, fearing that if she entered into these feelings fully, she might not come back out. Who knew where they would take her?

During those difficult days Ruth began to see a spiritual director. She was used to talk therapy and liked it, so she assumed that the answers she sought would come as she and her guide talked it out. She was wrong.

One day her spiritual director gently told her, "Ruth, you are like a jar of river water all shaken up. What you need is to sit still long enough that the sediment can settle and the water can become clear."

The image of a jar of muddy water gripped her and wouldn't let her go. *Yes*, she thought, *that's exactly what I'm like.* Eventually, her yearning to get clear impelled her to learn and practice solitude and silence.[1]

The Challenging Ease of Solitude and Silence

The related spiritual disciplines of solitude and silence—being alone and being quiet—seem easy at first. It doesn't take any special talent to be by yourself, not to talk to people, and not to consume spoken or written words. In fact, it's so simple it's almost impossible to believe that it could do you or anyone any good.

But the more you think about doing it, the more reasons arise as to why you can't. The calendar is too full. You can't let so-and-so down. What will your kids do without you? Where will you go, and what will you bring with you?

Pulling this off is going to be harder than you thought.

The more you count the obstacles, the deeper your unease grows. Are these *really* the reasons I can't do it, or is there something more? Am I not getting away to be still and alone because I'm so busy, *or am I so busy because I don't want to be still and alone?* And what will happen if I do?

Uh-oh. This *is* hard.

But when you take the plunge—you set your jaw and set your plans to get away with God—it becomes easy again. It's not a superficial easiness but a deep *ease* that grows as the quiet hours roll by. The muddy water settles. If your soul happens to be as vexed as Ruth's was, there may be some pain and some tears, but nothing that the Lord who is with you can't handle. You are not overwhelmed. The sediment comes to rest, and so do you.

In the end, most important, the water becomes clear. You can see through it . . . you see through *you*. You see you as God sees you, which means you see yourself through the eyes of his fathomless love. And once more, you get a good look at your Life Younique.

Retreat Annually

In addition to the moments of reflection and renewal you build into your life each day and week and season, I recommend that you schedule a solitary retreat once a year to take the place of your fourth consecutive quarterly planning session.

Paradoxically, stopping your striving to get away actually hastens you toward your destination. You go slow to go fast. Think of your annual retreat as the point at which you break the sound barrier—only the barrier that you're breaking is the deafening echo rippling between the noise within you and the noise around you.

One full day is sufficient for most people to take a decent look at their life, and it's far more time than most people give themselves to ponder their big picture in the presence of God. But I want to push you to block out a two-day solitary overnighter. I've found that two days is enough time not only to think carefully about my Vision Frame and Horizon Storyline but also not to think about anything in particular at all. The time that I'm *not* concentrating—the hours that I'm sitting on a porch or riding my bike or walking through the woods with no agenda, nothing to get through—makes the part of my retreat when I am concentrating far richer and more fruitful.

The practicalities of the annual retreat aren't complicated. Turn off your phone and leave it in the car when you arrive (you read that right). Seriously consider leaving any electronic device behind and going pure analog. If there's a TV where you're going, unplug it. Take one fun book or a craft or a bike as a way to take a break once in a while. Otherwise, bring your Bible, a journal or notebook, a pen, your Life Plan Snapshot, and *Younique*.

You might bring your past journals as well. One summer vacation I didn't bring any book with me but my Bible and some journals. Looking back at how God spoke and worked across the pages of my life was some of the most enriching reading I've ever done.

How to Review Your Life Each Year

After starting off your retreat with a healthy period of simply being still, the work begins. The annual retreat proceeds in three movements of unequal length with breaks between them and, if necessary, in the middle of them.

Movement #1: Your Past and Present

In the presence of God, take a good look at the year you just completed and where you stand today. First use the Four Helpful Lists exercise described in chapter 16 to get a bird's-eye view of your life right now. Then consider which LifeDrifts have been most prominent for you over the last year (see chapter 5). Expose the Life Lies you've been tempted to believe and reaffirm the Life Truths of the gospel that set you free.

Movement #2: Your Identity

This movement takes more time to complete. It involves reexamining your Sweet Spot and your Vision Frame and to the extent appropriate, reshaping them to better articulate your Life Younique.

Look Again at Your One Thing and LifeCall: Your personal mission statement doesn't have to remain untouched forever; feel free to tweak, refine, and let it shine over time. The longer you have a LifeCall, the more you're "taking photos" of your One Thing as you go through life. The more snapshots you take in various circumstances under different conditions, the better you see it, and the better you can describe it.

Coming to an even deeper "capture" of your One Thing reminds me of the famous American artist Andrew Wyeth, who painted the landscape around the Brandywine River in the part of Pennsylvania where I spent many of my formative years. Wyeth painted the same places over and over again because he believed that the more he painted them, the better he saw them and knew them. "Most artists look for something fresh to paint," Wyeth said, "Frankly I find that quite boring. For me it is much more exciting to find fresh meaning in something familiar."

In my case, after having *bringing clarity* as my Two Words for some years, I replaced them with *applying essence*. Those Two Words might seem obscure to you, but they are full of meaning to me. Yet it took me a significant amount of time living thoughtfully on the level of the previous statement before I discovered a deeper level underneath it.

Similarly, I've altered my LifeCore statements four or five times over the last fifteen years. For example, one of my values used to be Simplicity. Unfortunately, with all the things I had going on in my life, it wasn't particularly simple. I also didn't mean by "simplicity" a fixed cap on the quality or quantity of my material possessions, which is the way some use the term. Both these realities were evident to the people around me, so it accidentally made something of a joke of my value of Simplicity.

But I knew that I did value something that lay beneath the original label. The simplicity I meant was about narrowing my life, especially vocationally, to what really mattered. I've said "no" to more things than most people do. I often say that I don't work nearly as hard as people think I do—I don't do hard work; I do focused work. So I started to call this value Focus. I found that, paradoxically, my value of Focus is what created complexity in my life in the form of multiple vocational vehicles such as Auxano, Younique, and Denominee. The complexity came about because I was laser-focused on bringing break-thru clarity to people and organizations.

Look Again at Your LifeSteps: After reviewing your Sweet Spot, LifeCall, and LifeCore—and perhaps after a break—check whether your LifeScore storylines are well-named and well-defined. Then look at the Roles, Resources, and Replenishment Rhythms that form the substructure of your LifeSteps.

Look at your Role Map and consider whether it comprehensively encompasses the various roles you play in your life now. Significant vocational or relationship changes over the past year may require replotting the map to some degree.

Next, take a look at where you last left your Five Capitals. The first time you looked at these, you distributed seventeen imaginary "gold bars" among the five resource types to represent your life at that time, and you sketched what you would have liked to see your life look like in three years with thirty-four gold bars in hand. On your retreat, keep the target the same, but reevaluate your current situation. If one year has passed since you set your target, give yourself twenty-one gold bars to describe the present; if two, make it twenty-seven. If a full three years have passed, start over with seventeen gold bars for present resources and make a new projection for three years from now.

Finally, look at your Replenishment Rhythms. What are you currently doing to recharge, re-center, and refocus daily, weekly, monthly, and annually? Where are the gaps?

Movement #3: Your Direction

The movement of the annual retreat that usually takes the most time is the renewal of your LifeMap—your Horizon Storyline.

Start at the top with your three-year dream. If three years haven't yet passed since you first created it, consider whether it stands in need of adjustment. Your three-year vision is like a developing Polaroid photo. When you first capture it in words, it's blurry. Each year you see it develop more as it increasingly comes true and as you get a more precise idea of what you are hoping for. What you first saw becomes more vivid and clear. As appropriate, tighten your description to reflect that.

If a full three years have passed, contemplate whether you have arrived where you hoped you would be. It may be that your dream is yet unfulfilled and you'd like to renew it with tweaks for the next three years. Or else things may have changed so significantly that you're ready to go back to the drawing board and seek God for a new destination three years ahead. In either case, be sure to praise God for his faithfulness in the path he's taken you on so far, whether it's been joyous or sorrowful, or (as life usually is) both.

Then move to your one-year objectives. Did you meet these challenges over the last year? What came as a surprise? What did God teach you about himself and about yourself along the way? Following the guidance in chapter 16, set new objectives for the coming year.

Finally, define your new short-range vision—your ninety-day goal and your NOW-rhythms—as you do in a quarterly planning session.

 (By the way, if you'd like to see how I renewed my Life Plan during a getaway time to dream a new three-year dream, read the story at WillMancini. com/LifePlanUpdate.)

Return to the Temple

The power of the annual retreat is compounded as you take it year after year. It is like a temple to which you make pilgrimage that is adorned with precious artifacts of God's work in your life. Every time you go, you leave more riches there and expand the building. Every time you return, you enjoy and reappropriate what God has done to shape your Life Younique. Most important, every time you worship the Lord in that temple in solitude and silence, you encounter the God who loves you in a way you don't meet him anywhere else.

PART SIX

YOUR DESTINY
How to Fulfill God's Dream of You and for You

THE YOUNIQUE
VISION JOURNEY

In Moses' only prayer recorded in the book of Psalms, he wrote, "Teach us to number our days carefully so that we may develop wisdom in our hearts" (90:12).

I once owned Moses' plea so personally that I endeavored to practice it literally. I calculated the number of days of a projected average lifespan and subtracted the number of days I had already lived. Then I wrote the difference on a page of my journal.

Every day for ten years, when I started a fresh journal entry, I wrote a new number at the top of the page: the number from the day before, minus one. The series of numbers that ran across the pages was like a reverse odometer; every day it gave me an estimate of how many days I had left to make this life count.

That practice gave me break-thru appreciation of the priceless value of a single day. It's like a whole life in miniature. Each day I'm born afresh, yet I carry the heritage of all the days that have come before. When I go to sleep at the end of the day, that mini-life passes away to bequeath its legacy to tomorrow.

For those with eyes to see it, every day is a reminder of the mystery and majesty of life. Every day is an opportunity; we can shape it with our intentions, yet it is always full of surprises. And it always makes an impact on the days that follow.

So also is the one life we live on this earth. It is an opportunity to do and experience things that we both strive for and cannot conceive. It surprises us again and again. It is an inheritance we leave to all who come after. And it is fleeting—we must seize it while we can.

This last part of Younique contains some of my most treasured thoughts on what God teaches us about a life well-lived. It is about raising our eyes far past what we can see—by faith "looking forward to the city that has foundations, whose architect and builder is God" (Heb. 11:10). It is about casting our vision beyond the "beyond-the-horizon" to the rest of our lives.

We will begin by redeeming the "bucket list"—all the things you yearn to have happen for yourself and those around you between now and the day you die. Then I want to open your mind to imagine what might be your ultimate contribution—the single big thing God put you on earth to accomplish. And finally, I want to leave you with the maximum motivation to make the most of every day—every miniature lifetime—of your life.

Chapter 25

BUCKET LIST

The Essential Miniguide to Fulfilling Your Wildest Dreams

"Remember that life is not measured by the number of breaths we take, but by the moments that take our breath away!"

—Vicki Corona

Several years ago I checked a big item off my bucket list: a great escape to the island of Santorini, Greece—undeniably one of the most beautiful places on Earth.[1]

I'm not sure what first sparked my interest in visiting the Greek isles. Was it pictures in fifth-grade world geography, or was it one of those jet-way wall murals that haunts you forever? Maybe it was the setting of a movie I can't remember, or maybe a picture in my Greek textbook at seminary. (Wait, that book didn't have pictures!)

I guess it doesn't matter, because for as long as I can remember, I have had an Eden-echo in my soul, calling me there.

The idea of a "bucket list" was popularized by the 2007 movie *The Bucket List*. In the picture, two terminally ill men escape a cancer ward with a to-do list to accomplish before they "kick the bucket."

Do you have a bucket list? Have you recorded a set of life dreams to fulfill before you die? If not, why not start one? If so, when was the last time you checked something off?

How to Redeem Your Life Dreams

While basking in the sunset of my Aegean paradise, I reflected on what is required to propel us toward our dreams and the steps I took to get there. But before I share with you my strategy for bucket-list living, I want to address a major objection up front. Many believers have a frowning, austere inner warden. He clears his throat and glares down his nose whenever they think of doing something lavish for their own enjoyment. The warden is made up of the shadows of believers we've known, dead-and-gone spiritual giants we've read about, and infallible biblical admonitions such as "If anyone wants to follow after me, let him deny himself, take up his cross, and follow me" (Mark 8:34).

So, guided by this inner warden, they understandably wonder: *Is it selfish for me to dream big and set goals for self-fulfillment?* At first blush, I would say, "It absolutely can be!" For that matter, anything we do—including, by the way, even the most "spiritual" things—may be driven by hidden motives that are flesh-driven rather than God-inspired (see 1 Cor. 13:1–3, for example). So the better question is: *How do we discern whether a life dream is an act of pure self-indulgence or a way to glorify God, who "provides us with all things to enjoy" (1 Tim. 6:17)?*

I recommend you redeem your dreams by running every item on your bucket list through a four-question filter. I confess that I've seen my selfishness when I couldn't give a credible answer to any of these questions for one of my aspirations. This diagnostic keeps me grounded in God and reminds me where true happiness comes from: the love of Christ, who "died for all so that those who live should no longer live for themselves, but for the one who died for them and was raised" (2 Cor. 5:14–15).

Filter #1: How is the life dream facilitating deeper intimacy or special bonding with people? The simplest way to build a bucket list for God's purposes is to fill it with unique opportunities to build the most important of life's relationships. How might this work with your spouse or children? How about stressed or estranged relationships? With whom is God leading you to grow closer?

Filter #2: How is the life dream enabling personal re-creation or particular inspiration? God designed humans with rechargeable batteries. He commands special seasons and rhythms of Sabbath. How can a life goal renew your mind, heart, body, or emotions? Maybe in the course of your calling you need some special inspiration. How can your everyday work be forever enriched? How might an extended and even extravagant period of rest bring new vitality to your current life stage?

Filter #3: How is the life dream providing a general blessing or unique investment? God always blesses us to be a blessing. How can your giving be multiplied by your gaining? How can generosity be expressed through your experiences? What kind of investment into someone else does your goal make possible? If you travel, why not become an extravagant tipper? If you own a four-wheeler, who else can ride? If you are learning to kiteboard, who else can tag along?

Filter #4: How is the life dream promoting increased faith or gospel advancement? Achieving a goal can expand your capability and enlarge your perspective. Does your bucket-list item require a step of faith that will change how you live the rest of your days? Does it put you in contact with others whose faith inspires yours? Or will it bring you into proximity to people who need to hear the gospel and see it in your joy? A friend and pastor named Neil Tomba just rode his bike from coast to coast in thirty days, from Santa Monica to Annapolis. He used the experience to engage people in a dozen states and the District of Columbia with specific spiritual questions when they asked him about the trek. What looked like a novel bike ride was a noble missionary enterprise.

Five Kinds of Life Dreams

As you start writing your list—yes, literally write it; don't let it languish in the back of your skull—don't miss one crucial principle: the *No Perfect List Principle.* Don't try to get the list right; just get it started. Don't worry about dreaming too big or too small. Don't worry about what others will think. Don't worry about how many things you have written down. Just write, right now.

> Don't try to get the list right; just get it started. Just write, right now.

You can tap into a gush of inspiration at the intersection of the four storylines in your LifeScore and five kinds of aspirations. Instead of writing a single bucket list, write one for each of your storylines. We challenge participants in The Journey to come up with at least five "life wins" for each storyline in their first twenty minutes of reflection. You won't believe how well-rounded this makes your total collection of life goals.

Populate your lists with aspirations of five types—let the following aspirations be your inspiration.

Life Dream Type #1

A thing to do

- Attend the World Series
- Climb a fourteener in Colorado
- Go to a reunion concert with college friends
- Watch the entire *Star Wars* saga in one sitting
- Go sky-diving

Life Dream Type #2

A place to go

- See the Pyramids
- Check out every point of interest in your city that tourists visit and locals take for granted
- Visit ten Major League Baseball stadiums
- Hike the Grand Canyon
- Take a mission trip to Kenya

Life Dream Type #3

A skill to learn

- Take a photography class
- Impress people with ballroom dance proficiency
- Start taking piano or violin lessons
- Learn to speak Swahili
- Grow a bonsai garden

Life Dream Type #4

An objective to achieve

- Run a marathon in Vibram 5-finger shoes
- Do a cycling tour from Seattle to San Diego
- Save $100,000 in ten years
- Start an at-home business
- Spend three months a year donating time overseas

Life Dream Type #5

A possession to obtain

- Collect one of every Lincoln penny
- Buy a really powerful telescope
- Drive a 1969 Jaguar XKE for a weekend
- Have a home with a pool
- Own a kayak

The Major Obstacles to Bucket-List Living

It is crucial to examine your life for the five most common obstacles that keep you from setting life goals and going after them.

Obstacle #1: Busyness

Busy people are the most inclined to set goals toward a meaningful life, but ironically, busyness is deadly to actually achieving a meaningful life. An adrenalin addiction may keep us frantically living in the wrong direction. John Ortberg tells the story of a sage who changed his life by focusing on one piece of advice: "Ruthlessly eliminate hurry from your life."[2]

Obstacle #2: Imitation

Many people don't take the time to discern their dreams and instead strive after others' dreams by default. They hear an inspiring story; they follow family tradition; they go on a trip with a friend; they get a pool because the neighbors got one. While these situations certainly aren't bad, they can prevent a person from beautiful self-discovery in attaining something that God uniquely designed them to yearn for.

Obstacle #3: Fear

It can be scary to dream big, because any aspiration one might hope for illumines a gap between current reality and future possibility. For many people, this gap presents a problem: *Do I live with a gap—a hope, a goal, a desire unfulfilled—or do I try to close it knowing I might fail?* For many, the feeling of certain security is more attractive than possible failure. Dreamless living sets in.

Obstacle #4: Distraction

Everybody has small-bore fun things they like to do; one of mine is video games. These things are not a problem in themselves, but we can easily devote more time to them than we mean to. Recently my daughter and I were playing a game that records and publicly displays the amount of time that an individual plays. One of our opponents had logged *31 24-hour days*—the equivalent of a solid, sleepless month of gameplay. Every hour of low-investment-low-return fun sucks investment away from far more satisfying goals in our lives.

Obstacle #5: Expectation

The fifth obstacle is the expectations of others. They start with the deep-rooted expectations placed upon us by our family of origin—maybe your family didn't take certain kinds of vacations, for example. Another would be an expectation of workplace culture or a boss—maybe it's not customary to take more than one week off at a time. Layered on those are the expectations of your current family and other important relationships—maybe there's something you would love to do, but your spouse thinks it's crazy, or your friends would try to talk you out of your idealism. Unfortunately, others' expectations become the inhibitions that disconnect us from our aspirations. What *they* would say becomes what you say to hold yourself in place.

What goes unrecognized is the most powerful influence in your life, and what is not named cannot be overcome. Which of these obstacles casts a shadow over your heart? When you call it what it is and address it head-on, it is much more likely to shrink so you can climb over it on the way to your dreams.

Essentials to Living Your Life Dreams

So how do you press on in the tenacious chase of your dreams? How can you stay focused on the longer horizon but take small but real steps toward it each day?

When I approached these questions, I found four immovable factors. In summary:

DREAMS + TIME + MONEY + COURAGE = Your Life Goals Achieved

Let's walk through this simple equation.

Essential #1: "Dreams" are about having focused reflection to inspire.

Since most people don't have clear goals to begin with, the starting point for achievement is the ongoing journey of reflection. I'm not talking about something casual or soft but an intense, energetic, everything's-at-stake kind of reflection. Figure out the ideal time, place, and tools that you need to uncover the patterns that God has woven in your life and the desires he's placed in your heart. Where does he want you to go next? Write it down and revisit the list often.

Essential #2: "Time" is about long-term scheduling to accommodate.

What is the farthest in advance that you have ever scheduled anything? What kind of horizon are you living with every day? A few weeks, months, or years? How do you break the tyranny of today? Your willingness and ability to organize your time in the future will play a crucial role in personal vision planning. (The Horizon Storyline described in part 4 and the Life-Making Cycle of part 5 are transformative tools for this.) You need to schedule your time for focused reflection (Essential #1), preparation time for some of your bucket-list items, and time to do the items themselves.

Essential #3: "Money" is about prioritizing values to resource.

Your life dreams will require resources. Surely some goals do not necessarily have a direct connection to money (such as spending special one-on-one time with your kids), but most of your goals will have a financial factor. Your enemy, then, consists of the unintended leaks and sloshy handling of your money bucket. Obviously, different people have different amounts of cash to work with, but everyone has *some* opportunity to align the allocation of their funds with their personal values in order to fulfill their goals.

For example, I live in the Clear Lake area of Houston, which attracts a myriad of recreational boaters. I am not a boat guy myself, but what I have realized over the years is that a passion for boating can be expressed at all different income levels. Within minutes of my house I can drive by million-dollar properties with gorgeous yachts and mobile homes with boats that cost as much as the home. I can even find people whose boat is their home! Not everyone has the opportunity to have the biggest boat, but everyone has an opportunity to align their resources with their goals.

Essential #4: "Courage" is about repetitive risk-taking to commit.

The fourth essential swings away from the concrete aspect of cash to an intangible quality of the spirit. The greatest limiting factor in the end is not time and money, but courage. It is downright uncomfortable to do things you have never done before. The path of predictability is more attractive than we realize. That's why it's important to take risks step by step—small ones at first will develop your appetite for bigger ones. It's amazing to feel your risk tolerance grow over the years.

A simple example is the bucket-list trip to Santorini that I told you about. Several factors added to the risk of this trip, including the financial instability of Greece at the time. Part of me kept saying, "Do this later." Several people discouraged me from going. But I had carved out the time and I knew that delaying the trip would be an opportunity cost for other bucket-list items. So I took the leap, and I'm super-glad that I did! Seven years later I planned an even riskier trip: to leave Houston to live in the mountains for fourteen weeks one winter—steps away from snowboarding—without taking time off work.

So what's keeping your from checking off that next item on your bucket list? What routine are afraid to break? Whose opinion is weighing heavy on your decision? What area of your life paralyzes you like a six-year-old on the edge of the high-dive?

Maybe what you most need to overcome your obstacles is to consider again the mind-blowing invitation of Jesus: "Who among you, if his son asks him for bread, will give him a stone? Or if he asks for a fish, will give him a snake? If you then, who are evil, know how to give good gifts to your children, how much more will your Father in heaven give good things to those who ask him" (Matt. 7:9–11).

 (If you would like additional help designing and fulfilling your own list of 100 Life Dreams, join me for an online course entitled *Achieving Life Dreams*. Check it out at LifeYounique.com/courses.)

Chapter 26

DESTINY

How to Answer the Ultimate Question of Life

*"Do not be afraid to trust [God] utterly. As you go down the long
corridor you will find that He has preceded you, and locked many
doors which you would fain have entered; but be sure that beyond these
there is one which He has left unlocked. Open it and enter, and you
will find yourself face to face with a bend of the river of opportunity,
broader and deeper than anything you had dared to imagine in your
sunniest dreams. Launch forth on it; it conducts to the open sea."*

—F. B. Meyer

One of my very favorite parables that *wasn't* told by Jesus is the story of the three brick-makers.

A visitor walking down a road on the outskirts of town encountered three workmen engaged side by side in the same activity. "What are you doing?" he asked the first workman.

The workman looked up with an annoyed look on his face. "I'm making bricks," he replied curtly.

The visitor asked the next worker, "And what are you doing?"

The workman looked up with a determined look on his face. "I'm building a wall," he replied decisively.

Finally the visitor asked the third workman, "What are you doing?"

The third workman looked up with a rapturous look on his face. "I'm building a cathedral," he replied earnestly, "and it's going to be the most beautiful cathedral in the world."

In my work as a consultant with churches, I tell this story a lot. I love it because it illustrates how a compelling vision, the faith that it's coming true, and the knowledge of how we are contributing to it together transform the quality of our work and the joy with which we do it.

But when we talk about our Life Younique, the story leaves an important question unanswered: How did the third workman know the building was a cathedral? Why not a school or a factory or a homeless shelter or a bridge?

The only way any worker could know what he was making the bricks for is if the architect gave him a look at the blueprints.

Remember, this book is about "*designing* the life God dreamed for you." God doesn't treat you as a slave whose only responsibility is to follow orders not knowing why they're given. Admittedly, for a long season of your life, especially early on, it may go something like this. But over time, as your obedience grows, your intimacy with God grows, and your understanding and active involvement in the design of your life-project grows. After three-plus years of role-modeling and mentorship and living together, Jesus told his apostles, "I do not call you servants anymore, because a servant doesn't know what his master is doing. I have called you friends, because I have made known to you everything I have heard from my Father" (John 15:15).

I may not know what the building of my life ultimately looks like while I'm making the next brick. But the longer I go making bricks, the more likely the Architect comes over and I get to glance at the blueprints. Most workers never take their eyes off what they're doing, but if I'm willing to take a step back and talk with the Architect, he might show me. Sometimes he's waiting for me when I step back, sometimes not, and sometimes he interrupts me by surprise while I'm working. But—most important—to the extent I know the plan, he expects me to shape my work deliberately toward its completion.

Ultimate Contribution

The holy grail of the quest to know your Life Younique is to grasp and deliver your *ultimate contribution*. I picked up this term from the late leadership thinker J. Robert Clinton, who studied the lifelong journeys of consequential Christian leaders in his classic book, *The Making of a Leader*.[1] Clinton taught that in the later stages of a leader's life, he or she may be able to identify their most significant contribution and intentionally shape their activity to produce it.

Think of ultimate contribution as the cumulative output of your entire life, climaxing in your last and greatest achievement, expressed in a single idea. It is the ultimate reason you were put on earth. If your LifeCall is the trajectory of the arrow of your life soaring through the air, your ultimate contribution is dead-center of the target.

Five Biblical Examples

- For **Moses** it was leading God's people out of Egypt and becoming the personal conduit of the law of God.
- For **Joshua** it was leading the Israelites into the Promised Land by defeating the Canaanites in battle.
- For **Caleb** it was modeling whole-hearted faith and courage as a leader in Israel over forty-five years.
- For **Esther** it was using her privileged status to rescue the Jewish people from genocide.
- For the **apostle Paul** it was launching a worldwide missionary movement that included reaching Rome, the hub of the Roman Empire.

Five Historic Examples

- For **Joan of Arc** it was catalyzing an astounding comeback of the French monarchy against the English and Burgundians in the fifteenth century.
- For **Martin Luther** it was reforming the church from abuses of organized religion and awakening people to salvation by grace alone through faith alone in the sixteenth century.
- For **William Wilberforce** it was leading the British Empire to abolish slavery in the nineteenth century.
- For **Hudson Taylor** it was innovating missionary methods to reach inland China in the nineteenth century.
- For **Martin Luther King Jr.** it was serving as the prophetic mouthpiece of the civil rights movement in the twentieth century.

Five Contemporary Examples

- For **Max Lucado** it's bringing God's story to life as an author with a flare for poetic prose.
- For **John Piper** it's capturing people with the idea that God is most glorified in us when we are most satisfied in him.
- For **Kay Arthur** it's teaching the techniques of inductive Bible study to millions so they can mine the riches of God's Word for themselves.

- For **Alan Hirsch** it's helping the church in the West to reimagine its identity and practice the forgotten ways of the early church as a movement.
- For **Lee Mancini** (my mom) it's lifting the lives of others through mentoring that champions biblical womanhood.

I hope these fifteen examples help you catch the idea of ultimate contribution. My ultimate contribution, as far as I can discern it today, is to create transferable training and tools that keep the people of God emotionally connected to the mission of God. When I look back on my life on my deathbed or with the Lord on the day of judgment, I want to know that God used me to enable the church to experience redemptive movement as it navigated the transitioning culture of the early twenty-first century. Do you think that fixing my eyes on my ultimate contribution affects my priorities, choices, and actions in the present? You bet it does!

So what would you say your ultimate contribution is likely to be? If you are a little stuck, don't worry. This one takes time and "experience to grow."

Pay particularly close attention to Caleb's and my mom's statements above. What sometimes keeps us from recognizing our own ultimate contribution is the huge scale of the illustrations we know the best. The famous examples reach people nationally or globally and make an evident impact beyond their lifetime. By contrast, most people's ultimate contribution is found within a local scope—being a model saint, raising a godly family, leading a Bible study that influences many in one community. But that makes it no less grand in God's eyes if that's what he designed you to accomplish.

Four Ways to Discern Your Ultimate Contribution

Another difficulty that discourages us from thinking about our ultimate contribution is that we don't know how to start. We might assume that in every case it comes about by accident or miracle if it comes at all. Moses got his assignment at a burning bush. If you don't encounter a burning bush, how do you know what your ultimate contribution is and whether you will make one?

I am convinced that everyone has an ultimate contribution to make, but I'm equally convinced that not everyone discerns their ultimate contribution in the same way. In fact, I see four patterns of discernment that God employs to show people what their ultimate purpose is if they're willing to look and listen for it (table 26.1, also inspired by the work of J. Robert Clinton[2]). Two of these patterns primarily communicate God's will by looking inward at oneself and two by looking outward at the world around oneself—in both cases with God opening one's eyes.

Four Ways to Discern Your Ultimate Contribution			
		Revelation	
		One Big	Many Small
Focus	Inward	**Directed** (Mary the Mother of Jesus)	**Developed** (Peter)
	Outward	**Discovered** (Paul)	**Discrete** (Nehemiah)

Table 26.1

With the **inward** patterns, a person discerns their ultimate contribution by looking inward, understanding their identity with increasing depth, and considering the "names" bestowed on them by God through others. *Directed* **discernment** comes when God dramatically, directly, supernaturally reveals your ultimate contribution in a single burst. I can't think of a better example from the Bible than Mary, the mother of Jesus. God sent Gabriel the angel to tell Mary that her role in God's plan of redemption was to conceive the Son of God by the power of the Holy Spirit. It doesn't get more dramatic or "inward" than that!

Face-to-face conversations with angels are rare (even in the Bible), but a few people still receive directed discernment from God today in various forms. Directed discernment may allow for subsequent revelations that increase clarity as to ultimate contribution, as Abram/Abraham received (Gen. 12:1–3; 15; 17; 22:15–18).

Developed **discernment** is also about seeing yourself as God sees you, but unlike the directed variety, it is marked by an awareness that grows over time. Developed discernment involves deliberate, analytical meditation on your experience, frequently with the assistance of insightful companions and tools for reflection such as those of the Younique Life Plan Journey.

Jesus gave his disciple Simon a nickname, "Peter" ("bedrock"), because his ultimate contribution was to set the church on a sound footing (Matt. 16:17–19). But how that would play out practically wasn't obvious from the beginning. Peter's understanding of his Master's meaning developed gradually as he stepped—or fell!—into obeying the micro-calls the Lord gave him over time. The journey started with Jesus' multiple summons to follow in the early chapters of the Gospels, and it extended into Jesus' many instructions and challenges to Peter during his earthly ministry; the opportunities and threats facing the church in Jerusalem in the early chapters of Acts, including the integration of the Gentiles; and Peter's final post overseeing the church at Rome, which became the dominant city church of Western Christianity. One can almost imagine Peter at each of these thresholds saying to himself, "Oh, *that's* what he meant!"

While inward patterns involve looking inward at who you are, **outward** patterns involve looking outward at what you are to do—your consummate activity. ***Discovered*** **discernment** comes when God reveals a mission or a need that consumes someone with the compulsion to do something about it—in fact, to devote their entire lives to it. A great example is when the risen Jesus appeared to Saul of Tarsus, persecutor of Christians, commanding him to become the apostle to the Gentiles better known as Paul (Acts 9:1–16; 22:1–16; 26:12–18). From the perspective of ultimate contribution, the most important detail of Paul's calling is not that he had a vision of the risen Jesus, which most people don't receive (though that was extremely important to Paul for other reasons!). The important detail is that the former Pharisee saw Gentiles with new eyes and embraced a mission to make beachheads of the gospel among them for the rest of his life.

The second pattern of outward-facing discernment is ***discrete*** **discernment**, so called because it is a race run by many segmented laps of short-distance obedience over a long time. The person engaged in discrete discernment is, paradoxically, quite likely never fully to discern his or her ultimate contribution at all; it often becomes evident only at the very end of life or after death.

A great example of discrete discernment is Nehemiah. This senior official in the Persian emperor's court was overcome when he learned that the Jewish exiles who had returned home almost a century before were in awful shape and that the city of Jerusalem was still a disgraceful ruin. The ruined wall was the first need that he was called to meet. But its fifty-two-day reconstruction was just the beginning. He also found that local Gentile big shots exercised improper influence over the Jews, that rich Jews kept poorer ones saddled with oppressive debt, that the Sabbath was not being observed, that the temple was not adequately supplied with tithes and offerings, and that Jews were marrying Gentiles and raising children outside the faith. Nehemiah gave the rest of his life to correcting these problems one at a time (often more than once). At the end of his life, Nehemiah prayed that God would remember him for everything *but* building the wall (Neh. 5:19; 13:14, 22, 31). It wasn't until the end that

Nehemiah's ultimate contribution became evident: he restored the integrity of the Jews as the holy people of God amid their neighbors.

A person might discern their ultimate contribution by more than one pattern over the course of their life. (Indeed, a number of the individuals I mentioned could be classified in more than one way.) You might be *directed* by a dramatic revelation to a particular vocational focus in early or mid-career, but your grasp of the specific contours of that focus may be *developed* over time. Or you might proceed by *discrete* directions from God every few years until you encounter the *discovered* need that it is your destiny to address in a big way. Which pattern or patterns do you see in your life so far?

Types of Ultimate Contribution

Another obstacle that keeps people from thinking about their ultimate contribution is a kind of pseudo-humility, where we quickly recognize the kinds of major accomplishments that we would never make, but we downplay the kinds we can. The truth is, the nature of an ultimate contribution can vary widely. Some are tangible, like the founding of an organization, while others are less tangible, like the model of a holy life. None of these is more significant or essential to God's plans than another; if he is calling you to an ultimate contribution—and he is—it is important. And he will supply all that is needed in the process.

Table 26.2 outlines twenty-five ultimate contribution types—five each in five categories. They span the gamut from ideas to people to things. Consider which type most clearly corresponds either to your current vocational trajectory or to a hunch you have about your future.

Ultimate Contribution Types		
Category	Type	Definition
A Community to Grow	**Parent**	Builds a family whose successive generations and multiple branches model goodness with unusual effectiveness and reach. (Lyman Beecher)
	Mentor	Coaches, counsels, or shepherds individuals in a way that has ongoing influence and impact in their lives, which in turn impacts others. (John Newton)
	Facilitator	Generates community and shapes outcomes among a group of people in a transformative way through team-building, peacemaking, and collaboration. (Nelson Mandela)
	Philanthropist	Distributes a cache of wealth to supply a benefit to people over a long term. (Warren Buffett)
	Developer	Plans, funds, builds, or furnishes a large structure or a collection or complex of structures for human use. (Andrew Carnegie)
A Culture to Enrich	**Inventor**	Creates a new device or tool that improves people's lives. (Thomas Edison)
	Artist	Creates a great work of art, music, literature, or film or a body of such work. (Jane Austen)
	Artisan	Makes an artifact that is exceptionally pleasing and useful, or a body of such work, that requires highly developed skill. (Stradivarius)
	Entertainer	Brings pleasure or meaning to a large audience in a memorable way through the performing arts as a performer, producer, or part of a team. (Ella Fitzgerald)
	Conservator	Saves a natural or cultural treasure or resource from destruction, often rehabilitating it for future enjoyment or use. (John Muir)

Table 26.2a

Ultimate Contribution Types		
Category	**Type**	**Definition**
An Organization to Lead	**Founder**	Starts a new organization to meet a need or capture the essence of a movement. (John Wesley)
	Stabilizer	Helps a fledgling organization mature in stability, efficiency, and effectiveness. (Alexander Hamilton)
	Multiplier	Expands an organization or establishes an offshoot of it in a new territory or among a previously unreached group of people. (St. Patrick)
	Preserver	Defends an organization against forces that would unmake it and adapts it to survive to the next generation. (Abraham Lincoln)
	Renovator	Turns around a failing or almost dead organization. (Lee Iacocca)
An Idea to Conceive	**Discoverer**	Makes a major discovery that permanently expands human knowledge. (Marie Curie)
	Compiler	Gathers and organizes a large, even comprehensive collection of data or artifacts for others to study or reference. (Francis Collins)
	Thinker	Conceptualizes and describes reality in a way that revolutionizes how people view and understand the world or an aspect of it. (Isaac Newton)
	Presenter	Communicates knowledge, often conceived or discovered by others, as a writer or documentarian in a way that shapes how many people understand it. (Ken Burns)
	Communicator	Speaks to large groups of people in a way that informs, persuades, and inspires to an exceptional degree. (Billy Graham)
A Change to Activate	**Role Model**	Lives a model life, not a perfect one, that others want to emulate, often displaying an unusual zealousness for God. (Mother Theresa)
	Innovator	Creates a way of doing things in a particular field that sets a new standard of practice or technique for that field. (Henry Ford)
	Catalyst	Opens eyes in an organization, community, or society to a better way to live and function and inspires change in that direction. (Martin Luther King, Jr.)
	Promoter	Effectively distributes new ideas or artworks such that a large number of people engage and appreciate them. (Walt Disney)
	Victor	Leads people to defeat a formidable human, institutional, or national opponent, a social ill, or a disease in a contest with major consequences. (Dwight D. Eisenhower)

Table 26.2b

If you find yourself drawn strongly to two types, it is possible that they both pertain to your ultimate contribution. Maybe accomplishing one will result in the other. Or maybe you'll accomplish one earlier as a foundation for accomplishing the other later. Or maybe the two will reinforce each other over time.

An Encouragement to Pastors

I want to conclude this chapter with an encouragement to pastors who are reading this book. Pastor, may I invite you to see yourself as an Ultimate Contribution Coach? Would you encourage every believer you influence to uncover the big achievement for which God put them on earth?

Think about the potential of your platform: you have people's ears and eyes week after week, and God has given you that influence to leverage as you guide them toward the most important thing they'll do in their entire life.

A practical obstacle for many pastors is that they don't know their own ultimate contribution. Many settle for the general assignment of pastoring as the pinnacle of calling-clarity, but it isn't. If there are 250,000 pastors out there, there are 250,000 ways the unique gifts and ultimate contribution of each pastor are meant to play out.

Sadly, many pastors may not even believe they have an ultimate contribution to make, let alone have hope that they'll arrive at it. But you do and you can. And I want to give you an energy-jolt of encouragement and a new horizon to view. Every pastor—especially those approaching late career—faces a critical test that's also a golden opportunity.

The first love of my adventure-sport life is mountain biking. There is nothing like a technical downhill ride with smooth sections where I get to pedal fast. There are two very different reasons that my cadence gets really high. The first is when I know where I'm going and I'm eager to get there—that's when I *pedal with passion*. The second is when I don't know where I'm going, night is closing in, and I'm afraid I could get caught on the trail in the dark without making it to my destination—in that moment, I *pedal with panic*.

In the same way, I've noticed that pastors who haven't given any thought to making an ultimate contribution or who have talked themselves out of it with misguided humility are at risk of "ministering with panic" late in their career. I've seen them work to exhaustion, just barely hanging on with anxiety they cannot adequately name and no one rallying to assist them.

On the other hand, I am seeing more and more pastors go through The Journey and gain increasing clarity about their ultimate contribution and the confidence that comes with it. Even in the "fourth quarter" of their careers, these pastors "minister with

> The best part of watching pastors go through The Journey is the new freedom I see in them to imagine the greatness in others.

passion." The best part is the new freedom I see in them to imagine the greatness in others. It's a conviction that every sermon and every small group must call out and nurture the dreams of God for every man, woman, and child.

My heart's desire is that every pastor at whatever stage of their ministry career might lead with an eye on their ultimate contribution. I want it for the health of the pastor and for the strength of the church. Most of all I want it for the destinies of the unique people the pastor serves who are eager to make their mark for now and eternity. Church must bring a kingdom vision that dramatically raises our sight to the wonder of calling and contribution beyond a few volunteer activities that keep ministry programs running. And pastors can be used in amazing ways as God accomplishes this.

 (The topic of ultimate contribution is one where a coach can provide significant value. If you are ready to apply this chapter even more, check out the online course entitled *Your Ultimate Contribution Deep Dive* at LifeYounique.com/courses.)

Chapter 27

DEATH

The Five-Minute Practice That Turns Everyone's Greatest Fear into Your Life's Greatest Fuel

*"We must do the works of him who sent me while it is
day. Night is coming when no one can work."*

—Jesus

"Why do you write like you're running out of time?" So the cast of the Broadway blockbuster *Hamilton: An American Musical* asks of the title character, Founding Father Alexander Hamilton. On Twitter, a fan asked the show's creator, Lin-Manuel Miranda, why *he* writes like he's running out of time. Miranda's reply was blunt: "Because we all are."

That kind of candor about death screeches like grinding gears in our place and day. Consider:

- Infant mortality is vastly lower in our society than the norm. In all other eras and in many places today, losing at least one child to disease was practically a given.
- Routine conditions that kill adults prematurely and unexpectedly—from diarrhea to childbirth—are almost unknown as causes of death in the West.
- At the onset of Social Security in the United States, when the retirement age was set at age sixty-five, the average life expectancy was sixty-one years.[1] Since then, life-prolonging medicine made a decades-long period between working and death into a birthright—even the goal of life.

- Due to the pervasive presence of hospitals and residences for the elderly, many deaths happen out of sight, only in the presence of other elderly people and medical professionals.

Meanwhile, through digital media, the consuming public is fed a steady diet of made-up, well-lit, surgically manicured, Photoshopped, forever-young, high-energy faces as our daily companions. No one dies of cancer on a reality show.

As a consequence, very few live like they're running out of time. And it's not as though we needed the help of modern technology to avoid thinking about the inevitable. Humans have been doing it forever.

Long ago, Jesus shredded the folly of the person who stored up treasure for himself but was not rich toward God, oblivious to how his life would be demanded of him before his golden years (Luke 12:16–21). James echoed, "You do not know what tomorrow will bring—what your life will be! For you are like vapor that appears for a little while, then vanishes" (James 4:14).

People hate death and, therefore, fear it and avoid facing it. That's one reason why the heap of life planning books is consistently inadequate. They fail on two counts:

1. *Their summons lacks urgency.* What's another year of aimlessness if you have no terminus? If you're pretending you're going to live forever, there's no need to push the pedal on finding and living your Life Younique.
2. *Their summons lacks eternity.* If there *is* a sense of urgency in most of these books, it's to urge people to enjoy life in the near term, not to live a life of substance whose impact ripples beyond the end of your life and the end of the world.

A Serious Discipline for a Serious Call

I hate to say it, but Christ-followers today seem to avoid the Bible's urging to consider our impending deaths just as much as the world does. Think: When was the last time in group prayer that you heard someone ask, "Teach us to number our days carefully so that we may develop wisdom in our hearts" (Ps. 90:12)?

Many people who read my writings about church vision and strategy—or who encounter my high-octane "fiery red" and "sunshine yellow" energies in person—don't know that I harbor an inner mystic. I've been blessed beyond calculation by modern spiritual writers like Dallas Willard, Richard Foster, and others. Yet among these giants, I have rarely, if ever, found teaching on a haunting call that gripped me for many years as a young adult.

Picture this: when I was twenty-one years old, a semi-cocky Penn State senior eager to make bank in the Texas oil fields, something drew me to pace alone up and down the tombstones of a cemetery, feet damp with dew, praying. Not on one rare occasion, but many times.

I don't entirely know what I was doing there. But God mysteriously used those lonely trips to the graveyard to press into the wax of my soul a truth that I couldn't shake. It was evident to me that in light of my mortality, so much that sparkles in life is "meaningless, a chasing after the wind" (Eccl. 1:14 NIV). I knew that I would return to dust, and I didn't want the fruit of my life to endure the same fate.

Over the next fifteen years, through exhilarating successes and crushing failures, the Holy Spirit kept leading me to this lesson again and again, but I had trouble remembering it and living it out. Yet I found help along the way in a series of old spiritual writers who taught a spiritual discipline I never learned anywhere else: *the discipline of meditating on one's death.*

> What if tonight really *was* the last night of my life? Did I spend my last day on earth doing what I was put on earth to do?

I found an especially hair-raising version in William Law's *A Serious Call to a Devout and Holy Life* (1728). Law taught that when climbing into bed, you ought to pretend that you are climbing into your grave, and your last prayer of the day ought to commit your soul to God as if you're not going to wake up on earth the next morning.[2]

This morbid picture slapped me sober; I couldn't get it out of my mind. *A makeshift coffin was sitting in my bedroom.* What if tonight really *was* the last night of my life? Did I spend my last day on earth doing what I was put on earth to do?

I'm now convinced that the proverb, "Begin with the end in mind," is more than a slogan, and it applies to more than short-run projects. *If you don't begin your life with its end in mind, you can't plan anything.*

I advise participants in the Younique Life Plan Journey to write what I call their "Tombstone Tweet." You can do it too: take time in silence to imagine the end of your life, your obituary, your funeral (in cinematic detail—for example, who is attending?) and the epitaph engraved on your tombstone. Jot down notes. Then sum up your life in 280 characters or less.

What does your Tombstone Tweet call you toward? What yearning does it evoke in you? Does it fill you with a sense of urgency to live out your One Thing every day and make a lasting ultimate contribution before you run out of time?

Top Ten Panel: How Meditating on Your Death Gives You Clarity

1. *You stop mistaking activity for productivity.* The teacher in Ecclesiastes worked himself to exhaustion, and it profited him nothing because he had no transcendent purpose. Pondering his demise got him off the treadmill (Eccl. 2:17–26).

2. *You aggressively pursue the happiness that lasts for eternity over everything less.* Jonathan Edwards resolved "to endeavor to obtain for myself as much happiness in the other world as I possibly can, with all the power, might, vigor, and vehemence, yea violence I am capable of or can bring myself to exert in any way that can be thought of."[3]

3. *You squeeze every drop of usefulness out of the time you have before it's too late.* "See then that you walk circumspectly, not as fools but as wise, redeeming the time, because the days are evil" (Eph. 5:15–16 NKJV).

4. *You realize the limited number of your words and deeds in one lifetime . . .* and you concentrate them on what God would say and do (1 Pet. 4:7–11).

5. *You gain a discriminator when facing a big decision.* Ignatius of Loyola designed a prayer process for discerning God's will in an A-or-B choice. Steps include "making the present choice if I were at the moment of death" and to "picture and consider myself as standing in the presence of my judge on the last day, and reflect what decision in the present matter I would then wish to have made."[4]

6. *You refrain from doing things now that will embarrass you later.* Edwards resolved "to think much on all occasions of my own dying" and "never to do anything which I should be afraid to do if it were the last hour of my life."[5]

7. *You prevent regrets.* Thomas à Kempis predicted, "When that last moment arrives you will begin to have a quite different opinion of the life that is now entirely past. . . . How happy and prudent is he who tries now in life to be what he wants to be found in death."[6]

8. *You get back on course more quickly.* Thomas à Kempis also counseled, "I do not doubt that you would correct yourself more earnestly if you would think more of an early death than of a long life."[7]

9. *You become less discouraged and distracted by relationship hurts.* When Paul knew untimely death might be right around the corner, he put competition from rivals in perspective. Rather than get worked up about it, he enjoyed that they were preaching Christ, thereby fulfilling his personal mission beyond what he could do while imprisoned (Phil. 1:12–26).

10. *You humbly go for help to the only One who can make your plans a reality.* The watchword of your Horizon Storyline must be this prayer: "May the favor of the Lord our God rest on us; establish the work of our hands for us—yes, establish the work of our hands" (Ps. 90:17 NIV).

Why You Can Face What They Can't

As I said at the beginning of this book, I'm assuming that you are a follower of Christ who has been reconciled to the Father through faith in him. If that's so, you have a staggering advantage in life planning that others don't have: *you can lean into your death, while they must run away from theirs.*

Life design that isn't gospel-centered runs headlong into the black hole facing all humanity. Even if you were to shape your life absolutely perfectly, then at the very moment you put the cherry on top you would depart the edifice you spent your whole life building. You would not spend a single nanosecond enjoying the finished product of all your effort. You'd have no idea years afterward whether it was all worth it. The notion that "it's all about the journey" is no comfort when the journey's over.

To most of the world, death is the ultimate demotivator—something at best to be explained away or, more often, simply ignored. To some, like in Miranda's *Hamilton*, it's a frantic motivator—it causes them to work feverishly as if building a sandcastle on the shore while the tide is rushing in. But for the person in Christ, death is the great motivator, because "if we died with Christ, we believe that we will also live with him" (Rom. 6:8). The resurrection of Jesus from the dead makes death, our last enemy, into our fierce friend.

Death gives our lives urgency, because the time is short. But the resurrection gives our lives eternity, because the fruit Jesus bears through us will last forever (John 15:16).

My last exhortation to you is this. In light of the vanishing brevity of life and the yawning immensity of eternity, keep climbing the Clarity Spiral. Keep practicing the Life-Making Cycle. Keep leaning into your ultimate contribution. Make embodying your One Thing your supreme pursuit. Live like you're running out of time. Because your life will live forever.

NOTES

Introduction

1. Andy Stanley, *Visioneering: Your Guide for Discovering and Maintaining Personal Vision* (Colorado Springs: Multnomah, 2016).

2. Mark Batterson, *Soulprint: Discovering Your Divine Destiny* (Colorado Springs: Multnomah, 2011).

3. Tom Rath, *StrengthsFinder 2.0* (New York: Gallup Press, 2015).

4. Rick Warren, *The Purpose Driven Life: What on Earth Am I Here For?* (Grand Rapids, MI: Zondervan, 2012).

5. Ramesh Richard, *Soul Vision: Ensuring Your Life's Future Impact* (Chicago: Moody, 2004).

Chapter 1

1. A version of this chapter originally appeared in Will Mancini, *The Clarity Spiral: Four Essential Steps to Find and Align Your Personal Calling* (self-published, 2019).

Chapter 2

1. Dallas Willard, *The Divine Conspiracy: Rediscovering Our Hidden Life in God* (New York: HarperCollins, 1998), 283.

2. Eugene Peterson, *Run with the Horses: The Quest for Life at Its Best*, 2nd ed. (Downers Grove, IL: InterVarsity Press, 2009), 15–16.

3. Philip Yancey, *Reaching for the Invisible God* (Grand Rapids, MI: Zondervan, 2000), 163.

Chapter 3

1. An expanded version of this chapter with a thorough treatment of the four steps of life design is available under the title Will Mancini, *Clarity Spiral: The 4 Break-Thru Practices to Find the One Thing You're Called to Do* (self-published, 2019).

2. Os Guinness, *The Call: Finding and Fulfilling the Central Purpose of Your Life* (Nashville: Thomas Nelson, 2003), 107.

3. Benjamin Franklin, *Poor Richard Improved: Being an Almanack and Ephemeris of the Motions of the Sun and Moon for the Year of Our Lord 1750* (Philadelphia: n.p.), January, Rosenbach Museum and Library, Philadelphia, http://www.rarebookroom.org/Control/frappg/index.html (accessed June 6, 2019).

4. Richard P. Feynman, "Cargo Cult Science," commencement address, California Institute of Technology, 1974, http://calteches.library.caltech.edu/51/2/CargoCult.htm (accessed June 6, 2019).

5. Parker Palmer, *Let Your Life Speak: Listening for the Voice of Vocation* (New York: Jossey-Bass, 1999), 5.

6. I heard this phrase from a good friend, Brian McDougal, the executive pastor at Idlewild Baptist Church.

Part 2

1. Max Lucado, *Cure for the Common Life: Living in Your Sweet Spot* (Nashville: Thomas Nelson, 2005), 1.

Chapter 5

1. Commonly attributed to Blaise Pascal, unsourced. See, for example, https://mottod.com/quotes/7572 (accessed August 12, 2019).

2. Creating Your Life Plan with Donald Miller, www.creatingyourlifeplan.com (accessed October 29, 2018).

3. Mike Breen coined the terms "appetite," "ambition," and "approval" to describe the temptations of Jesus.

Chapter 6

1. Tom Paterson, *Deeper, Richer, Fuller: Discover the Spiritual Life You Long For* (New York: Howard Books, 2010), 194.

2. Alan Hirsch, *5Q: Reactivating the Original Intelligence and Capacity of the Body of Christ* (self-published, 100 Movements, 2017), 22. The tables that follow are adapted from those on pages 50–54, 99–116.

3. Ibid.

4. Ibid., xxxiv.

5. Richard Nelson Bolles, *What Color Is Your Parachute?* (Berkeley, CA: Ten Speed Press, 1984), 87.

6. Arthur F. Miller with William Hendricks, *The Power of Uniqueness: Why You Can't Be Anything You Want to Be* (Grand Rapids, MI: Zondervan, 1999), 31.

Chapter 7

1. Tom Paterson, *Living the Life You Were Meant to Live* (Nashville: Thomas Nelson, 1998), 188.

2. Peter F. Drucker, *Managing Oneself* (Watertown, MA: Harvard Business Review Press, 2008), 169.

3. Ibid., 170.

4. J. Robert Clinton, "Getting Perspective—Using Your Unique Timeline," BobbyClinton.com, 9–13.

5. Neil Cole, *Journeys to Significance: Charting a Leadership Course from the Life of Paul* (San Francisco: Jossey-Bass, 2011), 141.

6. John Acuff, *Start: Punch Fear in the Face, Escape Average, and Do Work That Matters* (Brentwood, TN: Ramsey Press, 2013). Bob P. Buford, *Halftime: Moving from Success to Significance* (Grand Rapids, MI: Zondervan, 1994).

7. Adrian Gostick and Chester Elton, *What Motivates Me: Put Your Passions to Work* (Lindon, UT: The Culture Works, 2014).

Chapter 8

1. Irving Fisher, "The Applications of Mathematics to the Social Sciences," *Bulletin of the American Mathematical Society* 36, no. 4 (April 1930): 229.

2. Edward Teller, Wendy Teller, and Wilson Talley, *Conversations on the Dark Secrets of Physics* (New York: Basic Books, 1991), 2.

3. The original quotation runs, "The only simplicity for which I would give a straw is that which is on the other side of the complex—not that which never has divined it." Mark DeWolfe Howe, ed., *Holmes-Pollock Letters: The Correspondence of Mr. Justice Holmes and Sir Frederick Pollock, 1874–1932*, 2nd ed. (Cambridge, MA: Belknap Press, 1961), 109.

4. Frederick Buechner, *Wishful Thinking: A Theological ABC* (New York: Harper & Row, 1973), 95.

5. Kevin McCarthy, *The On-Purpose Person: Making Your Life Make Sense* (Winter Park, FL: On-Purpose Publishing, 2013).

Chapter 9

1. Paraphrased from Chris Sperry, "Stay at 17 Inches," Baseball/Life, http://www.sperrybaseballlife.com/stay-at-17-inches (accessed June 27, 2018).

2. The idea that, on average, ten thousand hours of practice is necessary to achieve elite mastery in a field is popularized by Malcolm Gladwell in *Outliers: The Story of Success* (New York: Back Bay Books, 2008), chap. 2, NOOK.

Chapter 11

1. I heard this phrase for the first time from my good friend Jeff Harris. He is a pastor in San Antonio, and does a phenomenal job at leading from his values.

Chapter 12

1. David Bebbington, *Patterns in History: A Christian Perspective on Historical Thought* (Vancouver: Regent College Publishing, 1990), 21–67.

2. Walter Brueggemann, *Spirituality of the Psalms* (Minneapolis, MN: Augsburg Fortress, 2002).

3. C. S. Lewis, *The Last Battle* (New York: HarperCollins, 1956), 196.

4. John Calvin, Preface to the *Commentary on the Psalms in Reformation Reader* by Denis Janz and Shirley E. Jordan (Minneapolis, MN: Augsburg Fortress, 1999), 205.

5. Wikipedia, s.v. "Imprecatory Psalms," https://en.wikipedia.org/wiki/Imprecatory_Psalms (accessed September 21, 2018).

Part 4

1. For the purposes of this book, it was desirable to end with the teaching and tools on destiny. However, in The Journey we use destiny tools throughout the process. Specifically, we examine ultimate contribution as a Context Circle tool in the Sweet Spot, bucket list when working on LifeScore, and Tombstone Tweet before developing a three-year dream.

Chapter 14

1. I am especially indebted to my partner in founding Younique and creating the Younique Life Plan Journey, Dave Rhodes, for much of the material in this section.

Chapter 15

1. Aristotle, *On the Soul*, 3.7.

Chapter 16

1. Tom Paterson, *Living the Life You Were Meant to Live* (Nashville, TN: Thomas Nelson, 2003).

Chapter 17

1. Tim Ferriss, *Tools of Titans: The Tactics, Routines, and Habits of Billionaires, Icons, and World-Class Performers* (New York: Houghton Mifflin Harcourt, 2016), 389.

2. Maneesh Sethi, "How I Learned a Language in 90 Days," Lifehacker, July 9, 2012, https://lifehacker.com/5923910/how-i-learned-a-language-in-90-days (accessed June 8, 2018).

3. Brian P. Moran and Michael Lennington, *The 12 Week Year: Get More Done in 12 Weeks than Others Do in 12 Months* (Hoboken, NJ: John Wiley & Sons, 2013).

4. Pierre Bienaimé, "A Domino the Size of a Tic Tac Could Topple a Building," *Business Insider*, January 28, 2015, http://www.businessinsider.com/how-one-domino-can-topple-a-building-2015-1 (accessed June 8, 2018).

5. Peter Drucker, *Management: Tasks, Responsibilities, Practices* (New York: Harper & Row, 1973), 119.

Chapter 18

1. Budd Coates and Claire Kowalchik, "Running on Air: Breathing Technique," *Runner's World*, March 6, 2013, https://www.runnersworld.com/training/a20822091/running-on-air-breathing-technique (accessed June 14, 2018); "Budd Coates," Runner's World, https://www.runnersworld.com/author/210865/budd-coates (accessed June 14, 2018).

Chapter 20

1. This thought-experiment is drawn from Will MacAskill. Tim Ferriss, *Tools of Titans: The Tactics, Routines, and Habits of Billionaires, Icons, and World-Class Performers* (New York: Houghton Mifflin Harcourt, 2016), location 1,214 of 1,908, Apple Books.

Chapter 21

1. Dan Sullivan, "How to Stay at the Top of Your Entrepreneurial Game," Strategic Coach, https://resources.strategiccoach.com/the-multiplier-mindset-blog/how-to-stay-at-the-top-of-your-entrepreneurial-game-2 (accessed June 29, 2018).

2. Gina Trapani, "Work Smart: Do Your Worst Task First (Or, Eat a Live Frog Every Morning)," *Fast Company*, March 22, 2010, https://www.fastcompany.com/1592454/work-smart-do-your-worst-task-first-or-eat-live-frog-every-morning (accessed November 1, 2018).

3. Senior pastor and seminary professor Tommy Kiedis has written a three-hour retreat series where he uses the photography metaphor of the magic hour or golden window in relationship to finding the most productive use of your day. For more information, go to https://www.leaderslifeandwork.com/books/the-leaders-magic-hour.

4. Áine Cain, "A Day in the Life of the Richest Person in the World, Jeff Bezos—Whose Company Is Worth $1 Trillion and Who Still Washes the Dishes after Dinner," *Business Insider*, https://www.businessinsider.com/jeff-bezos-daily-routine-2017-7 (accessed November 1, 2018).

Chapter 22

1. Jesus did tell Jairus to "only believe" when the mourners outside Jairus's house laughed at Jesus for announcing that Jairus's daughter wasn't dead (Mark 5:36; Luke 8:50). But Jesus' point was that the man would get his daughter back if he simply persevered in believing that Jesus had the authority and willingness to solve the problem. "Only believe" in this context can't be generalized into the notion that expressing agreement with Jesus' gospel of eternal salvation is enough to inherit what it promises all by itself. See Matthew 7:21–27 and James 2:14–26 for classic statements of this principle.

2. "Eisenhower's Urgent/Important Principle," Mind Tools, https://www.mindtools.com/pages/article/newHTE_91.htm (accessed June 29, 2018). You may be familiar with this principle attributed to Dwight D. Eisenhower, which he derived from former Northwestern University president J. Roscoe Miller.

3. Percy C. Buck, *Psychology for Musicians* (London: Oxford University Press, 1944), 102.

Chapter 24

1. Ruth Haley Barton, *Invitation to Solitude and Silence: Experiencing God's Transforming Presence*, 2d ed. (Downers Grove, IL: InterVarsity Press, 2010), 25–30.

Chapter 25

1. This chapter contains content that originally appeared on WillMancini.com under the following titles: "Summer Dreamin': How to Use a Bucket List for a More Meaningful Life," "The Bucket List for Believers: 4 Ways to Redeem Your Dreams," "5 Kinds of Aspirations That Will Help You Design Your Life," "The 5 Major Obstacles to Personal Vision," and "4 Essentials to Achieving Your Life Goals."

2. John Ortberg, "Ruthlessly Eliminate Hurry," *Christianity Today*, https://www.christianitytoday.com/pastors/2002/july-online-only/cln20704.html.

Chapter 26

1. J. Robert Clinton, *The Making of a Leader: Recognizing the Lessons and Stages of Leadership Development*, 2d ed. (Colorado Springs: NavPress, 2014).

2. J. Robert Clinton, "Ultimate Contribution—a Life That Counts," BobbyClinton.com, 7–9.

Chapter 27

1. Javier Escamilla, "The Social Security Dilemma," https://web.stanford.edu/class/e297c/poverty_prejudice/soc_sec/hsocialsec.htm (accessed August 1, 2019).

2. William Law, *A Serious Call to a Devout and Holy Life* (London: J. M. Dent & Co., 1906), 339.

3. Jonathan Edwards, "Resolutions," in *Letters and Personal Writings*, Volume 16 of *Works of Jonathan Edwards Online*, ed. George S. Claghorn, 754, http://edwards.yale.edu/research/browse (accessed May 9, 2018).

4. Saint Ignatius of Loyola, *The Spiritual Exercises*, trans. Louis J. Puhl, SJ, 186–87, http://spex.ignatianspirituality.com/SpiritualExercises/Puhl (accessed May 8, 2018).

5. Edwards, "Resolutions," 753.

6. Thomas à Kempis, *The Imitation of Christ*, trans. Aloysius Croft and Harold Bolton, book 1, chapter 23, http://www.ccel.org/ccel/kempis/imitation.ONE.23.html (accessed May 9, 2018).

7. Ibid., book 1, chapter 21, http://www.ccel.org/ccel/kempis/imitation.ONE.21.html (accessed May 9, 2018).

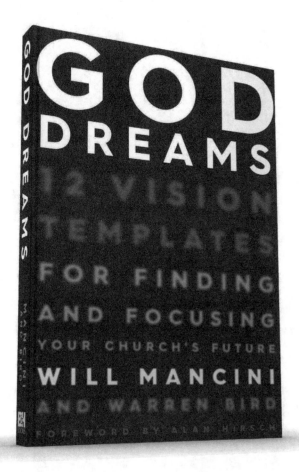

If you liked the book, you will love the planner. Master your next 90 days.

LifeYounique.com/planner

*"The bad news is time flies.
The good news is you're the pilot."
– Michael Altshuler*

Deliver gospel-centered life planning.
Through **your** church.

It's amazing to watch a room full of people discover their special calling and put it work almost instantly. In just a few months we will have over 1,000 people involved with Younique.
– Scott Kindig
Pastor of Kingdom Initiatives
Community Bible Church
San Antonio, TX

A sleeping giant is slowly awakening as our people understand and live out their personal calling in community. Younique has become central to our discipleship culture.
– David Loveless
Pastor of Disciple and Leadership Initiatives
First Baptist Orlando

Learn More at LifeYounique.com

Clarity isn't everything. But it changes everything.

Check out **WillMancini.com** to learn more about the entire ecosystem of break-thru books and tools developed for individuals, churches, ministries and denominations.

YOUNIQUE

IT'S YOUR CALL

Go Ahead

MORE VALUE. Every church.